COMPANION TO THE
BRITISH
ARMY
1939–1945

Architect of victory thanks the workers. Monty thanks Scottish factory workers for producing the weapons his Army Group needs to win the battles of NW Europe. (Author's Collection)

COMPANION TO THE
BRITISH
ARMY
1939–1945

GEORGE FORTY

The
History
Press

Cover Illustrations: Front: British infantrymen double through the narrow streets of Flushing, keeping a lookout for snipers (IWM SFD 15). Back: What an infantryman carries with him into battle c. June 1944 (IWM B 9005 & B 9006).

First published in 1998
This edition published in 2009

The History Press
The Mill, Brimscombe Port
Stroud, Gloucestershire, GL5 2QG
www.thehistorypress.co.uk

British Library Cataloguing in Publication Data.
A catalogue record for this book is available from the British Library.

ISBN 978 0 7524 5240 1

Typesetting and origination by The History Press
Printed in Great Britain

CONTENTS

ACKNOWLEDGEMENTS

I must thank the staff of the MoD Library for their usual courteous and unfailing support – how fortunate we are to have such a precious resource and long may it prosper!

Most of the photographs come from the Imperial War Museum Department of Photographs and I must thank them also for their help and kindness. The same applies to David Fletcher, Curator and Librarian of the Tank Museum, Bruce Robertson and others who have given me photographs to use – some of those marked 'Author's Collection' have been in my possession since I wrote my very first book on the 7th Armoured Division nearly twenty-five years ago.

Finally I must thank my son Jonathan, who has been responsible for many of the drawings and charts, the Royal Signals Institution for allowing me to use their table of radio sets, the Dorset Military Museum, Airborne Forces Museum, RA Institution and the Tank Museum Library, for their help with organizational tables.

ABBREVIATIONS

Given below are a selection of abbreviations used by the British Army during the Second World War. Only authorized abbreviations could be used, plus those in general use, such as lb, yd, mph, etc. Different abbreviations were used by the US Army and there was no Allied standardization until after the war had ended.

accommodation	accn	colonel	col
administrative order	admin O	column	colm
advance or advanced	adv	commanding officer	CO
aide de camp	ADC	command post	CP
airborne	ab	commando	cdo
aircraft	ac	communications	comms
ambulance	amb	company	coy
amendment	amdt	confidential	confd
ammunition	amn	construct or construction	constr
anti-aircraft	AA	coordinate	coord
anti-gas	AG	corporal	cpl
anti-tank	A tk	craftsman	cfn
armoured	armd	crossroads	x rds
armoured car	armd C		
armoured recovery vehicle	ARV	decontamination	dcn
artillery	arty	defence, defended, defensive	def
assault	aslt	defensive fire	DF
		demolition	dml
battalion	bn	depot	dep
battery	bty	detachment, detach	det
boundary	bdy	district	dist
bombardier	bdr	distribution	distr
bridge	br	division	div
brigade	bde	driver	dvr
brigadier	brig	dropping zone	DZ
		drummer	dmr
camouflage	cam		
captain	capt	echelon	ech
carrier	carr	embark	emb
cavalry	cav	enemy	en
centre line	CL	engineer	engr
chemical	chem	establish	estb

estimated time of arrival	ETA	light aid detachment	LAD
estimated time of departure	ETD	liaison officer	LO
evacuate	evac	lieutenant	lt
		light	lt
field	fd	line(s) of communication	LofC
field marshal	FM	locate, location	loc
flight	flt	low power	LP
follow, followed, following	fol		
formation	fmn	machine gun	MG
forming up place	FUP	magazine	mag
forward	fwd	maximum	max
forward observation officer	FOO	major	maj
frequency	freq	mechanized	mech
		medical	med
gallon	gal	medium	med
general staff	GS	memorandum	memo
general	gen	message	msg
group	gp	military	mil
guard	gd	minimum	min
guardsman	gdsm	miscellaneous	misc
gunner	gnr	mobile	mob
		mortar	mor
headquarters	HQ	motor, motorized	mot
heavy	hy	motorcycle	MC
high explosive	HE		
high power	HP	necessary	nec
howitzer	how	night	ni
hygiene	hyg	non-commissioned officer	NCO
		nothing to report	NTR
identification, identify	ident		
including, inclusive	incl	observation post	OP
independent	indep	objective	obj
infantry	inf	officer	offr
information	info	operation	op
intelligence	int	operation order	OO
		organization	org
junction	junc	other rank	OR
killed in action	KIA	parachute	para
		patrol	ptl
labour	lab	paymaster	pmr
lance corporal	LCpl	petrol, oil and lubricants	POL
landing craft infantry	LCI	pioneer	pnr
landing craft tank	LCT	platoon	pl
leader	ldr	point	pt

position	posn	strength	str
pounder	pdr	support	sp
private	pte	subject	subj
provost marshal	PM	supply point	sup P
		survey	svy
quartermaster	QM	switchboard	swb
quartermaster sergeant	QMS		
(as used, for example, with		tactical, tactics	tac
CQMS – company . . . or		tank	tk
SQMS – squadron . . .)		target	tgt
		technical	tech
ration(s)	rat(s)	telegraph	tele
railhead	RH	telephone	phone
reconnaissance	recce	temporary	temp
relief	rel	top secret	TOPSEC
rendezvous	RV	transport	tpt
rifleman	rfn	traffic control post	TCP
regiment	regt	troop carrying vehicle	TCV
regimental sergeant major	RSM	troop(s)	tp(s)
regimental police	RP	trooper	tpr
reserve	res		
restricted	restd	unclassified	unclas
road	rd	unserviceable	unsvc
sapper	spr	vehicle	veh
searchlight	SL	vehicle collecting point	VCP
section	sec	verbal order	VO
self-propelled mounting	SP	veterinary	vet
serjeant/sergeant	sjt/sgt		
signal(s)	sig(s)	warning order	wng O
small arms ammunition	SAA	warrant officer	WO
soldier	sldr	war department	WD
sound ranging	S rg	war establishment	WE
squadron	sqn	water point	WP
staff sergeant	SSgt	weapon	wpn
start line	SL	wounded in action	WIA
starting point	SP	workshop	wksp
sten machine carbine	SMC		

Men of the Commonwealth swiftly joined the 'Mother Country' against a common enemy. This photograph shows the confident men of the Rajput Regiment ready to start a patrol in the Ngakyedyank Pass in Burma. (IWM – IND 2917)

Prime Minister Winston Churchill visiting Royal Artillery heavy gun crews training at their anti-invasion gun positions, near Parkstone, Dorset, July 1940. The gun is a 9.2 in howitzer. (IWM – H2269)

INTRODUCTION

This is the second 'World War II Handbook' I have written for Sutton Publishing, the first being my attempt to cram the build-up, training, organization, weapons and equipment of the vast American Army of the Second World War, into a couple of hundred pages. Although it was difficult enough on that occasion, I misguidedly thought that it would be easier trying to do the same with the somewhat smaller British Army of the same period. It wasn't and I am quite certain that the reader will find many omissions for

which I apologize in advance – but it is a vast subject to cover in such a little book so I could only include the bare essentials.

I am of course not the first to attempt such a project. The American Army was well to the fore, producing their excellent training manual (TM 30–410) entitled Handbook on the British Army early in 1943. Fortunately there was an old, well-thumbed copy in the MoD Library, so I was able to read it and have quoted from it in some cases. However, the main problem with that excellent TM

Members of the BEF getting to know their French comrades during the strange 'Phoney War' period that preceded the German assault in the West. (Author's Collection)

is that it only portrayed the British Army of the early war years, before it had been modernized and altered by battle experience. Therefore it was a study of the Second World War British Army from a somewhat old-fashioned viewpoint. In addition, it contained information concerning the Royal Navy and Royal Air Force, which clearly need not be included this time. Indeed, the TM appeared to draw heavily on a most marvellous book, which I had read when a very young schoolboy, entitled *Britain's Wonderful Fighting Forces* by Capt Ellison Hawkes RA, which was published before the war by Odhams Press Ltd. So, for example, the section on AFVs dealt with the early lights, cruisers and infantry tanks, stopping with the early marks of Churchill, thus not covering Cromwell, Challenger, Comet, etc., or any of the amazing 'Funnies' of 79th Armd Div, which helped so much towards the success of the Normandy landings. Infantry anti-tank (a tk) weapons were far more concerned with the obsolescent Boys a tk rifle and the 2 pdr, with little information on the 6 pdr and no mention whatsoever of the 17 pdr or of SP a tk weapons, because obviously they had not yet come into service so could not be included. The same applied to much other equipment and to many vehicles and weapons, while there was

little mention of the activities of the British Army outside temperate climes, again for obvious reasons.

I have tried, in this volume, to give a more balanced and complete picture of the British Army in wartime from the early days of the BEF, through the years of defeat and struggle in the early 1940s, culminating in the eventual Allied victory, in which the officers and men of the British Army and their Commonwealth comrades played such an important role. The Commonwealth soldiers deserve far more coverage than I have been able to give them, but I hope that they will not feel I have forgotten them. They, the Australians, Canadians, Indians, New Zealanders, South Africans and all the rest, made a mighty contribution that must never be forgotten.

As far as the main general descriptions of the individual soldier, his weapons and equipment are concerned I have tried to base everything on the army that went into NW Europe in 1944, but at the same time not forgetting what went before and what came after, so the 'Forgotten Armies' that fought in Italy and Burma are mentioned as well. The format follows the same sequence as that in the *US Army Handbook*, so past readers will, I hope, be on familiar ground.

George Forty
Bryantspuddle

CHAPTER 1

HISTORICAL BACKGROUND

THE BRITISH PEOPLE GO TO WAR

'At 11.0am on September 3rd 1939, Britain entered a new era. The transition from peace to war was swift and dramatic. The country had put on uniform. The sky over the cities was dotted with balloons. Everywhere, people were digging trenches, filling sandbags. Gas masks were given out. There was a rush for black paper and cloth to screen windows and skylights. Grim, grey vehicles thundered along the roads on mysterious errands. There was in the air a feeling of change, complete, inevitable, tremendous.'

(Opening paragraph of *The British People at War* published by Odhams Press Ltd in 1942.)

300 YEARS OF HISTORY

The formation of a permanent regular army in Great Britain had taken place over 300 years before the Second World War began and ever since those days it had occupied a rather uncomfortable position in British society, owing its allegiance to the Crown, yet being under the effective control of Parliament. Invariably reduced to a ridiculously small size during peacetime – thanks to political fears that a large standing army would threaten civil liberty – it had nevertheless performed incredible feats of endurance and bravery, winning and then helping to maintain a vast, worldwide Empire. It has to be emphasized, however, that apart from the First World War, the country had relied more upon British-officered mercenary levies

to perform these miracles, rather than upon large numbers of her own regular soldiers. Nevertheless, the British Army had a remarkable record of success, losing only one major war (American War of Independence 1775–83) in the last 300 years, and, in more recent times, being engaged as an unsupported nation at the turn of the century in the South African War, then as a member of the Allied Powers in the First World War, the greatest war the world had ever known, in which the Motherland and its Empire suffered well over

Never again! The horrors of trench warfare in the 'War to end all Wars' are graphically illustrated by this macabre photograph of a corpse outside a dugout at Beaumont Hamel, November 1916. (IWM – Q2041)

Not yet time to say goodbye to boots and saddles! Until full mechanization took place, interwar exercises meant tanks and horses having to get along together. (Tank Museum)

a million military battle-deaths. Now, only some twenty years after the 'War to end all Wars' had ended, the world was about to be plunged into an even greater conflict.

However, this time Britain was a little better prepared. It had been obvious to most people even before the Munich Crisis of 1938, that another war with Germany was inevitable. Despite maintaining a policy of appeasement, Britain and its main ally, France, had embarked upon a programme of rearmament from the mid-thirties, which became more and more hurried and frenetic when it was realized just how far behind Germany they had fallen. Nevertheless, between the spring of 1936 and the autumn of 1939, while the Royal Navy and Royal Air Force enjoyed a

period of intense expansion and modernization, the fortunes of the army were, to quote the official history, '. . . altogether less happy. This was the period in which the Army became the "Cinderella Service".'[1] Despite this lethargy, the British Army eventually began to modernize, albeit very slowly, as is evidenced by the 1935–36 Army Estimates, which allowed for a paltry £4 million increase in budget, of which just £270,000 was allowed for the provision of tracked vehicles including tanks. Despite the fact that 'gurus' of armoured warfare such as 'Boney' Fuller and Basil Liddell-Hart had long been expounding their theories on how the

1. See N.H. Gibbs, *History of the Second World War – Grand Strategy*, Volume 1 (HMSO, 1976)

next war would be fought, only Adolf Hitler's Germany had been listening. The attitude of mind towards mechanization that pervaded the British Army at that time can be gauged by the apology made to the Cavalry by the then Secretary of State for War, when introducing the 1936–37 Estimates, in which he likened the 'unpalatable' decision to mechanize eight of their regiments to being like '. . . asking a great musical performer to throw away his violin and devote himself to the gramophone'. Such stupidity at such a high level would ensure that Britain had only two incomplete armoured divisions in September 1939, as compared with Germany's six.

Despite all the problems, 1937 saw a rearmament programme begin that was on a scale far larger than anything attempted since the end of the First World War. It was proposed to spend £1,500 million over five years, three times as much as was being spent when Hitler came to power and a 50 per cent increase on the previous year's expenditure. During the Chamberlain administration there was, however, a school of thought which argued that Britain should only participate in a continental war using her sea and air power. However, neither the British nor the French General Staff agreed and shortly before the war, the broad strategic policy was summarized by both parties as follows:

'We should be faced by enemies who would be more fully prepared than ourselves for war on a national scale, would have superiority in air and land forces, but would be inferior at sea and in general economic strength. In the circumstances, we must be prepared to face a

'Peace for our time'. Prime Minister Neville Chamberlain with his French counterpart Edouard Daladier, visiting the two dictators Adolf Hitler and Benito Mussolini in Munich in September 1938 to sign the Munich Pact. (IWM — NYP 68066)

major offensive directed at either France or Great Britain or against both. To defeat such an offensive we should have to concentrate all our initial efforts and during this time our major strategy would be defensive.'[2]

They went on to say that it might be possible to conduct counter-offensive operations against the Italians in both North and East Africa, thus reducing Italy's will to fight without undue cost! Subsequent policy would be directed against holding Germany and dealing decisively with Italy, while building up military strength to a point when it would be possible to take the offensive against Germany. Diplomacy would be used to ensure the active support, or at worst, the benevolent neutrality of other world powers, especially the USA. No mention was made of Japan, but in the last few weeks before war was declared in Europe, relations between Britain and Japan were under strain. However, for the time being, the Japanese had enough to contend with in China, while they – the Japanese – were deeply suspicious of Hitler's long-term objectives after his agreement with the USSR.

The Anglo-French military strategy was thus aimed at maintaining the integrity of French terrority. If the Low Countries were involved then the Allies would attempt to stop the enemy as far forward as possible. It would be necessary, therefore, for the British to send an Expeditionary Force to fight on the Continent, but it would be considerably smaller than the one sent in the First World War. Many politicians did not like this commitment, although there was general agreement for the need to maintain an adequate army in the Middle East. Egypt and the Suez Canal were considered to be of prime importance, while Palestine was necessary as a buffer to an invasion of Egypt from the north. India and the Far East were not thought to be in any immediate danger.

NATIONAL SERVICE

Conscription had ended in December 1918 and the massive British Army – larger than ever before in its history – had been rapidly whittled down, so that by the early 1920s there were under 250,000 men serving, thinly spread all over the Empire. The Territorial Army (TA), which had been created in 1908, had also been greatly reduced and its weapons and equipment were now seriously outdated. As has been explained, the Munich Crisis finally jolted the country out of its lethargy, mechanization, modernization

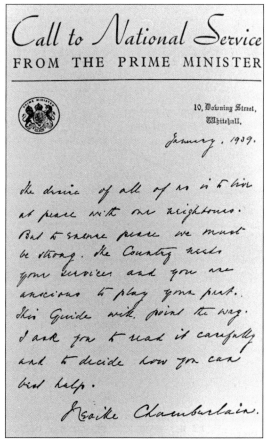

A 'Call to National Service' from the Prime Minister. (Author's Collection)

2. Gibbs, *History of the Second World War.*

Men of Gen Montgomery's 21 Army Group learn all about France as they wait to embark for the D-Day assault on Normandy. (IWM – B5207)

and expansion all being put into effect. The strength of the British Army, as given by the Secretary of State for War in April 1939, was: Regular Army 224,000; Territorial Army Field Force 325,000; and Territorial Army Anti-Aircraft Units 96,000, giving a total of men under arms of 645,000. However, much of the regular army was in India, or scattered in small garrisons worldwide, so more forces had to be built up at home. It had been agreed in March 1939 to double the size of the TA and the following month it was decided to re-introduce some conscription. Parliament passed the Military Training Act on 27 April 1939, more than 200,000 men between the ages of 20 and 21 registering in June 1939. These men, known as the Militia, were allowed to state their preferred choice of service, between the navy, army and air force,

and were drafted accordingly. During the middle of July the first batch of militiamen, numbering 34,000 for the army, were called up by age group, while the additional recruiting for the TA between April and September 1939 brought in some 36,000 extra men. To these were added the men of the Army Reserve (men who had returned to civilian life having completed their service with the Colours, but who were still liable to recall in case of emergency) and the Supplementary Reserve (mainly technicians), called out by proclamation on the outbreak of war and numbering a further 150,000. Thus, on 3 September 1939, the British Army numbered approximately 1,065,000.

Liability was extended on 6 September 1939, when the war was just a few hours old, Parliament passing the National Service

(Armed Forces) Act, which not only merged all these forces into a single entity but also made all physically fit males between the ages of 18 and 41 liable for military service. This was followed in 1941 by another Act, which extended the upper age limit for men to 51 and also made women liable for military service. In fact, only a few men over 41 were ever conscripted, and none over 45. By October all these measures had ensured that a million men were under intensive training, the cost of an infantryman's uniform being approximately £20 and comprising eighty items!

By the end of 1939, 727,000 men had registered; in 1940 the figure was 4,100,000 and in 1941 a further 2,222,000 were called up. From then on the numbers dropped sharply, as the only eligible men left were those in reserved occupations, plus each new generation as it reached the minimum call-up age. The armed forces, which in 1938 had numbered just 381,000, rose after only one year to 2.25 million and by D-Day (June 1944) nearly one-third of the entire male population of working age was serving in the forces. By April 1945 the British forces had reached a peak figure of just under 5 million, of whom 3 million were serving in the army. They made up some 47 divisions (11 armoured, 34 infantry and 2 airborne) of which 11 (2 armoured and 9 infantry) saw no combat as complete divisions.

Britain Stands Alone

Once the 'Phoney War' was over and the Battle for France had begun, there would be few bright patches in the early war years, with defeats all over the world being more the order of the day, until Britain stood virtually alone in its embattled islands. Most of the men of the once-proud BEF had been miraculously rescued, although the majority of their heavy equipment – including most of their precious tanks – had been lost. Fortunately the Germans did not react immediately, so Britain was allowed time to dig in and to build up her forces. One of the most important decisions at this time was to create an Anti-Aircraft (AA) Command of five TA divisions, which would prove vital against the enemy bomber threat. The regimental system remained the cornerstone of the army, for both infantry and armour, although there was inevitably some cross-posting when the casualties mounted. Mechanization had brought new roles for existing units – such as medium reconnaissance for the now fully mechanized cavalry regiments, while new units like the Reconnaissance Corps were also formed to provide recce units for infantry divisions. Specialized troops, such as paratroops, glider-borne troops and commandos, all came into being, but the three main supporting arms – artillery, engineers and

Evacuation of Dunkirk. A line of soldiers, up to their necks in water, struggle out to one of the 'little ships'. (IWM – M 4154)

The Battle of Britain. HM The King visiting an AA gunsite – note the immaculate guncrew in their well-pressed battledress, clean steel helmets, gas mask containers, etc. (IWM – C69)

Newly joined reservists, volunteers and National Servicemen all had to be trained. Here new recruits learn all about engines on their way to becoming fully trained drivers. (Author's Collection)

signals remained predominant, the Royal Artillery (RA) having the largest proportion of manpower among all the supporting arms and services. In addition to field artillery, they were also responsible for all AA, coastal and some a tk units.

COMMONWEALTH FORCES

Prewar, the two prime duties of the British Army were Home Defence and Empire Defence, the latter relying primarily upon the Royal Navy, which required well-protected bases in all parts of the world. Protecting these bases was an army responsibility, the size of such garrisons depending upon how quickly they could be reinforced. Some were small and relatively isolated, such as the fortress command of Malta. The major

An Askari AA gunner about to load his AA gun, 'somewhere in Burma' – another example of Commonwealth assistance. (IWM – K 8810)

dominions of course maintained their own armies, which were, like the British Army, small professional bodies, recruited on a volunteer basis. Although this book is primarily about the British Army it would be unforgivable to omit the forces of the British Commonwealth, which still covered one quarter of the world's surface. As in the First World War, India, together with the 'old' dominions of Australia, Canada, New Zealand and South Africa, plus all the other colonial parts of the Empire, had immediately joined Britain against the Axis, only Eire choosing to remain neutral. Their commitment was just as generous as it had been during the First World War, despite the understandable reluctance of some of the governments to repeat the levels of sacrifice. The global nature of the conflict meant that the Australians and Indians lost more soldiers against the Japanese than they did against the Germans and Italians. Canada, on the other hand, played a major part in the war against Germany, first in Italy then in NW Europe, while North Africa then Italy were the main battlegrounds for the South Africans.

In most cases, the Commonwealth forces were organized and equipped on British lines, using mainly British or US (Lend-Lease) equipment, although in some cases such equipment was produced within the Commonwealth country. Thus, when describing such weapons, vehicles, uniforms and equipment, I have deliberately included information and photographs of as many of these gallant Commonwealth warriors as possible, as a small tribute to the immense part they all played in securing victory. The numbers serving in these various armies were just about equal to those who served from Great Britain, namely, 4½–5 million men and women, including a staggering 2½ million from India, the largest volunteer army in history.

Victory in Europe! Some cheerful 'Desert Rats' display a battle-won trophy on VE-Day. (Tank Museum)

OVERSEAS SERVICE

The need for regular soldiers 'Empire-wide' had been resolved in peacetime by the 'linked battalion' system. One battalion, known as the Foreign Service Battalion, was always abroad – up to eighteen years of foreign service was not unusual – while a second battalion, the Home Service Battalion, remained in the UK, being fed with drafts from the Regimental Depot and sending drafts to the battalion abroad, as and when needed. Within the Indian Army there was one British battalion in every Indian brigade, a policy that had been instituted following the 1857 mutiny. Fortress garrisons, such as Malta and Gibraltar, were similarly manned by Foreign Service Battalions. In the rest of the colonial and mandated territories, the

forces were maintained by the principle of having a nucleus of British troops (largely for training purposes) with native levies recruited and built up around them. Most were highly efficient, but inadequately armed, and all had proved their bravery in the First World War.

THE 1944 ARMY

In describing the uniform, weapons, vehicles and equipment of the British Army I have decided, in the main, to base this book on the army that emerged as a main combatant in NW Europe. This is deliberately at variance with the *Handbook on the British Army 1943* (TM 30–410), which was produced by the US Army early in 1943 to give an overall

The Glad Hand for Montgomery. A young worker breaks through from the crowd to shake Monty's hand during his visit to Ministry of Supply factories before D-Day, March 1944. (Author's Collection)

picture of the British Army for their troops coming over for the Second Front. Although an excellent primer, this manual, as previously stated, understandably gave a rather old-fashioned picture of the British forces and did not include some of its important newer weapons – such as the 17 pdr a tk gun and the PIAT (Projector Infantry Anti-Tank) light a tk weapon. Armoured fighting vehicle coverage was also out of date, with the obsolete 'Queen of the Desert', the Matilda II being included. In line with most of the Allied armies, the British used a large range of Lend-Lease items from the USA. These have been mentioned but not described as full details can be found in the companion volume the *US Army Handbook 1939–1945* (The History Press, 1997).

CHAPTER 2

MOBILIZATION AND TRAINING

MAKING A CITIZEN ARMY

At the outbreak of war the British Army comprised the Regular Army and the TA, to which was being added the conscripted manpower. Initially, this was as a result of the Military Training Act of April 1939, which was aimed directly at creating the five extra TA divisions of AA Command. In the UK, the army was organized into eight geographic commands and districts (see Chapter 3), within which were a number of regular and territorial divisions, most of which were needed to form the British Expeditionary Force (BEF) that would cross the Channel in September 1939. Added to this were of course the regular units spread throughout the Empire, but they were miniscule when compared with the vast conscripted armies of the continental powers like Germany and France. The nation had to be turned swiftly into an 'armed camp', a vast training machine had to be organized, equipped and then put into action to deal with the ever increasing flood of recruits that full conscription brought in.

TRAINING POLICY

'Training is a wide subject and its necessity to an army in peace and war is unquestioned. However well-equipped, however perfect the plan, an army will not succeed unless the officers and men which it comprises are well trained both individually and as a body.'

This is the opening sentence of *Training in the Army*, which was to have been published as a volume in the series of British official histories of the Second World War, but was only ever produced in draft form. Nevertheless, it does outline in considerable detail how all forms of training were carried out. In its opening pages the fundamental statement is made that there is nothing to equal actual engagement with the enemy for learning the best way to fight: 'Everything else is make-believe. It follows therefore that the more practically and realistically troops are taught when they are not fighting the better they will perform when they are, and the impact of battle will be less strange to them.' Although this was fully appreciated from the outset, it was initially hampered by the shortage of arms and equipment.

Post Dunkirk, a new conception of realistic training also began to appear under the name of 'Battle Drill' (more fully covered later) although this was not officially adopted until mid-1942. The Battle School at Barnard Castle was then transformed into a School of Infantry, while a separate School of Advanced Handling and Fieldcraft was taken over by the War Office from Western Command. CinC Home Forces was charged after Dunkirk with the dual tasks of defending Great Britain against a probable invasion and of preparing an army to become an invasion force itself.

One of the many continuing problems on Britain's tiny crowded islands was to find sufficient and appropriate accommodation and ground for housing and practising a large army. Military camps, barracks and installations were initially few and scattered, while there was neither the space nor the time to build vast camps as was possible in the USA, with ranges and training areas on the doorstep. So hotels and private houses were requisitioned to make do until more camps could be built. However, there were never enough and it was a policy of 'make do', which was very expensive on the manpower needed to run the requisite scattered administrative facilities.

During the latter part of 1942 there were enormous changes. The mood of the country was now on the offensive and the tempo and spirit of training changed to make trainees, as the War Office history puts it, 'more offensively minded', the main difficulty, initially anyway, being how to deal realistically with all that was required by a modern army in the field, when the once-proud BEF had been evacuated from Dunkirk and to all intents and purposes no longer existed.

Pamphlets The Directorate of Military Training (DMT) also had the unenviable task of writing the pamphlets for use by not only the training organization but also the army as a whole. It is very easy to work out the ideal sequence – fight a battle, discover what has been learnt from it, write it all down, then print and distribute the findings, together with the procedure to be followed. Thus those having to fight future battles will benefit from the lessons as to what to do and what not to do. As one can imagine, this was extremely difficult to achieve, although many pamphlets were indeed written and issued, and proved extremely valuable, but inevitably mistakes were made.

General Training

Primary Training Centres and Wings

Formed under the aegis of the Director of Military Training (MT 2) and later known as the General Service Corps, which came

Fighting fit and fit to fight! Assault course training was a feature of Primary Training at PTCs. (Author's Collection)

into being in June 1942, it was responsible for most General Military Training (GMT) at Primary Training Centres (PTC). It was at these PTCs that recruits received their initial six weeks basic infantry training, to give them a comprehensive grounding in general military subjects such as drill, rifle and pistol shooting, PT, gas training, elementary map reading and tactics. Recruits were also tested by a 'personnel selection board', who decided for which of the arms of the Service each recruit was best suited. Requirements did not always match 'first choices', so recruits might well go to a second or even third choice. Some received this training in Primary Training Wings (PTW) attached to Corps Training Centres however; whether at PTC or PTW, the syllabus (devised by the War Office) was

Officers of the Coldstream Guards on a TEWT (Tactical Exercise Without Troops) at Fleet's Corner, Dorset, in March 1941. (IWM – H 8480)

common to all. Details of Tests of Elementary Training (TOETs), which were common to all arms, are given in Annex 'A' to this chapter.

OFFICER TRAINING

The rapid expansion of the army meant that potential officers had to be selected and trained urgently. At first, the policy was to create numerous small officer cadet units all over the country, where the emphasis was placed more on technical efficiency and physical endurance rather than on character and leadership. After two years, however, it was found that officer production units had to become more homogeneous and were better controlled by a common doctrine from one military training branch in the War Office. Potential Officers (PO) would usually

be selected, at the Corps Training Centre stage and sent to a War Office Selection Board (WOSB). If selected, a PO would then go to a pre-OCTU (Officer Cadet Training Unit) where a final decision was made. A PO could spend up to nine weeks there or be sent to OCTU after a week. Others, deemed unsuitable at any time, would be Returned to Unit (RTU). The OCTU course length varied according to the degree of technicality; for example, at an Infantry OCTU it was seventeen weeks, while at the RE OCTU it was thirty weeks.

Staff Training The enforced expansion also led to a shortage of trained staff officers so more had to be produced in a hurry. However, it was quickly realized that time did not allow the course to be as long as

PT was also an important part of training for war. And once troops were abroad – like these in Egypt – they had to get themselves acclimatized. (IWM – E225)

'Tough Tactics' in action. APTC staff of the Eighth Army taught the soldiers unarmed combat. This photo also gives a good close-up of the 'sword' bayonet for the SMLE rifle. (Author's Collection)

Gas training went hand-in-hand with other training, although this looks suspiciously like a posed photograph! (Author's Collection)

prewar, so merely the essentials were taught. This worked well in practice and students with ability soon excelled. There were three Staff Colleges – at Camberley, Haifa (Palestine) and Quetta (India) – but no Senior Staff College nor Combined Services Staff College, both of which would probably have been an advantage, while a common form of Staff Duties (SD)[1] between the Services did not come into being until after the war.

TECHNICAL TRAINING

It soon became apparent in some of the more technical arms, such as the RAC, RA and REME, that each should have some form of central training establishment, each commanded by a major general (who later became a deputy director under DMT). Their task was to organize all the training of their particular arm and to use all available instructors and equipment so that the instruction was properly co-ordinated and a common policy maintained throughout their arm.

ARMOURED TRAINING

Undoubtedly, mechanization and the re-equipping of the horsed cavalry with armoured fighting vehicles, together with the expansion of the RTC, produced one of the largest training loads. Prewar, there had been three cavalry training regiments (3rd at Edinburgh, 4th at Colchester and 6th at Maidstone), but these all closed during 1940. Armoured training had taken place at the RTC depot at Bovington, while those cavalry regiments that were in the process of mechanization were being converted by instructors (either RTC or newly trained cavalry) attached to their units. On the outbreak of

war, seven RAC training regiments came into being and were followed by a further four in the first year of the war, including one especially designed to deal with the production of NCOs and POs. A complete list is as follows:

51st Training Regiment (the Cavalry Depot) at Catterick
52nd Training Regiment (the RTR Depot) at Bovington
53rd Training Regiment at Tidworth
54th Training Regiment at Perham Down
55th Training Regiment at Farnborough
56th Training Regiment at Catterick
57th Training Regiment at Warminster
58th Young Soldiers Training Regiment (NCOs and POs) at Bovington
59th, 60th and 61st Training Regiments at Tidworth

Initially, they were spread around the country from Bovington to Catterick and Barnard Castle. However, from 1942 onwards, all were gradually brought north and centered on Catterick, which was also the location of the RAC Centre from 1943. For example, the 54th went to Barnard Castle and the 57th to Catterick. This was done to make room for the mass of Allied troops who would be concentrating in the south prior to D-Day. Towards the end of the war (May–August 1945) numbers were naturally cut down until only the following remained:

54th (armoured regiment)
57th (armoured regiment)
59th (armoured car)
61st (armoured regiment)
Recce Training Centre – now became the 62nd Training Regiment RAC, all in the Catterick–Barnard Castle area.

Army Armoured Fighting Vehicles School (AAFVS) Coupled with the setting up of training regiments there was a huge

1. Staff Duties; that is, the way in which the Staff carried out all their work; for example, writing documents, undertaking Staff procedures and generally carrying out their duties on behalf of their commander.

Gen Sir Bernard Montgomery listening to a D&M instructor at the AAFVS, Bovington, during a visit in April 1944. (IWM – H37667)

expansion of the AAFVS at Bovington and Lulworth in order to provide the instructors needed by units and by the new training organization. The AAFVS had replaced the RTC Central Schools in 1937, the new organization comprising Driving & Maintenance (D&M) and Wireless Wings at Bovington and a Gunnery Wing at Lulworth. The general training pattern that emerged in the thirties was governed by the fact that the RTC units manned the heavily armoured 'I' tanks for infantry support, together with the medium tanks for the medium tank brigades, while the cavalry crewed the armoured cars, light tanks and six-wheeled trucks for use in the reconnaissance and protection roles. Problems were compounded by the

multiplicity of types of AFV (for example, thirty-five different types of AFV were taught at the AAFVS between 1939 and 1945), guns and equipment in service, plus a desperate shortage of accommodation. The training was initially carried out using largely the reserves of dedicated, trained officers and men that the RTC (now the RTR) had built up in peacetime, thanks to its inherently sound and thorough methods of instruction.

At the RAC Training Regiments recruits received a 24-week concentrated course that prepared them to be able to take their place as trained crewmen in field units. Men were trained as drivers, gunners, wireless operators, driver mechanics, fitters, electricians, clerks and storemen, in the required proportions

Potential tank drivers learn the ropes, as well as the tricky job of keeping their footing on a tiny light tank, on the Bovington training area in Dorset. (IWM – H266)

Mobile reconnaissance troops of the Northumberland Fusiliers on training, driving through a Dorset village in 1939. (IWM – H3686)

Churchill tanks on battle manoeuvres on Salisbury Plain. (IWM – BH 15693)

as laid down by the War Office. Their first eight weeks were taken up by GMT, as at PTCs, and introductory lessons in D&M. At the end of this period of GMT, they were earmarked for a trade, but before starting a detailed training course everyone was given three more weeks of D&M plus a similar period of elementary gunnery. The aim of this extra training was so that they could, in an emergency, join a tank crew, no matter what their basic trade. After this, drivers did six more weeks driving, gunners six weeks advanced gunnery, while the remainder went to their respective trade schools. The last four weeks of the course were devoted to collective training in which, with the aid of lectures, sand-table and outdoor exercises, they learnt about the functions and handling of RAC units.

ARTILLERY TRAINING

Training Regiments At the outbreak of war, four field, three anti-tank, four signal and one survey regiments were formed. To these were added twenty-two of the existing RA militia depots, four of which, each training 840 field artillery personnel, became three field training regiments and one medium/heavy training regiment. AA personnel in nine militia training depots (each had a capacity of 705 militiamen) were converted to six

Potential tank gunners training on an indoor pellet range at Catterick, North Yorkshire, October 1940. (Author's Collection)

Bofors gun crews practise against a flight of Bristol Blenheim light bombers, somewhere in the UK. (IWM – H146)

HAA and three LAA training regiments. In addition, there were four searchlight training regiments, each of which had 1,203 men under training. The total in 1939 then stood at thirty training regiments as follows:

8 Field	6 HAA
1 Medium/Heavy	3 LAA
3 Anti-Tank	4 Searchlight (S/L)
4 Signals	1 Survey

Their task was to train reinforcements to keep pace with normal wastage and to supply the needs of new units. However, in 1940 the need for more AA and S/L units caused a change of function in many training regiments – one HAA, LAA and S/L training regiments trained reinforcements, the rest, with ever increasing additions, trained new units. Each training regiment now trained 600 men for one month of basic training and, at the same time, gave four-week refresher courses for officers and NCOs from existing operational regiments. In addition, there was a growing demand for extra personnel to man coast artillery units, and four new training regiments were formed. By the end of 1940, there was a total of sixty RA training regiments.

In 1941 the AA Training Establishment (AATE) took over responsibility for AA training from commands. Fifty-four training units were formed. The introduction of ATS into HAA units led to the formation of the first mixed training regiment (HAA); these were later increased to seven. By September 1943 some 200,000 reinforcements had passed through the AATEs and 250 AA

Training continued in other theatres – such as these soldiers of the BEF keeping on their toes, training on their Bren LMG. (IWM – F3704)

batteries and 40 regiments had been converted from infantry battalions to AA. In addition, the mobile and battle training organization had dealt with 100 HAA and 90 LAA regiments. In early 1942 an AA Mobilization and Training Centre was formed to provide mobile training for AA regiments from AA Command who were in the process of mobilizing for overseas. Also in 1942 it was decided that all R Signals personnel in AA signal sections would be replaced by RA personnel. By 1943 all training organizations were fully functioning, a special feature of the year being the training of young artillerymen (aged 17½–18) who had enlisted voluntarily. They were given an extended period of corps training to turn them out as either efficient signallers, specialists or gunner drivers, or as potential officers or NCOs with an all-round knowledge of the duties of a field artilleryman. By the summer of 1943 Air Defence Great Britain had reached its peak and there was no longer a need for AA training regiments to train new units. A shortage of manpower occurred in 1944 and this caused a decrease in the number of training establishments, so that by April there were only twenty-four training regiments. The shortage was offset by reductions in AA commitments and the posting in of large intakes from the RN and RAF for retraining, while coast artillery personnel were retrained as a tk gunners in order to form a reserve for NW Europe. A further reorganization in training regiments took place in 1945, to deal with increasing field and decreasing AA requirements. From April three training regiments were involved entirely in training infantry personnel, while another became a mountain training regiment. By the end of the war there were thirteen training regiments – two field, one field/medium/heavy, one HAA, one self-propelled, one driver, three signal, one specialist RA, one specialist mixed and two coast.

The main RA instructor training establishments were:

School of Artillery   Established at Larkhill in 1919. After an initial depletion of staff to meet outside demands, the school grew continually so that by 1943 its war establishment was over 2,000 and it could train 590 officers and 700 ORs at any one time as instructors. It comprised an HQ, Gunnery, Equipment, Tactics, Air and Survey Wings, a Radar Section and a Photographic Research Branch.

School of AA Artillery   Originally at Biggin Hill, it moved to Manorbier in September 1939. It comprised Gunnery, Radar and Searchlight Wings. In 1940, as a result of trials to test the suitability of women for employment on AA instruments and firing guns, it was responsible for the subsequent formation of mixed AA regiments. The total number of students who passed through the school during the war was 29,638.

Coast Artillery School   Located at Shoeburyness. By 1942 it comprised Gunnery, Searchlight, Wireless (Radar) and Administrative Wings plus a Workshop and a Coast Training Regiment. With the decreased threat of invasion, its training load diminished to under 50 per cent.

RA MT School   Initially at Lydd, it moved to Rhyl in May 1940. By 1944 it comprised two wings – Mechanical Traction Wing and Workshop Wing. One of its main functions was to produce instructors for all types of vehicles including basic tank and SP training. Its total wartime output was 3,800 officer and 8,000 OR instructors and 3,700 MT tradesmen.

School of Aircraft Recognition   Established near Bishop's Stortford, it moved to Deepcut in 1944. By the end of the war over 4,000 instructors had been trained here.

Engineer Training

School of Military Engineering (SME)

Prewar, the SME at Chatham was located in barracks that did not allow much room for expansion. Its main role was the supplementary training of young officers during and after their Cambridge course (RE officers were all sent to Cambridge University prewar after leaving the RMA, for a two-year degree course in Mechanical Science). Other courses were run for regular officers and NCOs in heavy bridging and various field engineering subjects, while summer courses were run for the TA. In 1939 the SME expanded the number and scope of its courses; a new MT School was opened (210 officers attended courses there in 1940). A large number of field engineering courses were run including some for the infantry and extra bridging courses were added. There were considerable difficulties in finding the necessary instructional staff, with regulars being posted out to field units and the SME having to provide large detachments for the defence of the Thames and Medway area. Subsequently, air raids made satisfactory training impossible, so the SME moved to Ripon in November 1940 and was then able to expand. Capacity was soon doubled despite the difficulties caused by its isolation and a shortage of adequate bridging sites.

The heavy German bombing of the UK

made it necessary to train large numbers of men in the entirely new technique of bomb disposal (680 students on 44 courses in 1942 alone). Bridging courses were brought up to date so as to cover new equipment such as the Bailey bridge, while other new courses included assault engineering, air photographic interpretation, a tk and booby traps. Once the USA entered the war a US attachment was sent to SME and stayed there for over a year. Between July 1942 and December 1943 the highest numbers were trained; a new Infantry Mines Wing was formed together with very large numbers of both field and engineering courses being run, until it became very difficult to obtain suitable men for training, despite special demands on the Ministry of Labour and considerable public advertisement. At the end of 1943 SME establishment was revised to deal with new courses such as draughtsman's and surveyor's clerk (both male and ATS); special courses for infantry pioneer platoon officers and sergeants; mechanical equipment courses; and Bailey bridge special user courses. After May 1945 emphasis on courses was switched to a more Far Eastern basis covering such subjects as improvized bridging, Jeep tracks and air portability.

Corps Training

The immediate problem was dealing with very large numbers of recruits – 100,000 joined the RE in the first twelve months of the war. Fortunately, plans had been prepared for the formation of three extra training battalions (including one for chemical warfare (CW) training) for training of the militia who had begun to arrive in quantity. They opened up and were immediately joined by a fourth to train Lines of Communication (LofC) recruits. The training period had been cut drastically and was fixed at fifteen weeks for field and eleven for LofC, who did not do 'wet bridging'.

Further expansion followed as soon as staff could be found and by April 1940 there were nine training battalions (including three CW and three MT training depots). These units, plus Transportation & Movement Control Training Centres, had a total output of 40,000 recruits per year, so there was still a large deficit who could not be given corps training. This was partly alleviated by forming specialist units direct from civilian firms and employing them in France with the BEF just three weeks after drawing their uniforms and with virtually no military training.

In January 1942 an extra two weeks military training was added to the basic sapper recruit syallabus, bringing the course to seventeen weeks. However, the introduction of the GS Corps in June 1942 altered the training battalion course by cutting out the need for the majority of GMT, so the course was reduced to twelve weeks. Large numbers of skilled men were also transferred from other arms in both 1941 and 1942, as a result of the findings of the Beveridge Committee on the employment of skilled men in the forces. Course structure remained constant in 1942–43, despite heavy intakes (for example, 51,000 trained in 1943 alone), but the shortness of the course made it impossible to train a sapper fully up to the standard of a pioneer. This was partly rectified by the introduction of a four-week continuation training period in the field companies of reserve divisions, while the training battalions concentrated on individual training and the basic essentials of engineer training. However, it was always necessary for overseas theatres to give continuation training peculiar to local conditions before a recruit could be regarded as a fully trained sapper. When RE field units were given wireless, a six-week driver operators course was introduced at the MT Training Depot, to be taken by selected drivers after their basic driver training.

Between 1943 and May 1945 recruit training carried out by corps training units

Mock invasion of South Wales. Mobile units of the invading army are breaking down resistance on the outskirts of a Welsh town in their Morris Commercial C8/GS 4×4, July 1941. (Author's Collection)

was supervised by the Chief Engineer Home Forces. From May 1945 training concentrated on Far Eastern requirements.

TRANSPORTATION TRAINING

On the outbreak of war it quickly became clear that the training facilities at the Railway Training Centre (RTC), Longmoor (which included the 8 miles of the Longmoor Military Railway), was inadequate and in November 1939 a second RTC was formed at Derby making use of the LMS Traffic School and an 11-mile section of a branch line (known as the Melbourne Military Railway). At their peak, both centres catered for a monthly intake of 800 and their combined strength was some 15,000 all ranks. By the summer of 1941 the training load had fallen and so RTC Derby was closed, although the Melbourne Military Railway and Bridging School were retained, while a separate Technical Training and Depot Establishment was set up at Longmoor. In July 1942 the RTC was redesignated the Transportation Training Centre. In 1943 a Port Operating Technical Training Wing was set up at Penarth, then after two moves (to Barrow and Cairnyan) it was finally located at Marchwood near Southampton.

OTHER ENGINEER TRAINING

The Survey Training Centre Formed in 1940, it dealt with all survey training, its total strength averaging 1,000. It was joined in 1942 by an Apprentice Tradesman Boys Company. By December 1943 survey training was concentrated temporarily on the particular tasks likely to be met during the coming invasion.

Mine warfare As the use of mines grew and grew, mine training for all arms became well nigh impossible, especially as no comprehensive pamphlets existed until the middle of 1943, while by December 1943 so many different types of mines had been found that it became impossible for other arms to learn about them all. The policy was then to divide everyone into three categories: skilled (RE only); semi-skilled (small trained detachments in almost every arm); and unskilled (the remainder). The training was assisted by the fact that it was no longer necessary to have training battalions to teach CW, which, in July 1943, became an all-arms responsibility.

Bailey bridging Seventy sets of model Bailey bridge were produced at the start of 1944 and proved most successful for training as long as there was sufficient for every man to have at least three bays of bridge to train with. It was found possible to save an enormous amount of practical training work by using these models.

Hardening training The evacuation of almost all wounded personnel from BAOR to the UK produced another problem, namely the giving of hardening training to the lightly wounded in order to enable them to return to active duty. A six-week course was therefore run with the field companies of 55 (West Lancs) and 61 Divisions, both in UK, to harden them and bring them up to date with latest practice.

SIGNALS TRAINING

School of Signals Before the war, signal training was concentrated at Catterick – the School of Signals, a training battalion and a depot battalion. The School of Signals was part of the Signal Training Centre (STC), an army school directly under the War Office, existing for two main reasons: to provide higher technical training for officers and NCOs of Royal Signals, and to train officers and NCOs of all other arms as unit signal instructors. It played no part in training recruits. Although its commitments were increased considerably once war was declared, no major effort was made to expand the school between 1939 and 1942, while the increased use of wireless throughout the army as a whole meant that more time had to be devoted to Regimental Signalling Instructors Courses and less to the scope of courses in the Royal Signals Wing. By 1942 this had been reduced to just five courses: officers advanced line; officers advanced wireless; NCO ditto; and Foreman of Signals.

A Tactics Wing was created to give both senior officers and company commanders a clear understanding of the tactical handling of a force in the field and the purpose for which communications were required by commanders at varying levels. Considerable expansion followed in 1943, including the work of the newly created Publications Section. In the Regimental Wing, where courses were divided into different categories, major expansion took place and there were many changes. For example, Category 'A' had been Cavalry and this had been transferred to the RAC School at Bovington. Later, its place was taken by Category 'D', which handled the Reconnaissance Corps personnel after its creation. A new Category 'A' was formed to cover students from RA (A tk, AA and LAA), RE and REME. The number of students handled on courses now exceeded 4,000 and extra accommodation had to be provided. There was also the continual problem of obtaining modern equipment and transport for instructional purposes, due to the ever growing demand by units of 21 Army Group who were fighting the battles. Another problem was the need for instructors to become familiar with new equipment before they were called upon to instruct on it – very often, a new wireless set arrived only a few days before the beginning of a course! The number of new courses constantly required can be judged by the fact that between January and August 1944 they were called upon to create nine new courses to meet the urgent operational requirements of 21 Army Group. An entirely new responsibility also emerged during this period, namely carrying out user trials on newly designed equipment and the emergency fitting-up of special Signals vehicles urgently required by 21 Army Group (including ACVs).

Another extremely important matter that required much effort was to standardize signals training throughout the army, especially with regards to voice procedure. As with the other corps, post-1944, there was a change-over of training to put more emphasis on the special needs of warfare in the Far East.

Signal Training Units

Between 1939 and 1942 the Royal Signals grew from some 34,000 – of which only 10,000 were regular officers and soldiers – to approximately 150,000 all ranks. In the first month of the war the corps training organization expanded to three STCs, comprising eleven battalions and two OCTUs, followed by the formation of a special operators training battalion in March 1940. A third holding battalion joined No. 2 STC in June 1940 and also formed that month were a special NCO training battalion and a Railway Signals Training Battalion (disbanded the following year); two special battalions to train artillery signal sections were formed in October 1940; and in January 1942 No. 5 Operators Training Battalion was formed to cope with the continued expansion. In July 1942, following the formation of the GSC, as in other arms the three depot battalions vanished and in fact became Nos 1 and 6 PTC. Then, three months later, the whole training organization was reshuffled, the 'BRICK' system of training being adopted. This was all the more necessary because of the technical advances made in telecommunications equipment as the war progressed, while the general mechanization of the army also had its effect on the signals training problem. Wireless sets and line equipment became more and more complicated, so technicians needed longer in training.

As with the RA, ATS personnel were introduced into signals training in October 1942, but the numbers were small compared with the ATS trained in the ATS Signal Training School, which had been formed as early as October 1940 and had grown considerably by 1945.

To summarize, the training establishments needed to start the general expansion of the corps were just not there when war began, while the requirement for training cadres rose almost immediately to its maximum on the outbreak of war. Fortunately, the slow build-up in the West, before Germany attacked, came to Britain's aid. Undoubtedly, had it not been for the 'breathing space' provided by the 'Phoney War'[2] it would have been impossible to catch up.

2. The 'Phoney War' is the name given to the strange period of inaction on the Western Front, from after the Germans conquered Poland (completed by 21 September 1939) until they invaded France and the Low Countries (10 May 1940).

Infantry Training

All-Arms Basic Training

Before September 1919 all infantry training took place in the infantry regimental depots and usually lasted some four months. These depots were transformed into Infantry Training Centres (ITC) on the outbreak of war. Officers received training at the Small Arms School at Hythe, but there was no School of Infantry, indeed this was not formed until the end of 1942. In addition to its own training tasks, the infantry had the responsibility of providing all-arms basic training – namely, six weeks basic training at PTCs or in the PTWs of ITCs. This was a vast undertaking.

Infantry Schools

The School of Infantry Formed at the end of 1942 from the GHQ Battle School, which the CinC Home Forces had set up at the start of that year. It taught three main courses: platoon commanders (28 days); company commanders (21 days); occasionally COs courses (21 days). Initially, instructors were selected from promising young infantry officers, none of whom had battle experience. However, by 1945 some 75 per cent had seen combat and most came straight back to the school from the field. There were also liaison staff who visited operational areas and brought back valuable information for application to training. Some 4,500 officers and 10,000 WOs and NCOs were trained there. Initially, it was located at Barnard Castle, then in early 1945 it moved to Warminster, where it amalgamated with the NCOs School from High Legh. In February 1943 the Infantry NCOs Classification Centre began at Bodmin, with the aim of classifying the large number of surplus NCOs in the army. Mainly TA, these personnel held substantive rank, but could not be found employment in the unit because of their apparent short-comings. Those showing promise were found suitable useful employment, while those who failed were 'disposed of elsewhere'. Having completed its job, the centre was closed at the end of March 1944, then turned into the Infantry NCOs School, which was transferred first to Gravesend then to High Legh. During 1944 an 'NY' Cadet Company was formed with the purpose of giving extra military knowledge to NCOs who had been graded 'not yet suitable' for commissioning by WOSBs.

Battle Drill. With so many men to train and so few instructors with any experience, the tendency was to produce drills for all tactical situations. This policy initially served its purpose in that it enabled students to be taught to do something rather than nothing when faced with a problem. However, in time the drills tended to become the masters and not the servants, commanders being inclined to act blindly and without first appreciating the situation. For security reasons, no special activities were carried out in connection with D-Day, although all senior airborne commanders did so before the Arnhem operation.

All-arms training. Demonstration troops at the School of Infantry included an infantry battalion, an armoured squadron, a field battery, an engineer platoon and a machine gun company. These were used for day-to-day demonstrations, while the school also had call on a complete field regiment RA and an RAF squadron.

The Small Arms School (SAS) Located at Hythe, with an additional wing at Bisley for training snipers, the SAS taught a wide variety of weapons, including: 2 in mortar, PIAT, machine carbine (e.g. Sten), numerous grenades, Lewis gun (re-introduced), Ross rifle (Home Guard), Vickers MMG, 20 mm AA (Oerlikon, Hispano and Polsten). Aircraft

Tank recognition training using dummy tank periscopes to give the students a more realistic view of the targets. (IWM – UK 328)

and tank recognition were also taught, while a special AA wing was eventually formed.

Infantry Heavy Weapons School The Netheravon Wing of SAS became the Heavy Weapons School, where the .303 Vickers MMG and the 3 in mortar were taught in separate wings at the outbreak of war. In 1942 they started teaching the 2 pdr a tk gun, which was replaced in due course by the 6 pdr. In October 1942 a new mortar wing opened to teach the 4.2 in mortar.

Advanced Handling and Fieldcraft School Established in North Wales in August 1942 to teach officers and senior NCOs the prac-

tical use of infantry weapons (including 3 in mortars and carriers), in addition it also taught fieldcraft. A sniper wing and a mountain training wing were added in 1944–45.

ITCS AND PTCS
Before the outbreak of war there were sixty-four regimental depots, equipped to handle a total intake of 18–19,000 recruits a year but never actually having to deal with such numbers. In addition, they were mainly located in large towns without any access to suitable training areas. It was appreciated that a more flexible system would be needed in wartime, and in 1941 the number of ITCs was reduced, the regimental ITCs

Men of the 5th Northants of 3rd Inf Div after their escape from France, training hard with Bren carriers near Christchurch, 12 March 1941. (IWM – H7972)

being merged into twenty-five numbered ITCs. Furthermore, as there were certain basic military subjects common to the early training of recruits of all arms, it was decided that all recruits should be enlisted into the GS Corps and carry out a common syllabus of six weeks primary training, during which selection procedure would take place to determine the type of employment for which the recruit was best suited. PTCs were formed in July 1942, where recruits spent their first six weeks; if selected for the infantry they would then be posted to the parent ITC to carry out infantry corps training. This system continued unchanged until the end of the war, and at its peak, during 1944, nearly 200,000 recruits were being trained at ITCs and PTCs.

RESERVE DIVISIONS

Formed in December 1942, the function of reserve divisions was to hold personnel who had completed corps training before drafting overseas. The aim was to relieve the field army at home as far as possible of draft commitments, so that it could be built up to establishment and be able to undergo uninterrupted intensive training. There were initially four such divisions: 48 and 77 Divisions in Northern Command; 76 Division in Eastern Command; and 80 Division in Western Command. In 1943 they were reduced to three, 77 Division becoming 77 (Holding) Division with a special role of re-classifying men such as those who had returned from overseas under the six-year rule, returned POW, etc. In September 1944 they were again reorganized and redesignated as follows: 38 Infantry (Reserve) Division took over from 80 Division; 47 Infantry (Reserve) Division took over from 78 Division; 48 Infantry (Reserve) Division and 45 Infantry Holding Division took over from 77 Division. This organization remained until the end of the war.

The Royal Army Service Corps (RASC)

Early in the war a wide range of schools and specialist training establishments were developed and controlled through a variety of headquarters, so there was a lack of co-ordination below War Office level. It was not until November 1943 that the HQ RASC Training Establishment was formed at Aldershot. Initially, it controlled the Officers' Training School, the Waterborne Training Centre, No. 14 Training Battalion (Artificers), the Specialist Transport Training School and three Supply Technical Training Centres. To these were added the WOs and NCOs School, the Petroleum Technical Training Centre and No. 12 Composite Training Battalion (including Clerks, Animal Transport and Boys Training Companies). Initial driver training remained the responsibility of No. 3 Training Brigade and No. 2 Driver Training Centre, both under direct War Office control.

Prewar, the RASC training units comprised the RASC Driving School and the Heavy Repair Shop (for artificer training) both at Feltham, the Militia Training Battalion at Crookham and the RASC Training Centre at Aldershot. In September 1939 this organization was superseded by the formation of Nos 1 and 2 Training Centres, which later became Nos 1 and 2 Training Brigades, RASC. A month later a number of Driver Training Centres were formed that became

No. 3 Training Brigade. Four RASC Mobilization Centres were also formed early in the war to control unit mobilization.

The Royal Army Ordnance Corps (RAOC)

TRAINING BATTALIONS
Five RAOC training battalions were formed at which the initial regimental training of all recruits was carried out, to start with by enlisting the services of recalled officers and NCOs. However, technical instruction was not so easy because of a lack of qualified instructors, the untried Ordnance Field Organization and an absence of instructional literature. By the end of 1940, besides the training battalions and OCTU, the Training Establishment RAOC consisted of an HQ and various specialized branches that covered the entire RAOC spectrum: A – Ordnance procedure, including WOs course and assistant instructors; B – ammunition, training of officers as inspecting ordnance officers, training ammunition examiners and ammunition storemen; D – MT, dealing with maintenance and driving; F – engineer and signal stores and armaments; G – MT clerks, storemen, drivers and training of field parks; H – laundry officers training and storemen for base and mobile laundries; R – regimental training for officers and ORs.

Examples of RAOC Training Establishments:

The RAOC Training Establishment Air raids forced it to move from Portsmouth to Leicester in September 1940; later it moved to Derby.

RAOC Officers' School Many new officers had come into the RAOC from civil life rather than from the ranks and were therefore ignorant of the army, of the technical working of the corps and of Staff Duties, so an officers' training school was formed at Rushton Hall, Kettering, where large numbers of officers – mostly ordnance mechanical engineers – were given general courses similar to OCTU. In August 1941 the accommodation at Leicester was much enlarged so a major increase in officer training was possible.

THE CHANGE TO REME
By far the largest change to affect the RAOC came in August 1942, when all RAOC (E) personnel left for Aborfield to join with other Ordnance Mechanical Engineering instructional units to form what ultimately became the REME Training Establishment. In addition, that autumn all primary training was centralized so the five training battalions were changed, three becoming PTCs, one a second Clerks & Storemen's School (a third being formed at the same time), while the fifth became a holding battalion.

In general terms, RAOC training became more specialized as the war progressed, new courses being run and new training establishments being formed to cope. One of the most notable achievements of the Training Establishment was the production of an excellent series of lecture precis and handbooks on equipment and weapons. To give some idea of the size of the training load, during the war period the RAOC Training Establishment trained a total of 12,200 officers and 320,450 ORs.

ROYAL ELECTRICAL & MECHANICAL ENGINEERS (REME)

Until 1 October 1942 the inspection, maintenance and repair of the majority of the army's technical equipment was the responsibility of the RAOC (E). REME was then formed and these tasks were henceforward

undertaken entirely by the new corps, under the direction of DMT. In September 1939 the strength of the RAOC (E) was 300 officers and 1,800 ORs. By the summer of 1945 when the peak strength of REME was reached, there were 7,500 officers and 160,000 in the new corps.

REME TRAINING ESTABLISHMENTS
In 1943, in addition to the Training Establishment at Aborfield, there was: the Army Radio School and No. 2 Radio Mechanical School; an Armoured Training Centre; the Officers' Training School; and three Technical Training Centres (Nos 1, 4 and 11). Certain command changes took place in 1944, with the result that by the end of the year HQ REME Training Establishment (commanded by a brigadier) had under its direct command: the REME School; the Army Radio School; Technical School; and the other Training Establishments. REME training was probably the most complex of all, as the training of armament artificers shows. They were Staff Sergeants, specially selected Class I tradesmen with a sound practical engineering background. They were always in demand and supply was never equal – hardly surprising when one considers that no fewer than ten *different* categories were required to cope with field artillery weapons, AA, vehicles (both motor vehicles and AFVs), wireless, radio, electrical (that is, electrical equipment, power installations and plant), AA instruments, field instruments and coast defence instruments. Courses on average were of thirty weeks duration.

OTHER TRAINING UNITS

These included:

(a). **Reserve divisions** As already mentioned under 'Infantry', for most of the time there were three, formed in late 1942 for training purposes only, so they were not field divisions but rather a mixture of units of different arms whose purpose was to give five weeks minor collective/crew training to all those who had completed their time at CTCs, before they went to their field units.

(b). **Holding units** These held men until they were needed as reinforcements to the field army.

(c). **Mobilization centres** These did for the technical arms what holding units did for the others.

(d). **Conversion training unit** Formed during the last two years of the war to train men converted from one arm or service to another.

LIAISON WITH DOMINIONS AND ALLIES

Close liaison was maintained on training matters with India and the other dominions and with the Allies, in particular the USA. Training took place abroad, not only in these countries but also in the various theatres of war, to acclimatize and adapt the British soldier to new environments and to train him, for example, in jungle warfare – clearly impossible at home. However, nowhere except for India was it necessary to turn raw recruits into fighting soldiers, as this had been done in the UK. The crowded conditions of troopships usually precluded any continuation training, so troops were inclined to forget things. Much of the pioneer work in the training of troops overseas was done in the Middle East, a whole range of schools and training establishments being set up there from 1939 onwards.

ANNEX 'A'

Tests of Elementary Training (TOETs)
(Common to All Arms) – 1943. (26/GS Publications/994)

Weapon or Subject	Nature of test	Details
Rifle	Aiming	Aiming rests used. Three aims at a 4a target at 200 yd. Two aims correct out of three.
	Aiming off	Aiming rests used. Test is to lay off one target's width from a Fig 3 target at 300 yd. Two aims correct out of three.
	Rapid firing	Using cover. Bayonets fixed. On command 'Rapid fire' pupil will fire five rounds at aiming disc held by instructor. Four out of five shots must be correct.
	Firing position	Bayonets fixed. Inspection in positions behind suitable cover.
LMG	Loading	Gun unloaded and one filled magazine. Firer on ground, butt on ground. Magazine in pouch. Test to be completed in 10 sec from command 'load' until left hand returns to butt.
	Aiming and firing	Firer lying behind gun, butt on ground until order to fire given. Gun cocked. Firer given 'Fire' or 'Bursts Fire'. Aiming disc held 1 yd in front of gun. Height of disc varied for each aim. All actions including sight setting must be carried out correctly.

	Immediate action	Object is to test actions of No. 1 when by No. 1 gun stops firing. On first by stoppage he should apply Immediate Action (IA). On second stoppage gas regulator must be altered by using combination feed tool from wallet. Forty-five sec.
	Handling gun	No. 1 will be tested in handling the LMG behind various types of cover. No time limit, but serious faults will entail failure.
Anti tank rifle	Magazine filling	Drill cartridges in clips. Empty magazines. 20 sec allowed to fill magazine from word 'Go'. Must be carried out correctly twice out of three times.
	Aiming and firing	As for Practice 2, Part 1 A tk rifle course. Firing with .22 ammo at direct crossing tank. Four shots out of six must be in scoring area of target.
Gas	Oral tests	Three out of four to be answered correctly.
	Inspection tests	Include respirator drill, testing for gas, rolling gas cape. No time limit. Serious mistakes mean failure.
	Standard tests	(a). Student in prone position. Respirator carried as ordered by instructor. Test is to gain protection in 15 sec. (b). Personal decontamination, Parts 1 and 2. Part 1 should take about 5 min, Part 2 about 15 min.

Note: No TOETs are set for Bayonet, Grenades, TMC or SMC

Basic physical efficiency tests	100 yd	Marks	10 – 12 sec	
			8 – 13 sec	
			6 – 14 sec	
			4 – 15 sec	
			2 – 16 sec	
	High jump	Marks	10 – 4 ft 8 in	
			8 – 4 ft 4 in	
			6 – 4 ft	
			4 – 3 ft 8in	
			2 – 3 ft 4in	
	Running long jump	Marks	10 – 16 ft	(to be credited with
			8 – 15 ft	exact jump irrespective
			6 – 13 ft	of take-off position)
			4 – 12 ft	
			2 – 11 ft	
	Heaving 9 lb medicine ball (Assoc football)	Marks	10 – 34 ft	Position – standing feet
			8 – 30 ft	astride, ball in both
			6 – 26 ft	hands in front or above
			4 – 22 ft	body. Start throw by

		2 – 18 ft	bending trunk downward and swing ball down between legs, swing ball forward and release. One swing only.
One mile	Marks	10 – 5 min 30 sec	
		8 – 6 min	
		6 – 6 min 20 sec	
		4 – 6 min 40 sec	
		2 – 7 min	

Classification of results: Special 84 per cent, 1st Class 68 per cent, Standard 48 per cent. Percentage of classification is found by doubling the aggregate marks of the five tests completed. Two attempts allowed on all but running events.

CHAPTER 3

HIGHER ORGANIZATIONS DOWN TO ARMY LEVEL AND ARMS OF THE SERVICE

HIGHER ORGANIZATIONS

HIGH COMMAND

The situation in 1939 was that the very highest level of defence, strategy and planning for the three armed Services (Royal Navy, Army and Royal Air Force) was co-ordinated by the Committee of Imperial Defence (CID), which reported to the Cabinet via the Minister for the Co-ordination of Defence. However, on 1 September 1939 the Prime Minister (Neville Chamberlain) dissolved the CID. Instead, the Minister for the Co-ordination of Defence together with the three armed

Britain's great wartime Prime Minister Winston Churchill at the Yalta Conference, February 1945, with President Franklin D. Roosevelt and Premier Josef Stalin. Under the archway to the left is FM Sir Alan Brooke, the British CIGS from December 1941 for the rest of the war. (US National Archives)

Services ministers were all given seats on the War Cabinet. When Winston Churchill took over in May 1940, he formed an 'Inner War Cabinet', making himself Minister of Defence as well as Prime Minister. Churchill preferred to deal direct with the uniformed heads of the three Services, who together formed the Chief of Staffs Committee. Thus the ministers dealt only with the administrative and organizational matters via their respective ministries, while Churchill and the Service Chiefs dealt with operations.

SUPREME COMMAND
The Supreme Command of the British Army was vested in the Army Council, which was composed of a number of political, civil and military members, totalling seven (later ten) in all:

Political members
Secretary of State for War
Under Secretary of State for War
Parliamentary and Financial Secretary

Military members[1]
Chief of the Imperial General Staff (CIGS) (initially Gen Sir Edmund Ironside, then FM Sir Alan Brooke from December 1941 for the rest of the war)
Adjutant-General to the Forces (AG)
Quartermaster-General to the Forces (QMG)

Civil Service member
Permanent Under Secretary of State for War

All orders were issued in the name of the Army Council rather than by any one individual; the Secretary of State for War, however, was individually responsible for all

1 Later, these were joined by three more officers: the Vice-CIGS (who was responsible for operations, plans, intelligence and training); the Deputy CIGS (organization for war); and the Master General of Ordnance (MGO)

Army business to the War Cabinet. The Army Council transacted its business via the War Office (see chart opposite).

HIGHER ORGANIZATION
At the start of the war, the British Army consisted of the Regular Army, the TA and various reserve forces, divided in general terms into the Home Forces, AA Command, the British Forces in the Middle East, the British Forces in India as well as a considerable number of scattered commands throughout the world. These elements were all commanded from the War Office.

The Home Forces Home Forces had their own CinC with his own GHQ. They consisted of all field force formations in the UK, which were located within the existing peacetime geographic command structure of commands and districts. Initially, there were eight of these main administrative areas: Eastern; Western; Southern; Northern; Scottish; Aldershot (in 1941 renamed South Eastern Command); London; and Northern Ireland Districts (see page 38). In 1944 South Eastern Command disappeared altogether having been swallowed up by Southern Command. Below the command/district level the chain of command went through area, to sub-area, then down to formations. Home Forces were responsible for the defence of the British Isles and initially that meant protecting the country against impending invasion, which fortunately never came. Each of the commands and districts was commanded by a GOC, who had a staff similar in make-up to that of a corps (see Chapter 4), but on a larger scale.

The Home Guard Within the Home Forces there was also the Home Guard. Hastily organized in May 1940 as the Local Defence Volunteers (LDV), it was armed with a mixture of outdated rifles, old fowling pieces, shotguns, even improvised pikes, until a

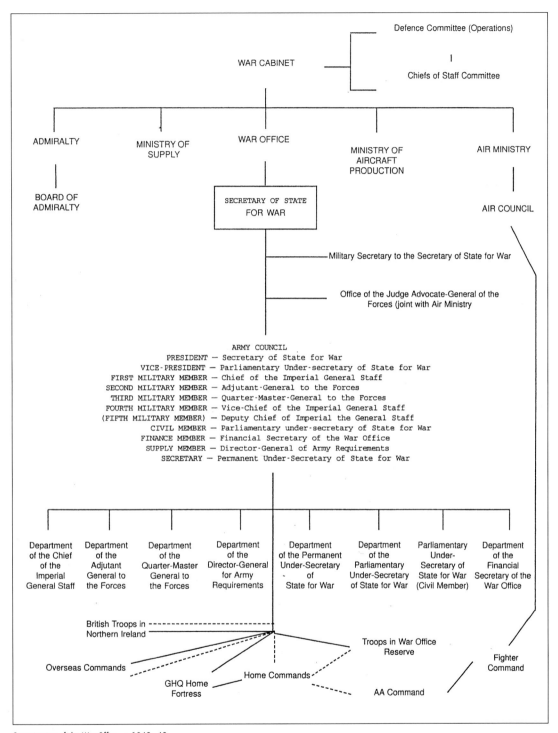

Organization of the War Office, *c.* 1942–43.

Military Commands and Districts, c. 1942.

consignment of half a million 0.30 P 17 Ross rifles arrived from the USA. Although never called upon to fight, 'Dad's Army', as it has since been popularly called, earned a special place for itself in Britain's military history. By November 1941, when the Government introduced military ranks and military discipline into the Home Guard, it numbered between 1½ and 2 million men. Nevertheless, it still consisted basically of volunteer, unpaid, part-time soldiers, formed into units for the local defence of communities, airfields, communi-cations, vital points (such as power stations, bridges, etc.) and for general observation purposes. In the case of invasion the Home Guard would have come to full-time duty. They were equipped generally with infantry weapons – rifles, some automatic weapons, a tk rifles, grenades, submachine guns, etc. Later in the war, the Home Guard not only protected AA sites and coastal artillery but they were also trained to man the AA and coastal guns, thus releasing regular troops for other duties. After D-Day it became clear that

Dad's Army. Men of the Poole Company of the Home Guard. Many are suitably bemedalled from service during the First World War, while others are clearly teenagers. The Home Guard stood down at the end of 1944. (Author's Collection)

the enemy was never likely to be in a position to invade the UK, so the Home Guard ceased to be needed. On 16 September 1944 it was announced that no more men would be directed into Home Guard service and that parades would in future be entirely voluntary. 'Stand Down' came shortly afterwards on 1 November, but was not finally completed until 31 December 1944.

Other Troops The only troops not under command of CinC Home Forces were: AA formations, who were part of AA Command (see Chapter 5); transportation troops held in reserve under direct War Office control; training units and training establishments (unless they were allocated an emergency operational role); those forces in Northern Ireland, who were commanded by the GOC British Troops in Northern Ireland.

The British Expeditionary Force (BEF) The field force troops were basically the regular

and TA divisions that would make up the BEF, which was despatched to France in some haste soon after war was declared. It comprised a total of over 160,000 troops and would be safely transported to France by 27 September 1940, without a single casualty. The CinC was FM Lord Gort, First World War hero and holder of the Victoria Cross (VC), three Distinguished Service Orders (DSO) and the Military Cross (MC). He commanded a force of three corps, together with GHQ troops, LofC troops and various reinforcements that arrived in May–June 1940.

When the men of the BEF returned from Dunkirk to the UK (over 338,000 men were rescued between 29 May and 4 June 1940), command of all British land forces in the UK reverted to GHQ Home Forces, through the Command/District structure already explained.

(a). **Overseas Commands** Overseas, within the spheres of British influence, there were various geographic commands:

HM The King meets his soldiers. King George VI spent many of the wartime days visiting units. Here he inspects men of the BEF in Dorset, prior to them leaving for France in September 1939. The senior officer nearest the camera is Gen Sir Alan Brooke, who commanded II Corps of the BEF before he became CIGS. (IWM – H12)

This immaculate 3 in mortar detachment of the BEF is being inspected at Orchies during the 'Phoney War' by French Gen Georges and FM Lord Gort, 23 April 1940. (IWM – F 3964)

Indomitable members of the BEF on their way to Dunkirk, using a 'borrowed' wheelbarrow to transport their kit. (IWM – F 4712)

GHQ Troops

Royal Armoured Corps
1st Light Armoured Reconnaissance Brigade   each two
2nd Light Armoured Reconnaissance Brigade   regiments
1st Army Tank Brigade (4th and 7th RTR)
plus four cavalry regiments not brigaded.

Royal Artillery
Two RHA regiments, four field regts, eight medium regts, three heavy regts and thee super heavy regts
1st AA Brigade (three AA regts)
2nd AA Brigade (one AA and two LAA regts)
4th AA Brigade (one AA regt and one LAA bty)
5th Searchlight Brigade (two searchlight regts).

Royal Engineers
Five field coys, one field park, one army field survey and three chemical warfare companies
Thirty-eight general construction companies, two road construction, one excavator, four tunneling and one workshop and park company
One field survey depot and two water-boring sections.

Infantry
One infantry battalion   Seven pioneer battalions
Four machine gun battalions   One garrison battalion.

I Corps

1st Division (1st Guards Brigade, 2nd Brigade, 3rd Brigade, each three battalions)
2nd Division (4th, 5th and 6th Brigade each three bns)
48th (South Midland) Division (143rd, 144th and 145th Brigade each three bns)
(Each division had three field regiments and an anti-tank regiment, RA, three field companies and a field park company RE).

Corps troops
Two field regts, two medium regts, an LAA regt, an LAA bty and a survey regt, RA
Three field coys, a field park and a field survey coy RE
Three machine gun battalions.

II Corps

3rd Division (7th Guards Brigade, 8th and 9th Brigade)
4th Division (10th, 11th and 12th Brigade)
5th Division (13th and 17th Brigade) in GHQ reserve on 10th May
50th Division (150th, 151st and 25th Brigade)   (Divisional troops as for I Corps).

Corps troops
Two field regts, two medium regts, an LAA regt and a survey regt, RA
Three field coys, a field park and a field survey coy, RE   Three machine gun battalions.

III Corps

42nd (East Lancashire) Division (125th, 126th and 127th Brigade)
44th (Home Counties) Division (131st, 132nd and 133rd Brigade)   (Divisional troops as for I Corps).

Corps troops
One RHA and one field regt, two medium, one LAA and one survey regt, RA
Three field coys, a field park and a field survey coy, RE   Three machine gun battalions.

Other troops

Formation	Comprised
12th (Eastern) Division	35th, 36th and 37th Brigade
23rd (Northumberland) Division	69th and 70th Brigade
46th (North Midland & West Riding) Division	137th and 138th Brigade
51st (Highland) Division	152nd, 153rd and 154th Brigade
1st Armoured Division	2nd and 3rd Armoured Brigade
52nd (Lowland) Division	155th, 156th and 157th Brigade
20th Guards Brigade	
30th Brigade	

These troops served under a variety of higher formations, *viz:*

Formation	Task
12th Division	Lines of Communication, BEF
23rd Division	GHQ, BEF, II Corps, then II Corps
46th Division	L of C, BEF, then III Corps
51st Division	GHQ, BEF, then II Corps, II Corps, 3 French Army, CQG (French), 9 Fr Corps
1st Armd Division	GHQ, BEF, then 7th and 10th French Army
52nd Division	GHQ, BEF
20th Gds Brigade	defence of Boulogne
30th Brigade	defence of Calais

Outline organization of the BEF (as at 10 May 1940). Source: *The War in France & Flanders 1939–1940*, Appendix I by Major F.L. Ellis (HMSO, 1953) (i). *Middle East Command* (MEC) GHQ was located in Cairo. It initially covered North Africa (Western Desert), East Africa and Syria. In 1942 Iran and Iraq were added (from CinC India).

(ii). *East Africa Command* Formed in August 1941 to cover all troops in the theatre.

(iii). *Persia and Iraq Command (PAIFORCE)* Formed in August 1942.

(iv). *India* GHQ was located in Delhi, under the CinC, who commanded all British and Indian personnel of all three armed Services. He was also the defence member on the Viceroy's executive council with, under him, a War Department (until July 1942 known as the Defence Department), plus three independent army commands (Northern, Eastern and Southern) and Western Independent District. In April 1942 Wavell abolished this ponderous structure, replacing it with three armies (North Western, Eastern and Southern) and a Central Command.

(v). *Malaya Command* Covering Malaya and Singapore, it ceased to exist after Japan's successful conquest in early 1942.

(b). **Armies** Army HQs existed abroad, as and when they were needed, under command of whichever Allied or British GHQ, controlled the particular area:

The CinC India, Gen Sir Claude Auchinleck, inspecting British soldiers who were serving with a West African regiment in Bhopal, March 1944. The picture provides a good close-up of British web equipment, while the soldier shaking hands with the CinC is carrying a 9 mm Sten Machine Carbine Mk 3. (IWM – IND 2953)

HE The Viceroy, FM Lord Wavell visiting forward areas in Burma in January 1945, to confer knighthoods on four generals. Here he invests Lt Gen Slim, the commander of the Fourteenth Army. (IWM – CI 872)

(i). *First Army* Formed for the US/British Operation *Torch* landings in November 1942, then went on into Algeria and French Morocco, then Tunisia, under the overall command of Gen Eisenhower's Allied Forces GHQ.

(ii). *Second Army* Formed in June 1943, took part in the Normandy landings and the NW European campaign, under Gen Eisenhower's Supreme Headquarters Allied Expeditionary Force (SHAEF).

(iii). *Eighth Army* Formed within MEC, replacing the Western Desert Force from September 1941. Took part in operations in North Africa, then Tunisia, Sicily and Italy.

(iv). *Ninth* and *Tenth Armies* Formed within MEC, but never numbered more than a few divisions, never saw combat as a formed body and were used instead to reinforce the Eighth Army.

(v). *Twelfth Army* Formed in May 1945, within Allied Land Forces South East Asia (ALFSEA) to command British troops fighting in Burma.

(vi). *Fourteenth Army* Formed in India in October 1943, under GHQ Delhi, fought in Burma until withdrawn to prepare for the invasion of Malaya, being replaced by the Twelfth Army.

An army consisted of army troops and two or more corps.

(c). **Army Groups** Whenever armies fought alongside one another in a particular campaign or operation it was necessary to form an army group. However, these were mainly Allied HQs. Examples of army groups are:

(i).   *15 Army Group* Formed on 11 July 1943 to command Seventh US Army and Eighth British Army for the invasion of Sicily, then on to the invasion of Italy.
(ii).   *21 Army Group* Formed in the UK on 9 July 1943 to command First Canadian Army and Second British Army for the forthcoming invasion of NW Europe.

An army group comprised GHQ Troops plus two or more armies, with LofCTroops and base installations. Taking 21 Army Group as an example, when they were in NW Europe in August 1944 it was calculated that some 56 per cent of the troops were 'fighting troops' and 44 per cent 'services'. The detailed percentages of the 660,000 personnel involved were as follows:

Fighting troops: RAC – 6 per cent; RA (including AA regiments of the RM) – 18 per cent; RE – 13 per cent; R Signals – 5 per cent; Infantry (including rifle, MG, motor, para and air landing battalions, commandos and glider pilot wings) – 14 per cent = 56 per cent.

Services: RASC – 15 per cent; Pioneer Corps – 10 per cent; REME – 5 per cent; RAMC, AD Corps and QAIMNS – 4 per cent; RAChD, RAOC, RAPC, RAVC, AEC, Int Corps, APTC, ACC, ATS, CMP, MPSC and some 'unspecified' – 10 per cent = 44 per cent.

The Divisional 'Slice' Before D-Day it was estimated that for every division ashore (approximately 16,000 men) there would ultimately be an additional 25,000 men in the theatre in corps, army, GHQ and LofC

troops. For 21 Army Group it was further calculated that this 'slice' would amount to approximately 41,000 men and 8,000 vehicles. Further, it was calculated that it would be accompanied to the Continent by 4,000 RAF personnel.

See Annex 'A' to this chapter for details of the insignia worn by such formations as army groups and armies.

FIELD FORMATIONS
Below army level, command was vested in corps, division, brigade and unit head-quarters. They are dealt with in detail in later chapters. However, within every corps, army and army group there were corps, army and army group troops who were, depending upon circumstances, available for the support of any of the divisions within the theatre of operations for a particular operation or phase of an operation. In order to give some idea of the size of such forces, here is an example of those allocated to 21 Army Group for the campaign in NW Europe, as at 23 May 1944:

RAC – four Armoured Car Regiments (2 HCR, Royals, 11 H and Inns of Court); two Armoured Delivery Regiment; GHQ Liaison Regiment.

RA – one RHA Regiment (4 RHA); four Field Regiments (6, 25, 150 and 191); twenty-one Medium Regiments (7, 9, 10, 11, 13, 15, 53, 59, 61, 63, 64, 65, 67, 68, 72, 77, 79, 84, 107, 121 and 146); four Survey Regiments (4, 7, 9 and 10); four A tk Regiments (62, 73, 86 and 91); five Heavy Regiments (1, 51, 52, 53 and 59); two Super-Heavy Regiments (2 and 3); twenty-two HAA Regiments (8, 86, 90, 98, 99, 103, 105, 107, 108, 109, 110, 111, 112, 113, 115, 116, 118, 121, 146, 165, 174 and 176); twenty-three LAA Regiments (4, 20, 27, 32, 54, 71, 73, 93, 102, 109, 112,

113, 114, 120, 121, 123, 124, 124, 126, 127, 133, 139 and 149).

INF – eight regiments (6 Border, 1 Bucks, 18 DLI, 2 Herts, 5 Kings, 8 Kings, 5 R Berks and the Glider Pilot Regiment).

(Source: Joslen, *Orders of Battle of the Second World War, 1939–1945*, vol. 2 (HMSO, 1960))

ARMS OF THE SERVICE

When taken collectively all branches of the British Army were known as the 'Arms of the Service' The fighting branches were known as 'The Arms', while the administrative branches were called 'The Services'. The principal branches in order of precedence[2] were as follows:

THE ARMS
Household Cavalry (H Cav)
Royal Armoured Corps (RAC)[3]
Royal Regiment of Artillery (RA)
Corps of Royal Engineers (RE)
Royal Corps of Signals (R Sigs)
Infantry Regiments (Inf)

2. All units of the British Army are allocated their place in the Order of Precedence of Corps etc. In general terms the Arms come before the Services, with the Household Cavalry (H Cav) taking precedence, *except* when the Royal Horse Artillery (RHA) have their guns on parade, when they will always be right of the line and march ahead of the H Cav.

3. On 4 April 1939 Mr Leslie Hore-Belisha, the Secretary of State for War, announced in the House of Commons that the newly mechanized regiments of the Cavalry were to combine with the RTC battalions in a single corps, to be known as the Royal Armoured Corps (RAC) with precedence immediately before the RA

Reconnaissance Corps (Recce Corps) – later became an integral part of the RAC
Army Air Corps (AO 21 of 1942) – see Annex 'B'

Details of the wartime Regular Regiments of the H Cav, RAC and Inf are contained in Annex 'B' to this chapter.

THE SERVICES
Royal Army Chaplains Department (RAChD)
Royal Army Service Corps (RASC)
Royal Army Medical Corps (RAMC)
Royal Army Ordnance Corps (RAOC)
Royal Electrical and Mechanical Engineers (REME)
Royal Army Pay Corps (RAPC)
Royal Army Veterinary Corps (RAVC)
Army Educational Corps (AEC)
Army Dental Corps (AD Corps)
Pioneer Corps (P Corps)
Intelligence Corps (IC)
Army Catering Corps (ACC)
Army Physical Training Corps (APTC)
Corps of Military Police
Military Provost Staff Corps (MPSC)
Queen Alexandra's Imperial Nursing Service (QAIMNS)
Auxiliary Territorial Service (ATS)
Officers' Training Corps (OTC)
General Service Corps (GSC)

It should be noted that the term 'Royal' has always been given to a regiment or corps as a special mark of favour for distinguished service. In addition, in most cases, the monarch (in the Second World War this was His Majesty King George VI) would then become the Colonel-in-Chief.

Annex 'A': Insignia

Examples of British GHQ, Army Group and Army Formation Signs

Formation	Sign	Remarks
GHQ Home Forces		Yellow winged lion in two yellow frames, in a red and blue circle, red half uppermost	
GHQ India		Five-pointed yellow star in a red and blue rectangle, red half uppermost	Represented the 'Star of India'
Central Mediterranean Force (CMF)		Shield with 'Torch of Freedom' rising from the waves	
Allied Forces HQ (Algiers & Naples)		White 'AF' on a blue background, within red circle	
Supreme Headquarters Allied Expeditionary Forces (NW Europe) (SHAEF)		Flaming Crusader's sword aflame in the darkness of occupied Europe, with the rainbow of peace above	
Supreme Allied Command (SE Asia)		Blue phoenix rising from red flames on a white background within a blue circle	
15 Army Group		White shield containing blue wavy lines, on a red square	
21 Army Group		Crossed yellow swords on a red shield bearing a blue cross	

continued opposite

Note: The insignia of the Allied Forces HQ (Algiers and Naples), SHAEF (NW Europe), Supreme Allied Command (SE Asia) and HQ 15 Army Group were all worn by both American and British troops, the latter being composed of Fifth US and Eighth British Armies in Italy.

Annex 'A' continued

Formation	Sign		Remarks
First Army		Upright sword on a white shield bearing a red cross	Crusader's shield
Second Army		Upright sword on a white shield bearing a blue cross	Crusader's shield
Eighth Army		White shield bearing a yellow cross set in a blue upright rectangle	
Ninth Army		Red charging elephant with small flagged castle on its back, in a black circle	Possibly chosen as army commander Gen 'Jumbo' Wilson
Tenth Army		Yellow Assyrian lion on a black rectangle	Chosen because it was formed in Iraq
Twelfth Army		White Burmese dragon sitting upright on top of 'XII', set on a red rectangle, with a black stripe at middle	Chosen as it was raised in Burma
Fourteenth Army		Red shield with white edge bearing a sword in middle, behind 'XIV' in white on a black band	

ANNEX 'B': ORDER OF PRECEDENCE

Details of Regular, Territorial, Yeomanry, etc., Regiments in the H Cav, RAC and Inf

Note: These do not include all the numerous training regiments that were formed. Regiments and abbreviations are given.

H Cav

The Life Guards	LG
Royal Horse Guards (The Blues)	RHG

Note: When the war began the two regiments provided: a horsed regiment for 1st Cavalry Division, which went to Palestine, and when this division became 10th Armoured Division, the horsed regiment became 1st Household Cavalry Regiment (1 HCR); a training regiment at Windsor, which gave up its horses in 1941 and became the 'Household Cavalry Motor Regiment', then 'Second Household Cavalry Armoured Car Regiment' and finally 2 HCR; and a small Reserve Regiment in London. After mechanization, the units became 1 HCR and 2 HCR and although the LGs commanded and staffed 1 HCR and The Blues 2 HCR, the two were actually composite units. They did not assume their separate identities again until 1 September 1945.

RAC

REGIMENTS OF HORSE

1st King's Dragoon Guards	KDG
The Queen's Bays (2nd Dragoon Guards)	Bays
3rd Carabiniers (Prince of Wales's DG)	3 DG or 3/6 DG
4th/7th Royal Dragoon Guards	4/7 DG
5th Royal Inniskilling Dragoon Guards	5 Innis DG

CAVALRY OF THE LINE

1st The Royal Dragoons	Royals
The Royal Scots Greys (2nd Dragoons)	Greys
3rd The King's Own Hussars	3 H
4th Queen's Own Hussars	4 H
7th Queen's Own Hussars	7 H
8th King's Royal Irish Hussars	8 H
9th Queen's Royal Lancers	9 H
10th Royal Hussars (Prince of Wales's Own)	10 H
11th Hussars (Prince Albert's Own)	11 H
12th Royal Lancers (Prince of Wales's)	12 L
13th/18th Hussars	13/18 H
14th/20th Hussars	14/20 H
15th/19th The King's Royal Hussars	15/19 H
16th/5th Lancers	16/5 L
17th/21st Lancers	17/21 L
22nd Dragoons	22 D
23rd Hussars	23 H
24th Lancers	24 L
25th Dragoons	25 D
26th Hussars	26 H
27th Lancers	27 L

The last six cavalry regiments were formed between 1940 and 1941 under AO 213/1940 and AO 7/1941, the cadres being provided as follows: 22 D – 4/7DG and 5 Innis DG; 23 H – 10 H and 15/19 H; 24 L – 9 L and 17/21 L; 25 D – 3 DG; 26 H – 14/20 H; 27 L – 12 L. Five saw active service – the first three in NW Europe (1944–45), while 25 D fought in Burma and 27 L in Italy. All six were disbanded in 1947.

REGULAR RTR

Royal Tank Regiment	R Tanks
1st to 12th R Tanks inclusive	

CAVALRY MILITIA

North Irish Horse	NIH

YEOMANRY REGIMENTS

Royal Wiltshire Yeomanry	RWY
Warwickshire Yeomanry	WY
Yorkshire Hussars	YH
Notts (Sherwood Rangers) Yeomanry	NSR
Staffordshire Yeomanry	SY
Cheshire Yeomanry	CY
Yorkshire Dragoons	YD
North Somerset Yeomanry	NSY
Derbyshire Yeomanry	DY
Royal Gloucestershire Hussars	RGH
Lothian and Border Horse	LBH
Fife and Forfar Yeomanry	FFY
Westminster Dragoons	WD
3rd County of London Yeomanry	3CLY
4th County of London Yeomanry	4CLY
Northamptonshire Yeomanry	NY
East Riding Yeomanry	ERY
Inns of Court Regiment	IC

TA ROYAL TANK REGIMENTS

40th to 51st inclusive	R Tks

INFANTRY CONVERTED TO RAC REGIMENTS IN 1941–42

107th to 116th RAC ⎫ a total of thirty-three
141st to 163rd RAC ⎭ regiments were converted

Most of these regiments saw action in various theatres. When the need arose to reduce the size of the RAC, then they were the first to be disbanded or re-converted. However, some remained until after the war. Full details of all converted regiments are shown in Appendix 1 to this Annex.

INF

BRIGADE OF GUARDS

Grenadier Guards	Gren Gds
Coldstream Guards	Coldm Gds
Scots Guards	SG
Irish Guards	IG
Welsh Guards	WG

INFANTRY ON THE LINE

There were sixty-four Foot Regiments in the infantry of the line, numbered between 1 and 91, the numbers being the old numbers by which the regiments were formerly known and the missing numbers being disbanded regiments, or alloted to junior battalions of existing regiments. Note: The Rifle Brigade had no number. The units shown with a * are additional battalions formed during wartime of the regiment shown immediately above.

(1)	The Royal Scots (The Royal Regiment)	RS
(2)	The Queen's Royal Regiment (West Surrey)	Queen's
(3)	The Buffs (Royal East Kent Regiment)	Buffs
(4)	The King's Own Royal Regiment (Lancaster)	King's Own
(5)	The Royal Northumberland Fusiliers	NF
(6)	The Royal Warwickshire Regiment	Warwick
(7)	The Royal Fusiliers (City of London Regiment)	RF
(8)	The King's Regiment (Liverpool)	King's
(9)	The Royal Norfolk Regiment	Norfolk
(10)	The Lincolnshire Regiment	Lincolns
(11)	The Devonshire Regiment	Devon
(12)	The Suffolk Regiment	Suffolk
(13)	The Somerset Light Infantry (Prince Albert's)	Som LI
(14)	The West Yorkshire Regiment (The Prince of Wales's Own)	W Yorks
(15)	The East Yorkshire Regiment (The Duke of York's Own)	E Yorks
(16)	The Bedfordshire and Hertfordshire Regiment	Bedfs Herts
(17)	The Leicestershire Regiment	Leicesters
(19)	The Green Howards (Alexandra, Princess of Wales's Own Yorkshire Regiment)	Green Howards
(20)	The Lancashire Fusiliers	LF
(21)	The Royal Scots Fusiliers	RSF
(22)	The Cheshire Regiment	Cheshire
(23)	The Royal Welch Fusiliers	RWF
(24)	The South Wales Borderers * Brecknock Bn	SWB
(25)	The King's Own Scottish Borderers	KOSB
(26)	The Cameronians (Scottish Rifles)	Cameronians
(27)	The Royal Inniskilling Fusiliers	Inniks

(28)	The Gloucestershire Regiment	Glosters
(29)	The Worcestershire Regiment	Worc R
(30)	The East Lancashire Regiment	E Lan R
(31)	The East Surrey Regiment	Surreys
(32)	The Duke of Cornwall's Light Infantry	DCLI
(33)	The Duke of Wellington's Regiment (West Riding)	DWR
(34)	The Border Regiment	Border
(35)	The Royal Sussex Regiment	R Sussex
(37)	The Hampshire Regiment	Hamps
(38)	The South Staffordshire Regiment	S Staffords
(39)	The Dorsetshire Regiment	Dorset
(40)	The South Lancashire Regiment (The Prince of Wales's Volunteer)	PWV
(41)	The Welch Regiment	Welch
(42)	The Black Watch (Royal Highland Regiment) * Tyneside Scottish	Black Watch
(43)	The Oxfordshire and Buckinghamshire Light Infantry	Oxf Bucks
(44)	The Essex Regiment * Buckinghamshire Bns	Essex
(45)	The Sherwood Foresters (Nottinghamshire and Derbyshire Regiment	Foresters
(47)	The Loyal Regiment (North Lancashire)	Loyals
(48)	The Northamptonshire Regiment	Northamptons
(49)	The Royal Berkshire Regiment (Princess Charlotte of Wales's)	R Berks
(50)	The Queen's Own Royal West Kent Regiment	RWK
(51)	The King's Own Yorkshire Light Infantry	KOYLI
(53)	The King's Shropshire Light Infantry	KSLI
(57)	The Middlesex Regiment (Duke of Cambridge's Own) * Kensington Regiment	Mx
(60)	The King's Royal Rifle Corps * Queen Victoria's Rifles * Queens Westminsters * The Rangers	KRRC
(62)	The Wiltshire Regiment (Duke of Edinburgh's)	Wilts
(63)	The Manchester Regiment	Manch
(64)	The North Staffordshire Regiment (The Prince of Wales's)	N Staffs

(65)	The York and Lancaster Regiment	Y & L	(No number)
	* Hallamshire Bn		* London Rifle Brigade
(68)	The Durham Light Infantry	DLI	* Tower Hamlets Rifles
(71)	The Highland Light Infantry		
	(City of Glasgow Regiment)	HLI	*AIRBORNE AND SPECIAL FORCES*

(65) The York and Lancaster Regiment   Y & L
  * Hallamshire Bn
(68) The Durham Light Infantry   DLI
(71) The Highland Light Infantry
  (City of Glasgow Regiment)   HLI
  * Glasgow Highlanders
(72) The Seaforth Highlanders
  (Ross-shire Buffs, the Duke
  of Albany's)   Seaforth
(75) The Gordon Highlanders   Gordons
  * London Scottish
(79) The Queen's Own Cameron
  Highlanders   Camerons
  * Liverpool Scottish
(83) The Royal Ulster Rifles   RUR
  * London Irish Rifles
(87) The Royal Irish Fusiliers
  (Princess Victoria's)   R Ir F
(91) The Argyll and Sutherland Highlanders
  (Princess Louise's)   A & SH
The Rifle Brigade (Prince Consort's Own)   RB

(No number)
  * London Rifle Brigade
  * Tower Hamlets Rifles

AIRBORNE AND SPECIAL FORCES
The Parachute Regiment   Para[†]
Glider Pilot Regiment   Glider[†]
Special Air Service Regiment   SAS[†]

Army Order 21 of 1942 established the Army Air Corps as an administrative and co-ordination centre for the Glider Pilot Regiment and the Parachute Regiment, then in 1944 the Special Air Service Regiment became the third regiment of the corps.

SUPPLEMENTARY RESERVE
Cambridgeshire Regiment   Camb
Herefordshire Regiment   Hrfd
Hertfordshire Regiment   Hert
Monmouthshire Regiment   Mon
Lovat Scouts   Lov

APPENDIX 1 TO ANNEX 'B'

Infantry Regiments converted to Regiments of the RAC in 1941 and 1942

Regt RAC	Infantry Battalion	Year converted
107th	5th Bn King's Own Royal Regt (Lancaster)	1941
108th	1st/5th Bn Lancashire Fusiliers	1941
109th	1st/6th Bn Lancashire Fusiliers	1941
110th	5th Bn Border Regt	1941
111th	5th Bn Manchester Regt	1941
112th	9th Bn Sherwood Foresters	1941
113th	2nd/5th Bn West Yorkshire Regt	1942
114th	2nd/6th Bn Duke of Wellington's Regt	1942
115th	2nd/7th Bn Duke of Wellington's Regt	1942
116th	9th Bn Gordon Highlanders	1942
141st	7th Bn Buffs	1941
142nd	7th Bn Suffolk Regt (*illustrated opposite*)	1941
143rd	9th Bn Lancashire Fusiliers	1941
144th	8th Bn East Lancashire Regt (*illustrated opposite*)	1941
145th	8th Bn Duke of Wellington's Regt	1941
146th	9th Bn Duke of Wellington's Regt	1941
147th	10th Bn Royal Hampshire Regt	1941
148th	9th Bn Loyal Regt	1941

Appendix 1 to Annex B continued

Regt RAC	Infantry Battalion	Year converted
149th	7th Bn King's Own Yorkshire Light Infantry	1941
150th	10th Bn York and Lancaster Regt	1941
151st	10th Bn King's Own Royal Regt (Lancaster)	1941
152nd	11th Bn King's Regt (Liverpool)	1941
153rd	8th Bn Essex Regt	1941
154th	9th Bn North Staffordshire Regt	1942
155th	15th Bn Durham Light Infantry	1942
156th	11th Bn Highland Light Infantry	1942
157th	9th Bn Royal Hampshire Regt	1942
158th	9th Bn South Wales Borderers	1942
159th	10th Bn Gloucestershire Regt	1942
160th	9th Bn Royal Sussex Regt	1942
161st	12th Bn Green Howards	1942
162nd	9th Bn Queen's Own Royal West Kent Regt	1942
163rd	13th Bn Sherwood Foresters	1942

Note: All personnel in these units wore the black beret with their own infantry regimental badge.

These two infantry battalions (7th Suffolks – marching past – and 8th East Lancs – being inspected) were photographed in Dorset shortly before they were converted to armour, becoming 142 and 144 Regt RAC respectively. (IWM – H 15337 and H 15329)

CHAPTER 4

NON DIVISIONAL UNITS, HEADQUARTERS AND THE STAFF

CORPS HEADQUARTERS

Below army group and army headquarters was corps headquarters, usually commanded by a lieutenant general. A corps normally consisted of two or more divisions, together with additional artillery, engineer, reconnaissance, signals, maintenance support, etc., all or part of which could be attached to divisions for specific operations or employed under corps control. Corps was a tactical grouping and should not be confused with Arms of Service (the Corps of Royal Engineers, the Royal Armoured Corps, etc.), where the term has an entirely different, non-tactical meaning. A corps might be transferred from one army to another depending upon the tactical situation.

War History There were thirteen corps HQ activated during the war and details of their insignia are given in Annex 'A' to this chapter. The first three to see active service were: I and II Corps – both part of the original BEF that went over to France in September 1939 – and III Corps, which arrived in March 1940 as reinforcements. I (Spearhead) Corps was also part of Second British Army's assault force on D-Day. IV Corps was part of Slim's Fourteenth Army in Burma, while V Corps took part in the ill-fated Norwegian campaign in 1940. Later, it joined First Army in North Africa, then Eighth Army in Sicily and Italy. VI and VII Corps were never formed. VIII Corps fought throughout NW Europe, from Normandy to the River Elbe. IX Corps saw active service with First Army in North Africa, while X Corps was formed just before El Alamein and spearheaded the Eighth Army breakthrough. XI Corps served only on the Home Front in the UK. XII Corps fought in France, Belgium, Holland and Germany as part of Second Army, while XIII and XXX Corps were both originally part of Eighth Army. Finally, XXV Corps was part of Ninth Army in the Middle East, but was redesignated as 22 Area in August 1944.

STAFF DEPARTMENTS

At all levels from GHQ down to brigade HQ there were three staff departments that assisted the commander in carrying out his onerous task of command. (These were General ('G') Staff, Adjutant General ('A') Staff and Quartermaster General ('Q') Staff.) In addition, they were there to help both the fighting troops and the services in carrying out their tasks. Complete co-operation between all members of an HQ and with the staffs of superior and subordinate HQs was essential. The staff officer was the servant of the troops and had to satisfy himself in the eyes of regimental officers that his contribution to the success of operations justified his presence on the staff. This confidence could only be achieved by efficient staff work, by frequent visits to units and by him carrying out his duties with sincerity and sympathy.

This ACV (AEC Mk 1 4×4) belonged to XXX Corps (note the Corps insignia on the mudguard), but was captured when part of the HQ was overrun by German panzers and later used by Rommel. Months later when the British retook Tobruk it was found and taken back into British service! (Author's Collection)

One of the ACVs belonging to 7th Armd Div Rear. This was also an AEC Mk 1. Note the vast amount of kit, camouflage nets, etc., stored on the roof and the canvas 'lean-to' rolled up on the side. (Author's Collection)

Newly arrived Eighth Army commander Gen Bernard Montgomery, with two of his corps commanders: Lt Gen Herbert Lumsden (X Corps) and Lt Gen Oliver Leese (XXX Corps). Lumsden was a dashing 12th Lancer whose corps was designated 'corps de chasse' after Alamein, while Leese took over the Eighth Army in December 1943, when Monty returned to UK for the Second Front. (IWM – E 18416)

Promises made had *always* to be carried out. This is especially important when it was realized that they acted in the name of the commander and not on their own authority. Staffwork thus called for loyalty, quick thinking, accuracy, commonsense, a pleasant disposition, imagination and an ability to decentralize. Maj Gen Sir Francis de Guingand KBE, CB, DSO, who was Montgomery's Chief of Staff at Eighth Army (1942–43) and 21 Army Group (1944–45), had this to say about being a successful army staff officer:

'There is certainly no black magic about becoming a successful Army staff officer in the field. Youth and brains are the important things. With a comparatively small amount of training and experience most staff appointments can be filled by non-regulars. . . . Montgomery backed youth and the "clever chap" (a favourite expression of his) and this policy paid him enormously.'[1]

ORGANIZATION OF THE STAFF
'G' Staff were concerned with operations, intelligence, tactical and training matters. 'A' Staff were concerned with all matters relating

1. *Operation Victory* by Gen de Guingand (Hodder and Stoughton, 1947)

to personnel and discipline. 'Q' Staff were concerned with supplies of all kinds, quartering and movements. These departments had their counterparts at every level, even at battalion, where the adjutant dealt with 'G' and 'A' matters and the quartermaster, the 'Q' matters. Headquarters also had representatives of the arms and services attached, who were thus able to give the commander and his staff expert advice as and when necessary and, in some cases, to command those elements of the arm/service within the formation. Examples of these representatives at, say, corps level would be:

Supporting Arms (located near or operating through 'G' Staff)

RAC	RE
RA	R Sigs

At corps level Commander Royal Armoured Corps (CRAC) would have been a brigadier and was available to advise the corps commander on all armoured matters. He may well also have exercised overall command over RAC units outside divisions (such as corps armoured car regiments). At lower levels this advice was provided by the commander and staff of the attached armoured formation. The same applied to the CRA, CRE and CR Sigs.

Supporting Services (located near or operating through 'A' and 'Q' Staff)

'A' Svcs	'Q' Svcs
RA Ch D	RE (engineer stores)
RAMC	RASC
RMP	RAOC
MPSC	REME
AEC	RAVC
AD Corps	P Corps
ALS (Legal)	ACC

Graves	NAAFI/EFI
Welfare Services	Civil Affairs
Civil Affairs	(with 'G' and 'A')
(with 'G' and 'Q')	

To give an example of the way the work was divided between staff officers, here is the breakdown of staff work for an infantry division staff (circumstances would determine whether all posts were filled):

'G' Staff

(a). *General Staff Officer, Grade 1* (GSO 1), also known as Chief of Staff, usually of lieutenant colonel rank. Main responsibilities were:
1. Policy as directed by the GOC, including training policy.
2. Coordination and general supervision of *all* work of Div HQ.
3. May well have to deputise for GOC in an emergency until another commander can be found.

(b). *General Staff Officer, Grade 2* (GSO 2), usually of major rank. Responsibilities were:
1. Orders and instructions as ordered by GSO 1.
2. Organization and working of 'G' (Operations & Intelligence) office.
3. Detail of officers duty roster for HQ.
4. Control and briefing/debriefing of liaison officers (LOs) at Div HQ.
5. Moves of Div HQ in conjunction with OC Div Sigs and Camp Commandant (officer responsible for local administration of Div HQ – layout, guarding, low-level duty rosters, etc.)
6. Road moves of the division, assisted by DAQMG (see below) for movement tables.

Montgomery, wearing an Australian bush hat, with his third desert corps commander, the brilliant Lt Gen Brian Horrocks, who commanded XIII Corps. He was badly wounded in 1943, but recovered to command XXX Corps in NW Europe. (IWM – E 16459)

An interesting group of British senior commanders with Montgomery, near Nijmegen in September 1944. On the far right (note his Desert Rat patch) is Maj Gen Verney (7 Armd Div). On Monty's left are: Second British Army Commander Lt Gen Dempsey, Maj Gen Graham (50 Div), Lt Gen O'Connor (VIII Corps) and Lt Gen Ritchie (XII Corps). (IWM – B 10388)

High-level planning taking place in Sicily, using the bonnet of a staff car. The group includes Montgomery, Alexander and (on right with foot on bumper) the dynamic American armoured commander Gen George S. Patton, Jr. (IWM – NA 5014)

(c). *General Staff Officer, Grade 3 (Operations) (GSO 3 (O))* was the understudy for the GSO 2 and usually of captain rank. Responsibilities were:

1. Operations as directed by GSO 1 and GSO 2.
2. Road moves as alloted by GSO 2.
3. Distribution of maps.
4. Supervision of 'G' draughtsmen (e.g. tabulations, charts and sketch maps).
5. Location Statement (Locstats) – every evening.
6. Circulation of situation reports (Sitreps).
7. Supervision of acknowledgement register for messages.
8. Codes and ciphers.

Maps, maps and more maps. In the mobile warfare in NW Europe the number of maps needed by any formation was enormous. Here the clerks of HQ 7th Armd Div sort through the latest consignment, 1 April 1945. (IWM – BU 3185)

A strange place for an office! These underground burial chambers provided excellent office space in Tobruk, November 1940 – and were relatively immune from bombardment. (IWM – E 978)

9. G' war diary.
10. Detailed orders for moves of the Orders ('O') Group[2]

(d). *General Staff Officer, Grade 3 (Intelligence) (GSO 3 (I))*, also of captain rank, was not only responsible for the collection and interpretation of relevant intelligence material, but also for ensuring that proper use was made of it. His responsibilities were:

1. Coordination of all intelligence (int) work in the divisional area.

2. Maintaining the situation map(s).
3. Maintaining the GOC's battle map.
4. Preparation of divisional int summaries.
5. Interpeting and making deductions from int information received.
6. Confirming uncertain information.
7. Reporting to GOC on requests for bomber support from brigades (known as Army Air Support Control (AASC)).
8. Liaison with the Air Int LO (AILO) on operational matters.
9. Ordering and interpretation of air photographs.
10. Distribution of int information gleaned from air photographs.
11. Maintenance of a diary showing identifications, (idents), enemy order of battle (en ORBAT), etc.,

2. The 'O' Group comprised the senior commanders to whom the GOC would give verbal orders – such as the brigade commanders, arms and service advisers, senior 'G', 'A' and 'Q' Staff. The composition would vary depending upon the nature of the operation.

less enemy artillery information which was dealt with by the IORA.

12. Liaison with IORA.

13. Arrangements for preliminary examination of prisoners and deserters – usually carried out by the IO.

14. Reporting enemy idents to higher authority.

15. Circulation of intelligence.

(e). *General Staff Officer, Grade 3 (Chemical Warfare)* (GSO 3 (CW)), again of captain rank. Duties were:

1. Advice on CW, including when necessary a CW appreciation of the situation.

2. Anti-gas training.

3. Study of the divisional area to assess the probable dangers from the enemy use of gas.

4. CW int in conjunction with int staff.

5. Examinations of specimens of technical interest in conjunction with anti-gas mobile laboratory.

6. Meteorological arrangements for CW.

7. CW map.

(f). *Intelligence Officer* (IO). He worked for the GSO 3(I) so his duties were very similar. One of them *always* had to be present at Div HQ. In principle the IO and his staff were primarily concerned with the detailed examination of prisoners, captured documents, enemy messages, etc., and with the keeping of int records.

Most 'O' Groups took place above ground; this is 7th Armd Div Tac HQ near El Alamein in September 1942. (Author's Collection)

(g). *Motor Contact LO* (MCLO). There were usually three of these officers who were primarily responsible for maintaining close liaison with brigades within the division, flanking formations, units on each flank, and of course corps HQ. They always kept in close touch with signal offices, calling for messages on outward journeys and reporting up-to-date information (such as locations) on their return.

(h). *Cipher Officer.* He was responsible to the OC Div Sigs for all matters concerned with cipher duties, including the cipher office. He and his staff were also always ready and prepared to help 'G' Staff when not involved in cipher duties.

'A' and 'Q' Staffs

(a). *Assistant Adjutant & Quartermaster General* (AA & QMG). He was responsible for all the administrative staff work of the HQ, both 'A' and 'Q', the coordination of the work of the services and was always in close touch with 'G' Staff. He was normally of lieutenant colonel rank.

(b). *Deputy Assistant Adjutant General* (DAAG). Normally a major, who was responsible for:
  1. Reinforcements.
  2. Medical services (with Assistant Director of Medical Services (ADMS)).

An early mobile command post as used in the Western Desert. The 'lean-tos' attached to the command vehicle provide extra office space. (Author's Collection)

3. Spiritual welfare (with the Senior Chaplain).
4. Graves.
5. Pay.
6. Personnel services, including discipline (with Deputy Assistant Provost Marshal (DAPM)), leave and POW.
7. 'A' and 'Q' War Diary.
8. Discipline (courts martial).
9. Morale.
10. Traffic control (with DAPM).

(c). *Deputy Assistant Quartermaster General* (DAQMG). Again normally a major and responsible for:
1. Supplies, petrol, oil and lubricants (POL), ammunition (with the Commander Royal Army Service Corps (CRASC)).
2. Ordnance services (with the Assistant Director of Ordnance Services (ADOS)).
3. Detailed quartering of troops in consultation with 'G' Staff,
4. Moves by road (with GSO 2).
5. Moves other than by road.

(d). *Catering Adviser*, who was responsible for:
1. Advising unit commanders on all matters concerning food preservation, cooking, preparation of diets and dietetic hygiene.
2. Arranging for the relief or transfer of ACC personnel throughout various units of the division (cooks were normally all ACC personnel, but under command of the unit to which they were attached).
3. Training ACC personnel in their specialist duties within the division.

GOC's personal staff

The Aide de Camp (ADC) was normally a young officer who had the following duties:
1. The personal comfort of the GOC.
2. When necessary, he acted as the GOC's personal staff officer.
3. On return from visiting troops he ensured that the Signalmaster (OIC Signal Office) knew the latest locations of the units visited.
4. Assistant to the Camp Commandant in his duties (he acted as Camp Commandant for the advanced Div HQ when it was formed)

In higher headquarters, such as at army level and above, the commander would also have his own personal staff officer, known as his Military Assistant (MA), whose duties were much wider in scope and not of such a personal nature as those of an ADC.

BRIGADE STAFF

The staff of a brigade (bde) was naturally smaller than that of a division, a smaller number of officers having to deal with all the 'G', 'A' and 'Q' matters. The senior staff officer, who was normally a major, was known as the brigade major (BM) and equated to the Chief of Staff in higher headquarters and performed similar duties. The other members of the brigade staff were (example is for an infantry brigade):

Brigade Intelligence Officer (Bde IO)
Three Motor Contact Liaison Officers (MCLOs)
Bde Sigs Offr (Communications)
Staff Captain (SC) ('A' and 'Q' matters)
Captain RASC
Brigade Transport Officer (Bde TO)

ANNEX 'A': INSIGNIA

Army Corps Formation Signs

Corps		Sign	Remarks
I		White spearhead on a red diamond	Chosen as it was the first 'Spearhead' corps in the army
II		Red fish on a blue and white horizontally striped rectangle	Chosen after its commander's name – Lt Gen Sir Alan Brooke
III		Green figleaf on a white square	Chosen after its commander's name – Lt Gen Sir Ronald Adam
IV		Black charging elephant on a red rectangle	Was part of Gen Bill Slim's Fourteenth Army in Far East, hence choice of elephant
V		White Viking longship with red cross on sail on a black background	Took part in the Norwegian campaign in 1940, hence choice of Viking ship
VIII		White charging knight on a red rectangle	Adopted in February 1943 as it comprised two armoured divisions
IX 1st		Black cat with hair and tail up on a red square	Both signs were to do with nine: nine lives for the cat, nine squares on the banner
2nd		White trumpet with nine squares on banner on a black rectangle	
X		White circle above a white line on a red square	Resembles the number 10 on its side
XI		Black and white chess 'castle' on a black diamond	
XII		Oak, ash and thorn trees in an oval on a black background	Chosen to link with the oak, ash and thorn in *Puck of Pook's Hill* by Kipling as it was raised in Pook Hill country
XIII		Red leaping gazelle in a white oval on an upright red rectangle	
XXV		Red heraldic lion on a yellow rectangle	Formerly the badge of HQ British Troops, Cyprus
XXX		Black leaping wild boar within a white circle on a black square	

CHAPTER 5

THE COMBAT ARMS

ARMOUR

THE PREWAR SITUATION

Thanks to the intransigence of the politicians and the entrenched 'anti-mechanization/ pro-horse' lobby that had still existed within the War Office even in the 1930s, Britain's armoured forces were in a sorry state just before the Second World War began. As well as being short of trained men to man the tanks and armoured cars, there was also a grave shortage of AFVs themselves and other associated hardware, and it was not until the very last days before the war began that anything really constructive was achieved. In 1936, for example, before rearmament began in earnest, the *total* British tank strength was just 375 AFVs, of which 209 were light tanks and all but 71 were classed as obsolete – remember the apology made to the Cavalry by the then Secretary of State for War about having to mechanize! (see Chapter 1)

On 4 April 1939 the dynamic Mr Leslie Hore-Belisha, then Secretary of State for War, who was largely responsible for giving the army a capacity for mechanized war (how different from his predecessor!), announced the formation of the Royal Armoured Corps, which combined into a loose 'association', the eighteen regular cavalry regiments that had so far been mechanized with the eight existing Regular and seven TA battalions of what had previously been known as the Royal Tank Corps and would thereafter be known as the Royal Tank Regiment. More units would join them as the RAC then rapidly expanded. These would be the men who would crew British armoured units in Europe and the Middle East, then later in the Far East and other theatres.

Tank Types As far as tanks were concerned, three types were then in vogue: small *light tanks*, armed only with machine guns, whose main task was to reconnoitre; medium sized, fast, lightly armoured *cruiser tanks*, whose main role was to exploit breakthroughs and spread havoc behind enemy lines; and heavily armoured, slow moving *infantry tanks* to support major deliberate assaults, etc., in what was still basically an infantry-orientated army.

The role of the light tanks was soon to be taken over almost entirely by armoured cars, while the main armoured formations in the British Army were either armoured divisions or independent tank brigades, both of which were in short supply, there being just two armoured divisions in existence (one in the UK and one in Egypt, the latter being woefully badly equipped), while a third was still only in embryonic form in the UK.

Initially, the grave shortage of hardware continued; in mid-July 1939, for example, less than two months before war was declared, there was a confirmed RAC requirement for 2,231 tanks, yet only 2,000 modern machines had so far been ordered and few had been built. As a War Office report of the time said, the newly formed RAC was, '. . . caught between wind and water'. The report also highlighted the state of AFV armament explaining that:

Light tanks, like this Lt Mk VIB belonging to 1 RTR and in the Western Desert in 1939/40, were used for a variety of tasks, in particular reconnaissance, but had thin armour and only machine guns with which to fight. (IWM — E 1501)

The next main class of British tanks were cruisers, like these A13 Mk IIs of 5 RTR, preparing to advance in France in 1940. (IWM — F 4606F)

Nicknamed 'Queen of the Desert', the Matilda Mk II infantry tank had thick armour and was more than a match for the Italians in the early part of the desert war. (IWM — BM 7175)

'. . . the changeover from the Vickers type MG to Besa[1] had only recently been decided. The only light tanks available in any numbers were the Vickers (machine gun) armed Marks VIa and VIb. The Mark VIc with Besa equipment was still in production. In the case of Cruisers (with Vickers armament) Marks I and II (A9 and A10) were in production and Mark III (the original A13 – also Vickers armed) was just coming into production. The Heavy cruiser (A15) existed only on the drawing board and no close support tanks were available . . . the Vickers armed Matilda I (which carried one Vickers MG and no anti-tank gun) was in service and the Infantry Tank Mark II (the original A12) was only just coming into production.'[2]

EXPANSION

Armoured Divisions The initial target was for the formation of just four armoured divisions, but in fact, as Appendix 1 (page 328) shows, a total of eleven (including one of specialized armour) would be formed, but two of these would not serve outside the UK and a further four would not last out the war for one reason or another. The basic organization of the armoured division, as agreed by the War Office in May 1939, was for a light armoured brigade of three regiments, a heavy armoured brigade, also of three regiments, and a support group (infantry, artillery, engineers, etc.), the division containing in total some

350 tanks of all types. This unwieldy, armour-heavy formation was to change its organization many times during the war (see Chapter 7) and in the end produce a more balanced armour/infantry grouping, with less tanks but more mobile infantry, properly supported with elements of the other arms and services, so that it could deal with any battle situation that might arise.

79th Armoured Division Special mention must be made of one unique British armoured division, also known as 'The Funnies', because it contained the largest concentration of specialist devices under the inspiring leadership of Maj Gen Sir Percy Hobart. From D-Day onwards, while the division remained under the direct command of 21 Army Group, portions of it were placed in support of the armies as operations required. Thus, it never fought as a division but rather 'farmed out' its component parts throughout British and Canadian formations. They played a major part in the success of the Allied landings and at one time or another the following brigades (plus one Canadian regiment) were under command with specialized equipment as shown:

27 Armd Bde – equipped with DD amphibious tanks (these were US Shermans, although much of the trial work on amphibious tanks had been done with British Valentine DDs).

30 Armd Bde – flail minesweeping tanks (these were also Shermans, although there had been initial development using Matilda Mk IIs, while Churchill tanks were also equipped with various mine clearing devices).

1 Assault Bde – AVREs (Armoured Vehicles Royal Engineers – based on Churchills – described in a later chapter).

31 Armd Bde – Churchill Crocodile flame-throwers – described in a later chapter.

---

1. Modern tanks of the period were normally armed with a mixture of machine guns and larger calibre weapons ranging from 20 mm up to 75 mm. The British stayed far too long with the tried and trusted Vickers .303 machine gun and the Ordnance QF 2 pdr as the main tank gun – and only changed to larger calibres when the American Lend-Lease AFVs began to arrive in late 1941.

2. Quoted in *History of the Royal Armoured Corps and its Predecessors 1914–1975* by Maj (Retd) K.J. Macksey MC.

33 Armd Bde – Buffalo (tracked amphibians of American origin).

35 Tank Bde – CDL (Canal Defence Lights) tanks – mainly based upon Matilda Mk II.

4 Armd Bde – DD amphibious tanks (see 27 Armd Bde above).

Canadian APC Regt – 'degutted' Canadian Ram tanks, known as Kangaroos.

Tank Brigades In 1939 the 1st Army Tank Brigade comprised the 4th, 7th and 8th RTR. Only the 4th and later the 7th would go to France, the 8th being left behind in the UK while 4 RTR had 50 Matilda Mk Is and the 7th had 27 Mark Is and 23 Mk IIs. These heavily armoured but poorly armed AFVs would give the hitherto invincible German Panzerwaffe a severe shock at Arras on 21 May, thus being largely instrumental in delaying the German advance sufficiently to save the BEF from being cut off from their escape route to Dunkirk. Nevertheless, all their precious tanks had to be left behind when the BEF was evacuated. Major expansion followed and by early 1942 there were eleven such formations, known as Army Tank Brigades (1st, 10th, 11th, 21st, 25th, 31st, 32nd, 33rd, 34th, 35th and 36th), available to be allocated to corps and divisions as required. As part of the policy to absorb armoured forces into the rest of the army (cf. the changes in organization of the armoured divisions already mentioned), five of these tank brigades (the prefix 'Army' was dropped) had, by mid-1942, replaced the third infantry brigade in the 1st, 3rd, 4th, 43rd and 53rd Infantry Divisions. However, this was found to be unsatisfactory and the 'mixed' division was abolished in 1943, although the role of the tank brigade – now mainly equipped with the Churchill heavy tank (see Chapter 9) – was still that of infantry close support and remained so for the rest of the war.

Although it had early teething troubles, the Churchill infantry tank proved most reliable and was well liked by crews. This Mk IV, mounting a 6 pdr gun in a new cast turret, is driving through the streets of Tunis on 14 May 1943, after the last Axis troops had surrendered. (IWM — NA 1177)

In August 1944 the independent armoured and tank brigades each contained three regiments/battalions of tanks (despite the changes in nomenclature brought about by the 'merging' of RAC and RTC into the RAC, RTR regiments were still invariably known as 'battalions') plus a proportion of signals and services, with an approximate strength of 3,400 all ranks. The 1,200 vehicles included some 190 medium or infantry tanks and 33 light tanks. In the five armoured brigades the basic tank was the American Sherman M4, while in the three tank brigades it was the Churchill, as already mentioned. All light tanks were Stuarts (American M3s and M5s). In two of the armoured brigades there was also a motor battalion. These independent brigades were primarily intended and trained for close co-operation with infantry divisions, but it was 21 Army Group policy (laid down by Montgomery) that they must also be equally capable of working with armoured divisions.

Other Armoured Units   Initially, within the BEF as sent to France in 1939, there was a total of eight cavalry regiments – 1st and 2nd Light Armoured Reconnaissance Brigades (each of two regiments), plus a further four cavalry regiments not brigaded. The mechanized cavalry were thus now either armoured car regiments, divisional cavalry regiments or light tank regiments. By early 1943 it had been found that the divisional armoured car regiment was unable to carry out adequately the functions of both close and medium

Best of the early cruiser tanks was the Crusader, seen leading this line of mixed AFVs that includes American-built Sherman M4s. This is a Mk II CS version, which mounted a 3.7 in howitzer as its main armament. (Tank Museum)

reconnaissance. A unit was needed that could not only fight for information but also, if necessary, protect the rear and flanks of the division during advance/withdrawal. This led to the establishment of an armoured recce regiment for every armoured and most infantry divisions, while the armoured car regiment became corps troops, with the task of carrying out medium reconnaissance only. Although usually more lightly equipped than the armoured regiments within the armoured brigade of the armoured division, the armoured recce regiment often became used as a fourth armoured regiment and in some formations was equipped with the same AFV (for example, the Cromwell Cruiser tank in 7th Armd Div in 1944). To perform these tasks within infantry divisions, a new corps – the Reconnaissance Corps – was formed in January 1941 and was formally absorbed

into the RAC on 1 January 1944. Its units, however, were very different from normal RAC units, being organized for dismounted action, but in each of their three recce squadrons there was a proportion of armoured cars and light recce cars.

Although Britain built a roughly similar quantity of tanks as did Germany during the war, they still needed Lend-Lease American tanks, such as the Sherman, to equip many of their armoured formations. This was due partly to poor tank design because, apart from some notable exceptions like the Churchill and the Comet, British tanks were, on the whole, lacking in the right mix of firepower, protection and mobility that made the tank such a potent force during the war. In June 1945 the RAC Directorate of the War Office listed its AFV holdings as being 9,994 armoured cars, 5,443 light tanks,

The A27M Cruiser Mk VIII Cromwell was very fast (40 mph), but had thin armour. These Cromwells belonged to 22nd Armd Bde and are lined up for an attack east of the Orne River, in July 1944. (Tank Museum)

Bombing up a Comet tank belonging to 3 RTR in NW Europe, towards the end of the war. The Comet was the best all-round British tank of the war. (Tank Museum)

13,667 cruisers and 2,823 infantry tanks. In addition, they estimated that 15,844 tanks and 1,957 armoured cars had been lost. These figures included the large numbers of American Lend-Lease AFVs supplied. For example, 7,489 light tanks and 17,181 mediums were supplied by the USA to British and Commonwealth forces during the war.[3]

3. Sources of these figures for US Lend-Lease AFVs are Richard Hunnicutt's definitive books on the Stuart and Sherman tanks, as published by the Presidio Press.

COMMONWEALTH ARMOUR

Mention must also be made of Commonwealth armour, which in general terms was organized as for British armoured formations and equipped with much the same types of AFVs. Australia, for example, formed three armoured divisions, which fought in the Pacific theatre, while the Australian infantry divisions in the Middle East contained divisional recce regiments – later designated 'Divisional Cavalry Regiments'. Canada formed no fewer than five armoured divisions and they fought in NW Europe and Italy, there being a total of thirty Canadian armoured units by the end of the war in the Royal Canadian Armoured Corps (awarded the prefix 'Royal' by King George VI in August 1945 in recognition of their outstanding war record). The Indian Armoured Corps was formed in May 1941 and basically consisted of all the old Indian cavalry regiments together with units from the UK, there being three Indian armoured divisions (31st, 32nd and 43rd) in 1942, while a fourth armoured division (44th) was formed in 1944. By March 1944 the New Zealand Armoured Corps consisted of three

armoured regiments, while the South African 6th Armd Div fought with distinction in Italy, the remainder of the SA armour being mainly composed of the highly effective armoured car companies (equipped with such excellent SA-built AFVs as Marmon-Herringtons) that fought in East Africa and the Western Desert.

BASIC ORGANIZATIONS

While the full, detailed organization of the armoured division is dealt with later, a few words on basic organizations during the middle of the war (1943–44) would be valuable here.

Armoured cars, like this Morris CS9/LAC belonging to the 11th Hussars, soon took over medium- and long-range reconnaissance from the light tanks. (I'm told that the parasol came from Groppis restaurant in Cairo!) (IWM — E 380)

Armoured and Armoured Recce Regiments and Tank Battalions All were similarly organized apart from minor details, so all were capable of performing the same role. Each had an HQ of four cruiser/infantry tanks; an HQ Squadron of four troops (AA (four tanks fitted with 20 mm guns), recce (eleven light tanks), intercommunication (eight scout cars) and admin); three tank squadrons each – an HQ (four tanks) and five troops of three tanks (total 19). Shortly before D-Day, 17 pdr 'Fireflies' (US Sherman with British 17 pdr gun) began to be issued and squadrons were reorganized into four troops of four tanks, including one 'Firefly'. Total tanks = 61 × med/inf and 11 × lt = 72. Strength 36 officers and 630 ORs. Outline organizations of armoured car and recce regiments (infantry divisions only) are shown below:

ARTILLERY

UBIQUE
Throughout the centuries artillery has been the primary supporting arm of the infantry and armour, earning for the RA the enviable mottoes *Ubique* (Everywhere) and *Quo Fas et Gloria Ducunt* (Where Right and Glory lead). Within the RA was the Royal Horse Artillery (RHA) although it retained its title and distinctive badge. The Gunners had the largest proportion of manpower among all the supporting arms and services – and rightly so because it manned such a wide range of different types of artillery, which at the start of the war included Horse, Field, Medium, Heavy, Super Heavy and A tk, all separately controlled, from AA and coast artillery. In addition, they later provided gun crews for merchant vessels and operated

Type	Armoured Car	Recce
HQ	3 × ACs	1 × AC
HQ Sqn	AA tp – 5 × ACs (fitted with 20 mm guns Intercomm tp – 12 × sc cars Admin tp	A tk bty – 8 × 6 pdr Mor tp – 6 × 3in mor Sigs tp Admin tp
Sabre Sqns each	SHQ – 4 × ACs 5 × troops each 2 × ACs and 2 × sc cars Hy tp – 2 × AECs Sp tp – rfn in half tracks	SHQ 3 × scout tps (ACs, LRCs & Bren carrs) Aslt tp – rfn in half tracks
No of Sqns in regt	4 × AC Sqns	3 × Recce Sqns
Total AFVs	Daimler ACs (basic car), AECs (hy tp), Staghounds (HQ car) – total AC = 67 Sc cars (Daimler or Humber) = 67	ACs (Humbers) 28, LRCs (Humbers) 24, Bren carrs 63
Strength	55 Officers and 680 ORs	41 Officers and 755 ORs

'Ubique' means 'Everywhere' and the Gunners certainly lived up to their motto. Here 25 pdrs are mounted on 'Z' craft to fire at Japanese positions some 6 miles away from the newly taken beach-head on the Akyab and Myebon Peninsula, 17 February 1945. (IWM — SEU 1395)

light aircraft as flying observation posts to spot targets and direct artillery fire on to them. The demand for air recce and airborne artillery fire direction led to the creation of Air Observation Post Squadrons, RA, as explained below.

TYPES OF ARTILLERY

(a). **Field (Fd)** The main artillery support at divisional level was the field regiment, mostly equipped with 25 pdr gun-howitzers, which had rapidly replaced the older 18 pdr. In the infantry division they were towed by 4×4 'Quad' motorized tractors, with separate ammunition limbers. Unlike the Germans, horsedrawn artillery was not used in any British fighting formation (with the exception of animal pack howitzers). In the armoured division self-propelled (SP) guns (such as the 25 pdr 'Bishop') were introduced, manned by the RHA, while the field batteries of the airborne divisions were equipped with Jeep-towed 6 pdrs or the earlier 3.7 in pack howitzer. (This was originally a mountain gun that could be mule-packed and, as already mentioned, was also used by field batteries in such inaccessible areas as New Guinea and other parts of the Far East.) Field artillery was very much the 'maid of all work' and provided accurate, close, immediate fire support whenever and wherever it was needed.

British 25 pdrs light up the desert sky as they support the Eighth Army's offensive, following their great victory at El Alamein in October 1942. (IWM – BM 20216)

The field artillery regiment had been extensively reorganized in 1938, the twenty-four guns being split into two twelve-gun batteries, each with three four-gun troops. The basic problem this organization raised was that the field regiment was intended to support an infantry brigade of three infantry battalions, thus the two batteries could not be divided between the three battalions without severe dislocation of the administrative and fire control systems. The BEF soon found out this problem and as a result the field regiment was reorganized into three eight-gun batteries, each of two four-gun troops. It would remain on this organization for the rest of the war. Ammunition carried in first line, per gun, was 144 HE, 16 smoke and 12 AP.

(b). **Medium (Med)** The mediums – such as 5.5 in gun-howitzers or the older 6 in howitzer – were corps artillery and normally employed in counter-battery work or other such tasks in which they could make full use of their longer range. They would be superimposed on to the immediate fire support of the field regiments in any fireplan. The medium regiment contained two batteries each of four guns, total of sixteen guns per regiment, tractor – towed. Ammunition carried in first line was 100 rounds per gun.

(c). **Heavy (Hy) and Superheavy (Superhy)** Like the mediums, these were either corps or army artillery, being guns like the 7.2 in howitzer, 9.2 in howitzer and 9.2 in gun. They would be superimposed, when available, in any fireplan, in the same way as the mediums. By 1944, in NW Europe, half of the heavy batteries in 21 Army Group were equipped with US 155 mm guns so that the four batteries in each regiment would be equally split with two of four 7.2 in howitzers each and two of four 155 mm guns each, making a total of sixteen guns and howitzers per regiment.

(d). **A Tk** Although the smaller calibre (for example, 2 pdr) a tk guns were an integral part of most infantry units and were thus manned by infantry soldiers, the larger calibre a tk guns (6 pdrs and 17 pdrs) and all SPs (for example, the Valentine Archer –

Waiting for the enemy. An A tk gun crew in Leuven, Belgium, have a smoke-break while waiting for the German panzers. (IWM — F4461)

see Chapter 9) were manned by the Gunners, each armoured and infantry division having an organic a tk regiment of four batteries. In infantry divisions these contained four batteries each of one troop (four guns) of 6 pdr and two troops (each four guns) of 17 pdr. In armoured divisions the guns were all 17 pdr.

(e). **AA** The basic division of AA units was into Heavy (HAA) and Light (LAA):

HAA The larger calibre AA guns ranged from the 3.7 in up to 5.5 in – the latter also doubling as coastal defence guns. Although HAA batteries were to be found in the field force, especially in rear areas, defending important installations, etc., by far the largest concentration of HAA guns was in AA Command in the UK, which also contained both LAA and SL regiments. In the field force each HAA regiment contained three batteries each of two troops of four 3.7 in guns – thus twenty-four guns per regiment.

LAA Within the field force, the AA support was mainly organic LAA regiments within armoured and infantry divisions, the guns being the 40 mm Bofors. These were used to defend vital points (VP) such as bridges, headquarters, supply and ammunition dumps, important road junctions, etc. LAA regiments contained three batteries each of three troops of six 40 mm Bofors – thus fifty-four guns per regiment.

AA Command Prewar, the AA defences of the UK were largely the responsibility of a small volunteer TA organization, which presented few problems. However, the rapid expansion of AA defences in 1938–39 as a result of the obvious success of aerial bombardment, especially against civilian targets in the Spanish Civil War (1936–39), put a great strain upon regular RA units as they were called upon to provide a large

Battle for Caen, a 17 pdr A tk gun crew on the corner of Le Bijude, July 1944. Note that the divisional insignia on the sleeves of their battledress has been blotted out by the censor. (IWM — XL 337146)

number of adjutants and permanent staff instructors. This expansion saw the formation of a separate AA Command, as part of 'Air Defence of Great Britain' (ADGB). The command consisted of three corps and twelve divisions, divided as follows: I AA Corps – five AA divisions; II AA Corps – four AA divisions; III AA Corps – three AA divisions. The corps and divisons were geographical commands and the units assigned to each varied according to their particular mission, thus the AA division was not like a normal tactical division but rather a formation charged with the AA defence of a certain area. Within the division were three or more brigades, together with certain service elements. The brigades were very flexible and

contained a mix of units equipped with heavy or light AA guns, searchlights, unrotating projectiles (rockets) or a combination of any of the four. The GOC-in-C was Gen Sir Frederick Pile, who had commanded the 1st AA (TA) Division from 1937–39, and his command's first challenge was supporting the RAF in the Battle of Britain when they played a significant part in containing the almost continual German air assaults in the summer of 1940. They were equally successful against the menace of the V-1 flying bombs and V-2 rockets in 1944–45. In addition to the AA guns, there were searchlights, predictors, height-finders, observation telescopes, telephones and of course the battle-winning new radar sets for early warning, all to be manned,

3.7 in AA guns firing at enemy aircraft during an air-raid on Alexandria, 22 October 1943. (IWM — NA 8094)

which required a large number of personnel. This produced a manpower crisis that was solved by employing ATS (called 'Co-ed Gun Girls' by the American troops stationed in the UK!). The women were specially trained and were not employed in fighting units outside AA Command. In addition to the ATS, the Home Guard also made up the shortfall from late 1941 onwards – in fact, by August 1944 a total of 118,649 Home Guards had been seconded to AA Command and made up nearly half of all gun and rocket crews.[4]

4. As quoted in *The Home Guard* by S.P. Mackenzie (OUP, 1995)

AA Brigades In 21 Army Group in NW Europe, these each contained two or more HAA and three or more LAA regiments, together with at least one battery of searchlights.

(f). **Coast** The main task of this branch was clearly to prevent enemy warships from raiding or bombarding shore installations. When the war began, and particularly after the fall of France when the threat of German invasion was at its height, coastal artillery had an important task to perform. However, as the threat receded so did the need for this branch. Coastal artillery sites were vulnerable to air attack as well as sea bombardment, consequently guns had to be protected by installing them in concrete gun emplacements (barbettes). Additionally, harbours had to be

Coastal artillery in action. A 9.2 in gun – part of the East Weares detachment of the Portland coastal defence battery – carrying out a night shoot. (IWM – H 11310)

defended against attacks by smaller vessels (such as German 'E' boats), this task being allocated to light quick-firing guns and cannons. Coastal batteries were also sometimes responsible for electrically controlled submarine mines and even land-mounted torpedo tubes. Radar was incorporated into coast artillery fire control from 1940 onwards, to support the existing observation posts and range-finding equipment.

(g). **Gunners in the Air** In October 1939 it was proposed that the RA should be equipped with a new type of light aeroplane '. . . to improve the application of artillery fire and to be piloted by Army officers'. Subsequently, on 1 August 1941, the first Air Observation Post (AOP) unit was formed,

entering the RAF order of battle as 651 Squadron. It contained a mixture of aircraft, although the ultimate intention was to equip it with American Stinson light aircraft. Two more squadrons were subsequently formed, numbered 652 and 653. The complement of each unit was eighteen RA officers, eighteen soldiers, an adjutant, an engineering officer and 112 ORs from the RAF. Forty-eight Stinson aircraft were ordered to equip the three AOP squadrons, but accidents in transit and other delays prevented their arrival and the squadrons were eventually equipped with British-built Austers (see Chapter 9). The AOP squadrons first saw action with the British First Army in Tunisia. The AOP soon became an indispensable part of gunnery, going on to fly in Italy and in the Far East. By the end of 1943 twelve squadrons had been formed, seven were subsequently used in NW Europe in 1944–45 and the rest worldwide. In NW Europe squadrons were provided on the scale of one per corps, plus one spare per army. Each contained three flights of four aircraft – total twelve.

(h). **Miscellaneous** Mention must also be made of other highly specialized artillery units, such as sound ranging and survey, who pinpointed the positions of enemy guns and mortars using such methods as aerial observation, flash spotting and sound ranging, the last of these techniques using bearings obtained from a network of carefully sited microphones. These methods, combined with the accurate calibration of guns and careful attention to all calculations, resulted in the RA's ability to put down consistently accurate and heavy fire, not only on enemy artillery positions but also on enemy troop/armour concentrations, HQs and communications centres, etc. As an example, the organization of the Survey Regiment in 1944 in NW Europe in 21 Army Group was two batteries, each comprising one observation troop, one sound ranging troop and one survey troop.

ARMY GROUPS, ROYAL ARTILLERY (AGRA)

Before leaving artillery units to look at tactical deployment, mention must be made of AGRAs, which were in vogue in 21 Army Group in NW Europe. They generally contained one heavy and three medium regiments. Some AGRAs also had one of more field regiments. The average strength of an AGRA was 4,400 all ranks and they were provided on a scale of one per corps plus one spare.

THE TACTICAL DEPLOYMENT OF A FIELD REGIMENT

The diagram overleaf shows how artillery at low level operated on the battlefield.

In a tactical situation the field regiment was divided into the following groups:

Group Composition

COs – those personnel who were needed to accompany the CO to the division/brigade commander's orders (for example, IO)

Recce – regiment/battery personnel needed to recce regiment, battery and observation post (OP) areas

HQ – regiment/battery personnel needed to man HQs and command posts (CP) and to complete the technical work and communications that had to be in place before the guns could open fire. Battery HQ groups were divided into the 'O' party for the OP area and the 'G' party for the gun position area

Gun – the guns and vehicles, plus the personnel to man them

Ammunition – reserve ammunition and one POL distribution truck to each battery. Usually they were centralized and moved under RHQ orders, unless batteries were operating independently

HQ – MT stores and technical personnel of RHQ and attached light aid detachment (LAD), who normally moved with the ammunition group under the RQMS

'B' Echelon – as in any other unit, moving under orders of RHQ

Before leaving to receive his orders the CO would lay down the RVs for all groups then, after receiving his orders, he would (with or without a personal recce) supervise the establishment of the OPs while his 2IC supervised the recce and occupation of the gun position area(s).

Deployment of Batteries Speed was essential, so as soon as the OC received his orders he

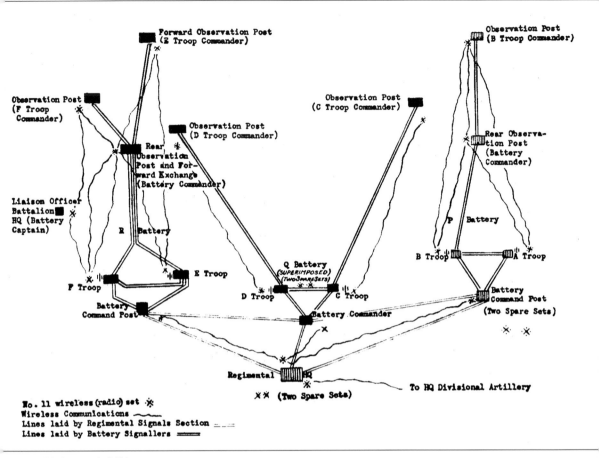

Tactical deployment of a field battery.

sent his Command Post Officer (CPO) to the gun position area to recce the CP and troop positions. 'G' party was then called forward and all preparations made so that the guns could open fire as soon as they arrived. Meanwhile, the OC had called forward the 'O' party and supervised the establishment of the OPs, communications were then opened up between them and the gun positions. Once the gun positions had been fixed, the Battery Captain (BC) arranged a track plan and, with the Wagon Line Officer (WLO), selected the wagon line area, where all the unwanted vehicles park. Then he arranged the AA and a tk defence of the gun position(s) and wagon lines. At the same time, guides went back

to the gun group RV, to bring up the guns, while all unwanted vehicles were taken to the wagon lines.

Control and Liaison Tactical control was the CO's primary responsibility and he would remain with the brigade/division commander he was supporting while his 2IC looked after the technical control (via the CPO and GPOs). The Forward Observation Officers (FOOs) would keep in touch with the forward units from their OPs. In an armoured division, the FOOs would be mounted in tanks of the same type as the unit they were supporting, so they could not be singled out by the enemy.

This example gives some idea of the complicated procedures that had to be employed to bring the guns into action. The heavier, longer range guns employed much the same principles, but everything was more complicated. The accuracy and efficiency of British artillery was the hallmark of the Royal Regiment throughout the war.

ENGINEERS

Just like the Gunners, the Sappers, as the men of the Corps of Royal Engineers (RE) were popularly called (and whose mottoes were exactly the same as those of the RA), performed a wide variety of tasks in support of the field army, such as: construction work on all types of defences (apart from the most basic); minc-laying and clearing; bridge-building (note that the actual bridge equipment was carried by special RASC units, who delivered it to the RE unit as and when it was needed; see also Chapter 9); demolitions; the building, operating and maintenance of camps, roads, railways, airfields, etc., including ports; specialized tasks, such as the purification of water – even the running of the military postal system was a Sapper task. As well as being highly skilled, technically trained tradesmen, Sappers were also taught how to fight and could, in extremes, be used as infantry, being equipped as they were with small arms. However, the fact that there were never enough RE personnel to tackle all the

Sappers at work by moonlight. Gaps had to be made through the German minefields before an assault – not a job for the faint-hearted! (IWM – E 18800)

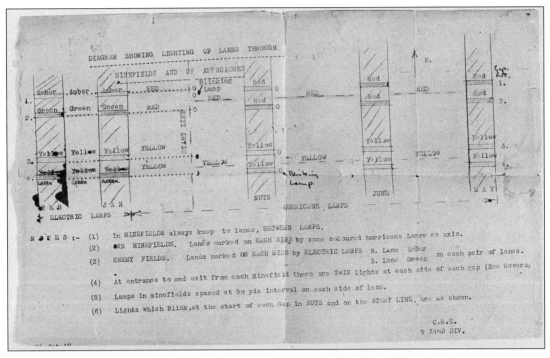

The Battle of El Alamein. This was the actual minefield lane diagram as issued by CRE 7th Armd Div. (Author's Collection)

The amazing mobile Bailey bridge. Here it was being demonstrated to Gen Mark Clark (CG US Fifth Army) and Gen McCreery (Commander Eighth Army) on 29 March 1945, in Italy. The Bailey was fitted with sets caterpillar wheels ('dollies') then pushed across the gap by a Churchill AVRE. (IWM — NA 23467)

technical jobs made this a very rare occurrence. The basic engineer unit was the field squadron/company and within the RE as a whole there were three types of unit:

(a). *Field and Fortress* Field units formed the engineer element of the fighting formations, while fortress companies only existed in such overseas locations as Gibraltar and Malta.
(b). *Line of Communications (LofC)* They provided engineer services in the base and LofC area.
(c). *Transport* They provided engineer units for the construction, maintenance and operation of docks, inland waterways and railways.

Thus, REs were normally distributed within the ground forces as follows:

(a). *Infantry division* – HQ Div RE (with Div HQ), one field park company, up to three field companies.
(b). *Armoured division* – HQ Armd Div RE (with Div HQ), one field park squadron, up to two field squadrons.
(c). *Corps* – three corps field companies, one corps field park company, one field survey company.
(d). *Army, GHQ and LofC* – nothing was fixed, but units normally included some or all of the following: army troops companies, engineer base workshops, engineer store base depots, workshop

Crossing the Irrawaddy River, Burma, December 1944. Rafts powered by outboards motors were used to ferry vehicles and men across the river at Tigylang. (IWM – SEU 1342)

and park companies, mechanical equipment companies, electrical & mechanical companies, forestry companies, quarrying companies, road construction companies, tunnelling companies, general construction companies, artisan works companies, aerodrome maintenance companies, welding companies, welding sections, well-boring sections, army field survey companies and transport units.

The following list of arbitrary facts and figures gives a graphic impression of the vast scope of engineer work on the battlefield.

(a). By May 1940 Sappers with the BEF had constructed 400 pillboxes covering 40 miles of a tk ditch along the Franco-Belgian border, plus forty-seven new

aerodromes and landing grounds for the RAF in France. At Dunkirk they built a pier by driving their lorries 150 yd into the sea and placing a plank walk on top, allowing 1,000 men an hour to be embarked into small boats.

(b). In the UK Sappers built camps for the incoming American and Canadian troops, new RAOC installations and vehicle parks, supply and ammunition depots, oil storage facilities, hospitals, even POW camps. Added to this was all the hard standing and hutting needed for RE stores, the Nissen and Romney huts being built in vast numbers. In addition, they again built airfields – including dummy ones – so their contribution to the Battle of Britain was considerable.

Mud, glorious mud! The men of this Bengal Engineer Field Company had their work cut out to keep the routes open into Burma in 1944. (IWM – IND 3612)

(c). Assistance with bomb disposal caused a new organization to be established of 120 mobile sections for the removal and sterilization of unexploded bombs. 13,000 men from the REs and Pioneer Corps dug out and rendered harmless over 35,000 unexploded bombs. Twenty-one Sappers were awarded the George Cross, the majority for bomb disposal work.

(d). In November 1942 it was decided to take over all movement control and to form Movement Control Sections RE over 10,000 officers and ORs were trained to form thirty-one such units worldwide.

(e). D-Day. Specialized armour, manned by the REs, played a major role on the beaches on D-Day – see Chapter 9 for further details of equipment, such as the Assault Vehicle Royal Engineers (AVRE); Special Landing Craft Obstacle Clearing Units were some of the first troops to land on the beaches. The Mulberry harbour at Arromanches, which played such a major part in the success of the landings, was assembled by an RE Port Construction Force; they had built 1,500 ft of the centre pier and 600 ft of the east pier by D+3. Despite damage from severe storms, by the time the Mulberry was no longer needed 2.5 million men, half a million vehicles and 4 million tons of stores had passed through it. (Also from the Normandy Mulberry onwards the Transportation Sappers built ninety-one railway bridges and put 7,000 miles of railway and 900 miles of canal back into operation!)

Special units To complete this pen picture of the ubiquitous Sappers, here are of some of the more specialized types of engineer units as found during the Second World War: postal, mobile bath & laundry (MBLU), salvage, bomb disposal and chemical warfare. The last of these were also trained as ordinary divisional field companies (except for bridge building), so that they could be quickly converted when necessary.

The strength of the REs increased from 90,000 in 1939 to over 280,000 in 1945. Despite this massive increase there were never enough Sappers to meet all the tasks they were given and they were always in short supply. They suffered 25,000 casualties during the Second World War.

SIGNALS

The Royal Corps of Signals (R Sigs), which had its roots in the Royal Engineers Signal Service, was responsible for all types of army communications (radio, wire, teleprinter and telegraph) down to the HQs of armoured regiments, infantry battalions, artillery batteries and similar sized units of other arms at the same level, below which wireless sets, telephones, etc., were manned by unit signallers. The R Sigs were also responsible for wire communications to RAF units allocated in support of the army, including the provision of such communications for the RAF (provided by Air Support Signals Units (ASSU)). Thus, when the BEF went to France, R Sigs units provided the signalling for its ten divisions and two corps. The R Sigs personnel were everywhere – for example, the last Allied troops to leave Paris just before the German encirclement were women of the ATS (Signals) and men of the Air Formation Central Telegraph Office. In the very mobile conditions of the Western Desert the commander and his wireless operator on the radio telephone in his armoured command vehicle were the pivot around which everything revolved, the principle of responsibility being that higher formations were responsible for communications with the next lower formations and for lateral communication between adjacent

Despite the increasing use of radio communications, line was still laid on occasions in the desert because it was so much more secure. Here a land line is being laid near Agedabia. (IWM — E 20899)

This wheeled command vehicle would have been a nerve centre for radio communications in the desert — note the tall radio mast on the roof. (Author's Collection)

lower formations. As the war progressed the need for co-operation between the signal units of all nationalities increased, while the corps played an important role in all operations in NW Europe and the Far East. They had many obstacles to overcome in order to maintain a high level of successful communications in the jungle areas, where wireless equipment was badly blanketed by the foliage and, at least initially, was not tropicalized initially (resulting in fungus and deterioration in insulation. The jungle also carried disease and death; by the end of the war, 4,364 signalmen had given their lives keep to the communications flowing.

ATS Involvement Women had been employed on signal communications duties during the First World War, so it came as no surprise that in the Second World War they were soon asked to make up the shortages in certain types of R Sigs tradesmen. Their contribution increased as the war progressed, until by 1945 there were over 15,000 so employed, that is, one woman to every ten men. By early 1944 they had taken over almost entirely the staffing of signal and cipher offices, the operation of switchboards, line circuits and many of the wireless circuits of the static and AA communications systems in the UK. In addition, more and more were drafted overseas and eventually ATS units were serving in the Middle East, Central Mediterranean, NW Europe and the Far East.

R SIGS UNITS

At each level – army, corps and division – there were R Sigs units each of battalion size, commanded by a lieutenant colonel, and comprising a number of companies (coy) – later called squadrons (sqn) – as follows:

(a). **Army level** An HQ and three coys, No. 1 being the construction coy; Nos 2 and 3 were identical operating and maintenance coys.

Coys were divided into sections, the number of which varied according to requirements. No. 1 coy contained line laying sections and a line maintenance section; Nos 2 and 3 comprised a teletype section, wireless sections, messenger sections and a tech maint section.

(b). **Corps level** Known by the same number as the Corps (so XII Corps signals unit was known as 12 Corps Signals), and contained an HQ and three coys, No. 1 being the construction coy, No. 2 the operating coy and No. 3 the corps artillery coy. They were subdivided into sections as follows:

> No. 1 (Construction) Coy – four line sections, one line maint section.
> No. 2 (Operating) Coy – three op sections, three wireless sections, two messenger sections (each a sergeant and twenty-four messengers).
> No. 3 (Artillery) Coy – signal sections for all corps artillery units.

(Note: If the number of formations/units in the corps altered, then the number of sections altered accordingly.)

(c). **Divisional level** As with corps, they took the same number as the division, (for example, 7th Armd Div Sigs). As well as maintaining communications to all units it also was responsible for the maintenance of all radio sets in the division and carried out first line repairs to signal equipment. Within the infantry division in the early war years it was divided into an HQ, an HQ coy and four coys. However, later in the war all divisional signalling regiments changed to calling their sub-units 'squadrons' rather than coys. The sub-unit tasks were initially as follows:

> No. 1 Coy provided communications at divisional HQ and to brigade HQs, artillery regiments and army tank

Sgt 'Topper' Brown, Royal Signals, was a wireless operator at FM Montgomery's HQ in May 1945. He was the man who transmitted the news to the German High Command that their surrender to 21 Army Group had been completed. (IWM — BU 5326)

brigade: A Sect – radio; B Sect – line; C Sect – radio; D Sect – despatch riders (DR); O Sect – operating.

No. 2 Coy provided communications for all artillery regiments, down to batteries: E, F and G Sects were attached to each field artillery regiment, while H Sect was the divisional artillery HQ staff section.

No. 3 Coy provided communications for infantry brigades, down to infantry battalions; also for the divisional recce regiment down to recce squadrons and for Command RE down to his field coys: R Sect was the recce regiment section; J, K and L Sects were each attached to infantry brigades (the number of sections varied with the number of brigades).

No. 4 Coy provided communications for the army tank brigade to tank battalions and from each battlion HQ down to squadrons: W Sect was the army tank brigade section; X, Y and Z Sects were attached to each tank battalion.

By the end of the war the breakdown was:

1 Squadron

A Troop – Main HQ wireless troop, provides wireless communications at main HQ, providing and manning sets to work on the following nets: div command (RT & CW); main corps (RT & CW); rear div RT; flank formations; TC (incl four outstations and a rover).

B Troop – Rear HQ wireless troop, provides wireless communications at rear HQ, providing and manning sets to work on the following nets: main div and brigade RT (Q); div command CW; rear corps; med net (incl three outstations); S & T net (incl four outstations and a rover; REME net (incl six outstations and a rover).

C Troop – Line troop, lays all lines from div HQ to brigades and flank formations on the right; lines from HQRA to RA regts; between main and rear div and locals at both main and rear. Carries 128 miles of field cable and is divided into four building and four line dets.

D Troop – DR troop, SDS to formations and units under div command and flank formations on the right. Contains eight DRs on MCs and thirteen in cars 5 cwt 4×4 (proportions may be varied).

O Troop – Operating troop, ops sig offices at main and rear HQ; divided into three op sub-troops (each capable of manning a sig office) and a cipher sub-troop. Cipher office responsible for issue of cipher equipment throughout div as well as cipher security.

2 Squadron (Note: OC was sig adviser to CRA). It comprised:

three field regiments RA signal troops (E, F and G), the OC troop being sig adviser to the field regt command. Each troop comprised a sig office det, four wireless dets, four charging dets, six linemen and four DRs. Each troop was responsible for: op of sig office at regt HQ; wireless communication from regt to batteries; line and SDS communications down to batteries; first line maint of sig equipment and charging for the regt.

H Troop (CRA's sig troop) provided wireless communications at HQ RA as follows: control station for CRA's command net; rear link to CCRA; control station for div artillery (Q) net; CRA's rovers; link to Air OP. It also provided: dets for a tk and LAA regts which incl rear link stas, charging and main facilities; small sig office at HQRA if required; first line maint of sig equipment and charging for HQRA.

3 Squadron

three infantry brigade signal troops (J, K and L), the OC troop being sig adviser to the brigade commander. Each troop comprised eight wireless dets, four charging dets, sig office det, nine linemen and five DRs. Each troop was responsible for: op of sig office at brigade HQ; wireless communication from brigades to battalions; line and SDS communications down to battalions; first line maint of sig equipment and charging for brigade.

N Troop (CRE's sig troop) comprised one LCV and rover set to provide rear link and forward control communications for CRE; first line maint of sig equipment and charging for engineers.

R Troop (Recce Regiment sig troop) comprised three wireless and four charging dets to provide rear links (RT & CW) to division HQ and the set at regiment A echelon; first line maint of sig equipment and charging for regiment.

The increase in communications work of all descriptions as the war progressed is very apparent by comparing these two lists of tasks. Organizational changes were affected mainly by four general causes: modifications in scales of communications required, new types of equipment, administration, and mobility.

Armoured Division Nowhere was mobility required more than in the armoured division where, although the basic system was similar to that of the infantry division, communications in such a mobile force were almost entirely by radio, there being, for example, over 500 radio sets in an armoured division, which included one in every AFV. (This figure naturally fluctuated with the reorganization of armoured divisions.) There could be more than fifty different radio networks operating in an armoured division at any one time, so the issue of frequencies for these radio nets to work on, the daily codes and callsigns to be used for security purposes and all the other essential work to keep communications open, represented a major and continuing task for the R Sigs personnel. Details of the main types of ground radio sets in use during the war are given in Appendix 5 (page 350).

Signal Office Every unit or formation had a signal office, which was the terminal for all types of communication emanating from or ending at the unit or formation concerned. The Signals Office was run by a Signalmaster, who was directly responsible to the CO for every aspect of its operations and the general efficiency of all R Sigs personnel. While on duty, communications personnel wore a distinguishing blue and white armband on their upper arm.

The Signal Troop The basic R Sigs sub-unit was the signal troop, which was the 'brick' with which signal regiments were built up, no matter whether they had a fixed or variable composition. Signal Troops varied in size from a captain's command with over 100 men down to a handful of men under a sergeant. There were two main categories: those designed for a specific purpose, such as troops affiliated to formations and units, and those that consisted of a number of detachments or tradesmen to be used for any general purpose, such as medium wireless troops and despatch rider troops. There were many

different types during the war although every effort was made to employ standard types of troops to avoid special establishments and equipment tables.

By way of example, the signal troop of an armoured regiment comprised just a sergeant and fourteen men: 1 Sergeant; 1 Corporal Electrician Signals; 1 Corporal Operator Wireless & Line; 4 Electricians Signals; 3 Operators Wireless & Line; 1 Driver Operator; 1 Driver Mechanic; 1 Instrument Mechanic; 2 Drivers IC

RADIO PROCEDURE
From the very outset of military radio communications, a set way of speaking on the radio had to be followed so that trans-

The enemy listens. Security was important all the time, especially on the radio. This early poster was drawn by Bruce Bairnsfather, the famous cartoonist of the First World War. (IWM — F 3641)

missions were kept simple, short and easy to follow, but at the same time giving away as little as possible to the enemy ('The enemy listens!' was one catchphrase). This involved, for example, the use of a phonetic alphabet. Radio procedure was altered at numerous times during the war, to make it simpler, shorter, more secure, etc. The phonetic alphabet provides an example of these changes:

Letter	Initially	Later
A	Ack	Able
B	Beer	Baker
C	Charlie	Charlie
D	Don	Dog
E	Edward	Easy
F	Freddie	Fox
G	George	George
H	Harry	How
I	Ink	Item
J	Johnnie	Jig
K	King	King
L	London	Love
M	Monkey	Mike
N	Nuts	Nan
O	Orange	Oboe
P	Pip	Peter
Q	Queen	Queen
R	Robert	Roger
S	Sugar	Sugar
T	Toc	Tare
U	Uncle	Uncle
V	Vic	Victor
W	William	William
X	X-Ray	X-Ray
Y	Yorker	Yoke
Z	Zebra	Zebra

Code and Link Sign System All radio networks used the code and link sign system, which was designed to deny information to enemy Intercept and Intelligence services. This was achieved by issuing daily, secret groups of three letters (known as code signs) to HQs of all formations and units down to company/squadron HQs and to all rear link

wirelesses down to regiment rear links. These code signs allowed identification by own troops, but prevented it to the enemy. They were changed daily at 0001 Z hrs. Sub-units merely added a figure to the code sign of the parent station and sub-sub-units a letter. (For example, if an armoured regiment HQ had allocated code sign 'ADG' to 'A' Squadron then 1 Troop would be 'ADG 1' and the troop sergeant would be 'ADG 1A – see example radio net below.)

Security At high level, cipher was used, which initially involved the Army Educatonal Corps (see next chapter), but soon after Dunkirk it was decided to transfer to the R Sigs full responsibility for the operation of ciphers, and for the provision and training of all cipher personnel. At unit level, simple codes were often employed to disguise map

A 7th Armd Div signaller using a morse key to send long distance messages by CW, under shade of his 'acquired' parasol – I wonder if Groppis ever ran out?! (Author's Collection)

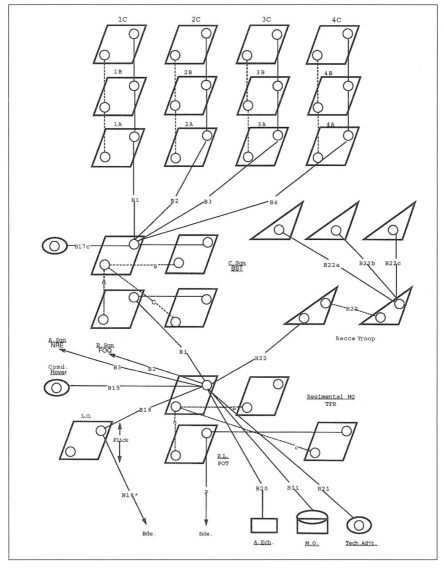

An example radio net.

references, orders, intentions, etc. They became more and more sophisticated as the war progressed and intercept became more skilled. SLIDEX, for example, was introduced in 1944, prior to the Normandy landings, and involved using a pack of cards on which there were grids of useful phrases, words, figures and letters, etc. – see example overleaf. There were in fact nine of the cards, labelled: RAC/REME, OPS/ SIGS, AIR(ASSU), MED, ST, RA, RE, Q(b) and UNIT. Each card had 204 rectangles.

The cards fitted into a special waterproof holder and were flanked by moveable celluloid horizontal and vertical cursors on which letter keys could be inserted using a chinagraph pencil, thus giving a means of referring to a given word on the grid in the same way one refers to a map reference using the grid.

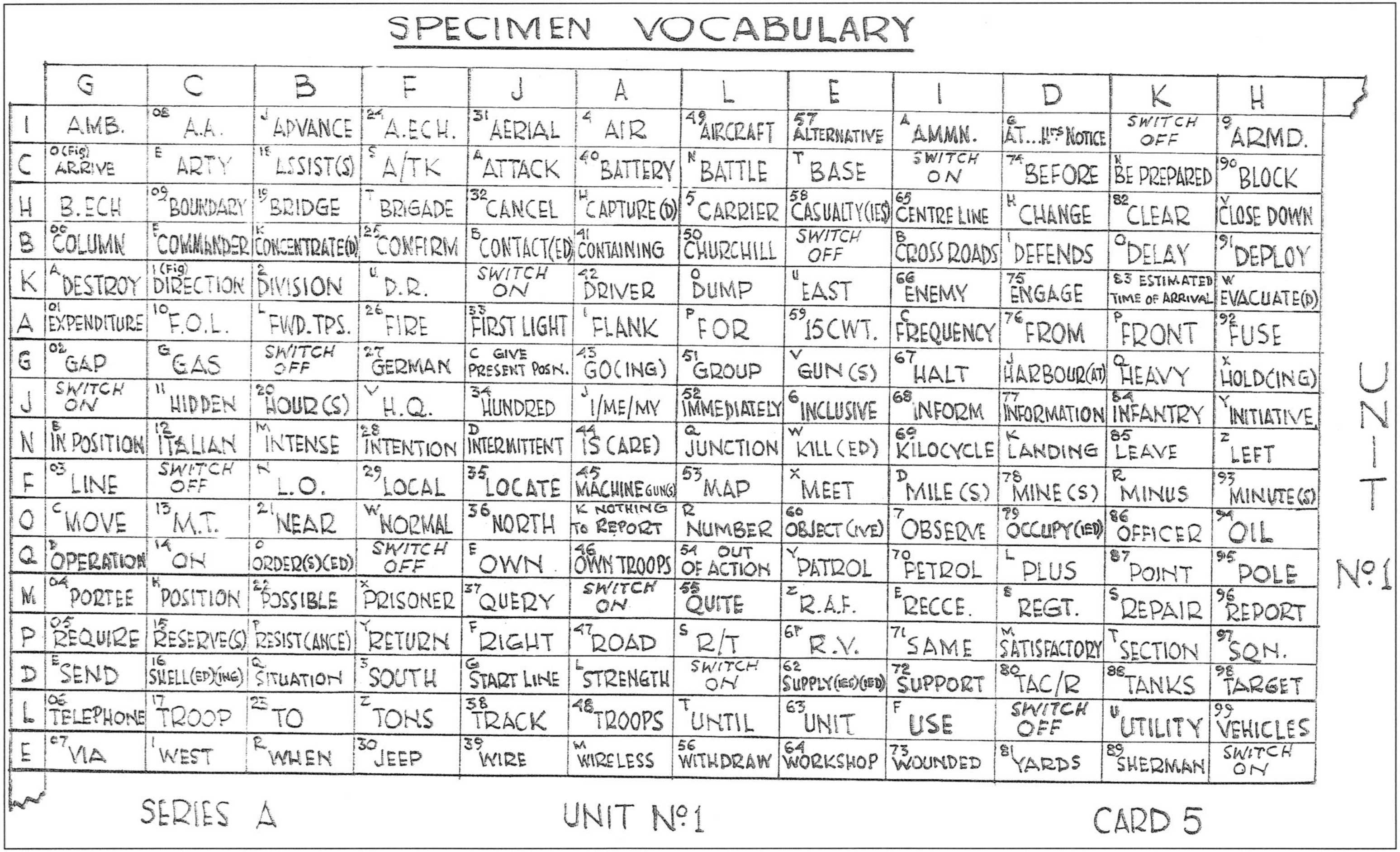

SPECIMEN VOCABULARY

UNIT No.1

SERIES A UNIT No.1 CARD 5

(Slidex card — 17 rows × 12 columns. Column key-letters across the top; row key-letters down the left. Cells marked "SWITCH ON" / "SWITCH OFF" are dummy/null cells.)

Row	G	C	B	F	J	A	L	E	I	D	K	H
I	AMB.	A.A.	ADVANCE	A.ECH.	AERIAL	AIR	AIRCRAFT	ALTERNATIVE	AMMN.	AT. Hrs NOTICE	SWITCH OFF	ARMD.
C	ARRIVE	ARTY	ASSIST(S)	A/TK	ATTACK	BATTERY	BATTLE	BASE	SWITCH ON	BEFORE	BE PREPARED	BLOCK
H	B.ECH	BOUNDARY	BRIDGE	BRIGADE	CANCEL	CAPTURE(D)	CARRIER	CASUALTY(IES)	CENTRE LINE	CHANGE	CLEAR	CLOSE DOWN
B	COLUMN	COMMANDER	CONCENTRATED	CONFIRM	CONTACT(ED)	CONTAINING	CHURCHILL	SWITCH OFF	CROSS ROADS	DEFENDS	DELAY	DEPLOY
K	DESTROY	DIRECTION	DIVISION	D.R.	FIRST LIGHT	DRIVER	DUMP	EAST	ENEMY	ENGAGE	ESTIMATED TIME OF ARRIVAL	EVACUATE(D)
A	EXPENDITURE	F.O.L.	FWD.TPS.	FIRE	GIVE PRESENT POSN.	FLANK	FOR	15 CWT.	FREQUENCY	FROM	FRONT	FUSE
G	GAP	GAS	SWITCH OFF	GERMAN	HUNDRED	GO(ING)	GROUP	GUN(S)	HALT	HARBOUR(AT)	HEAVY	HOLDING
J	SWITCH ON	HIDDEN	HOUR(S)	H.Q.	INTERMITTENT	I/ME/MY	IMMEDIATELY	INCLUSIVE	INFORM	INFORMATION	INFANTRY	INITIATIVE
N	IN POSITION	ITALIAN	INTENSE	INTENTION	LOCATE	MACHINE GUN(S)	JUNCTION	KILL(ED)	KILOCYCLE	LANDING	LEAVE	LEFT
F	LINE	SWITCH OFF	L.O.	LOCAL	NORTH	NOTHING TO REPORT	MAP	MEET	MILE(S)	MINE(S)	MINUS	MINUTE(S)
Q	MOVE	M.T.	NEAR	NORMAL	OWN	OWN TROOPS	NUMBER	OBJECT(IVE)	OBSERVE	OCCUPY(IED)	OFFICER	OIL
Q	OPERATION	ORDER(S)(ED)	ON	SWITCH OFF	SWITCH OFF	SWITCH ON	OUT OF ACTION	PATROL	PETROL	PLUS	POINT	POLE
M	PORTEE	POSITION	POSSIBLE	PRISONER	QUERY	ROAD	QUITE	R.A.F.	RECCE.	REGT.	REPAIR	REPORT
P	REQUIRE	RESERVE(S)	RESIST(ANCE)	RETURN	RIGHT	STRENGTH	R/T	R.V.	SAME	SATISFACTORY	SECTION	SQN.
D	SEND	SHELL(ED)(ING)	SITUATION	SOUTH	START LINE	TROOPS	SWITCH ON	SWITCH ON	SUPPLY(IES)(IED)	TAC/R	TANKS	TARGET
L	TELEPHONE	TROOP	TO	TONS	TRACK	WIRELESS	UNTIL	UNIT	USE	SWITCH OFF	UTILITY VEHICLES	SWITCH ON
E	VIA	WEST	WHEN	JEEP	WIRE		WITHDRAW	WORKSHOP	WOUNDED	YARDS	SWITCH ON	SHERMAN

Above, an example slidex card and, opposite, instructions on how to use.

SLIDEX.
UNIT CARDS.

(a) The lines dividing the spaces on the cursors are either red (issued by army) or black (issued by Div) or green (issued by unit). In the case of red or black cursors, the key is copied on to the cursor in the order of letters as given and the remaining four spaces on the cursor are completed by repeating the first four letters of the key. e.g:

Horizontal cursor   G C B F J A L E I D K H G C B F

Vertical cursor   I C H B K A G J N F O Q M P D L E I C H B

(b) Except when using unit cards, the first five spaces on the cursors have, in addition to the letters already referred to, a scrambled combination of the figures 1 - 5. A figure from each cursor is used to indicate the setting of the cursor in relation to the code card and these two figures are known as the "INDICATOR PAIR". The figure from the horizontal cursor is given first followed by the figure from the vertical cursor. In the diagram the "Indicator Pair" would be 41.

(c) Green cursors only contain the letters of the key and no figures - the last four spaces being left blank.
(d) Notice that the cursors may be moved in the frame and still leave a key letter at the beginning of every row and at the top of every column except in the case of Unit Card (green cursor).
(e) Normally, keys will be changed daily at 0001 Z hrs, but whenever the volume of traffic makes it desirable on security grounds, keys may be changed twice daily at the discretion of the Army Commander. In such cases, the time for the change during the day will be the same throughout an army and will be chosen so that approximately the same weight of traffic is thrown on each key.
(f) In the case of keys being changed <u>during</u> the day, the key for the first part of the day is written on the dotted side of the cursor and that for the second part on the "barred" side.

Key Rectangles,
(a) The recipient of a message using SLIDEX must of course have his cursors at the same setting as the sender's. To ensure that this is done, the top left hand rectangle on the card is known as the "KEY RECTANGLE".
(b) At the beginning of every conversation (not transmission) the sender names the Indicator Pair as the setting of the cursor,(except when using Unit Cards).

These keys were secret, issued regularly with other classified signals material (for example, wireless code signs, frequencies, etc.) and regularly changed to prevent them being compromised. Other codewords were merely used to make radio messages shorter and clearer – for example, the use of words like 'Sunray' for Commander, 'Shelldrake' for Gunner, and so on could prevent mistakes occurring when men were tired and communications difficult. (See 'Annex A' to this chapter for full list.) Other regularly used codes included a map reference points code, while morse code (CW) was used to send messages over greater distances, but had itself to be encoded to be secure.

MANPOWER SUMMARY

A comparison of strengths at the beginning and end of the war shows the enormous growth of R Sigs personnel:

When	Officers	ORs	Total
At outbreak of war	1,771	32,551	34,322
At end of war	8,518	142,472	150,990

Note: The ratio of officers to ORs did not vary very much, being 1:18 (approx.) in 1939 and 1:just under 17 in 1945.

INFANTRY

BACKBONE OF THE ARMY

The backbone of the British Army was the infantry and when war began it consisted of five regiments of foot guards, known collectively as the Brigade of Guards, and sixty-four infantry regiments of the line. The 'regiment' was of course an administrative rather than a tactical grouping. In peacetime

Digging in. All infantrymen had to know how to dig and usually got plenty of practice. However, they didn't often get as much time as the BEF did in France and Belgium during the strange 'Phoney War' period in 1939/40. (IWM – F 4201)

most regiments consisted of two Regular Army battalions (one at home and one abroad) and from two to five TA battalions. RHQ was generally suitably located in the regiment's recruiting area and recruit training was carried out at the co-located regimental depot. The infantry expanded massively during the war although no new regiments were formed, but rather additional battalions were added to existing regiments. When it came to allocating regiments to formations, then the infantry battalion was considered to be the lowest 'building block' and battalions were allocated usually without any regard

for regimental unity. There were numerous exceptions of course. For example, in the 51st Highland Division all the battalions in the three infantry brigades (152nd, 153rd and 154th) were Scottish, while the 131st Lorried Infantry Brigade at one time comprised 1/5th, 1/6th and 1/7th Queens.

Types of Infantry Battalion (Inf Bn) The infantry were undoubtedly the true 'maids of all work' on the battlefield and all had to be able to master a great number of basic skills (for example, fieldcraft, map reading, small arms, anti-gas drills, etc.) but

Having constructed their immaculate trench – which looks to be very reminiscent of those of the First World War – this group of infantrymen enjoys a singsong. Some members keep watch – one is even using a trench periscope. They would get a terrible shock when the Panzerwaffe swung into action. (IWM – F 4211)

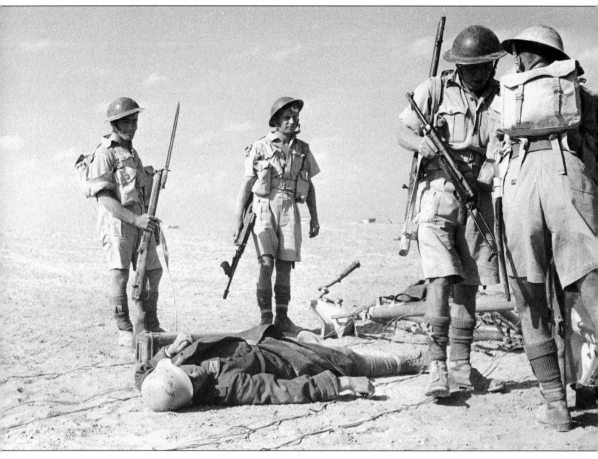

British infantry in the desert. The primary task of the infantry is well illustrated by this photograph, namely to close with the enemy and kill him. However, in this instance was it posed? (IWM — E 18475)

there was a degree of specialization within types of infantry battalions. For instance, the basic infantry battalion was known as a 'rifle battalion', but when they were regularly carried in permanently allotted RASC transport (3 tonners) they became a 'motorized battalion'. It was these motorized battalions that formed the infantry brigade in the armoured division. More specialized were the 'motor battalions', which were an integral part of armoured brigades (one per brigade) and were equipped with Bren carriers and later US half-track vehicles so that they could keep up with the tanks and had very

nearly as good a cross-country performance – the KRRC and RB became experts at this role and provided the majority of the motor battalions that gave immediate support to the tanks. Motor battalions had more firepower than any other infantry battalion. Early on in the war there were also separate machine gun battalions assigned as corps troops and based upon the Vickers .303 medium machine gun. They were also completely motorized. The Divisional Reconnaissance Regiment was also initially manned by infantrymen until the formation of the Reconnaissance Corps. It is also interesting to note that by 1943 the

A platoon of New Zealand infantrymen in a ruined village in the Cassino area of Italy. Note that, apart from US Thompson sub-machine guns, they are fully equipped with British uniforms, equipment and small arms. (War History Collection, Alexander Turnbull Library — DA 5375)

Waiting to enter Tobruk, January 1941. Infantry pause before the final assault as smoke from burning oil terminals fills the sky. (Tank Museum)

Indian infantry of 8th Inf Div, supported by a Universal Carrier, during the Battle of Rome in May 1944. Their uniforms and weapons (less the Thompsons) are British, but may well have been manufactured in India. (Armed Forces Film & Photo Division, New Delhi – WWII/5990)

average age of COs of infantry battalions had dropped from 40 to 30, with company commanders correspondingly younger.

Machine gun battalions comprised three MG coys each of 3 × Pls with a total of twelve MMGs (Vickers .303in) and a Heavy Mortar coy of 4 × Pls with a total of 16 × 4.2 in mortars.

INFANTRY DIVISIONS

By late 1939 there were some seven regular infantry divisions in existence, backed up by twelve 'First Line' and twelve 'Second Line' territorial divisions. From the debacle in France a number of depleted divisions emerged, to be amalgamated with existing formations in the UK and redesignated. This redesignation continued throughout the war as is explained in detail under each division as shown in Appendix 1, while other new divisions were formed, including specialist divisions such as the two airborne divisions.

Rushing through Flushing. British infantrymen double through the narrow streets of Flushing, keeping a sharp lookout for snipers. (IWM – SFD 15)

Thus, at one time or another there were forty-two active infantry divisions (including Guards and Airborne).

Despite their increased sophistication and mechanization as the war progressed, infantry remained the only carriers of weapons who, in theory, were never exhausted, could always 'go that extra mile' and could be counted upon to operate over any terrain anywhere in the world. As has been already stated, despite the success of armour and the effects of mobile warfare, the 'PBI' (Poor Bloody Infantrymen) still formed

the backbone of the British Army throughout the Second World War.

AIRBORNE AND SPECIALIZED FORCES

The Parachute Regiment After the success of German paratroops in the invasion of France and the Low Countries in May 1940, the British Army began to take an interest in this new form of warfare and the Parachute Regiment was officially formed in August 1942

Early paratroopers under training about the time of the Bruneval raid in February 1942. (IWM– CH 2604 via Bruce Robertson)

(Army Order 128 of 1 August), although a battalion of volunteer paratroopers had been formed earlier under Churchill's direct orders from No. 2 Commando. Three more para battalions were formed during 1941–42 and the four became the Parachute Regiment on 1 August 1942, with the motto *Utrinque Paratus* (Ready for anything!). After disaster during the assault on Sicily (because of high winds), they played a major role in the success of D-Day, but showed their vulnerability in the brave, but disastrous, Arnhem operations that autumn, when, although initially highly successful,

the vulnerability of lightly equipped airborne forces became very evident when linkup with the relieving tank column proved impossible. See Chapter 7 for details of the organization of the airborne division.

Gliderborne Forces Military gliders, to carry men, vehicles, materiel – even light tanks – were produced between 1940 and 1942 and a special Glider Pilot Regiment was formed to pilot the series of gliders such as the Hamilcar (specially designed to carry the Tetrach light tank). They were used with success on D-Day, capturing

British paratroopers, Bren gunners in their position in a wood at Arnhem, September 1944. They had been under heavy shell, mortar and machine gun fire for four days when this photograph was taken. (IWM — BU 1108)

Members of the Indian Parachute Regiment aboard an aircraft on the way to Rangoon where they were dropped on 1 May 1945. (IWM — SEU 2350)

Gurkha paratroopers, who were dropped on Rangoon on 1 May 1945. (IWM — FE 491765)

Sergeant glider pilots on an airfield in Oxfordshire enjoy a cuppa courtesy of the Church Army, during a break in practice for gliderborne operations in NW Europe. (Author's Collection)

strategic targets such as bridges and gun positions. They landed safely at Arnhem but too far away to be able to assist the paratroops. They also played a vital role in Burma, landing Gen Wingate's Chindits far behind Japanese lines. Wingate, with Churchill's blessing, mounted two Chindit operations, the second in February 1944 being the most successful when three brigades (two airlifted) crossed into Burma. The Chindits, despite their unorthodox means of transport, were basically infantrymen, so lacked heavy support just like all other airborne forces. A flight usually had twenty gliders each with two pilots who were trained to fight alongside their passengers on reaching their destination. The gliders themselves were RAF equipment.

Airborne divisions contained both paratroop and airlanding (gliderborne) battalions. Detailed organizations are dealt with in Chapter 7; to compare the two basic battalions see table opposite.

Some of Wingate's Chindits waiting to board their aircraft for forward movement to 'Broadway', the invasion field well behind Japanese lines in Burma. Note the cup grenade discharger on the end of the nearest marching man's rifle. (IWM — EA 20832)

Type	Parachute	Airlanding
HQ Coy	5 × Pls incl: 2 × Mor Pl (each 4 × 3 in mor) 1 × A tk Pl (10 × PIATS)	Sp Coy of 6 × Pls incl one with 4 × 3 in mor AA/A tk Coy of 4 × Pls: 2 × AA Pls (each 6 × 20 mm) 2 × A tk Pls (each 4 × 6 pdr)
Rifle Coys	3 each of 3 Pls	4 each of 4 Pls
Strength	29 Officers, 584 ORs	47 Officers, 817 ORs

Indian Paratroopers The Indian Army also had paratroopers, who were trained with the help of the British Army. The 20 Indian Paratroop Brigade, which consisted of two battalions (152 Indian Para Battalion and 153 Gurkha Para Battalion) plus a Para MG coy, was part of IV Corps. They were used in a ground role during the battle for Sangshak in March 1944 and suffered heavy casualties, but were reformed as a composite para battalion and took part in the capture of Rangoon, when, for example, on 1 May 1945 two battalions of Gurkha paratroops were dropped at the mouth of the Irrawaddy to the south of the Burmese capital.

SPECIAL FORCES AND COMMANDOS

Special Forces In October 1941 the Special Air Service (SAS) was formed in the Middle East, its name deliberately chosen to make the Germans think that Britain already had a large airborne force in Egypt. They worked closely with another clandestine group, the Long Range Desert Group (LRDG), who operated far behind enemy lines. The 1st SAS Regiment was formed in 1942 and 2nd SAS was raised in early 1943. They fought in Sicily and Italy, then returned to the UK to form an SAS Brigade that, after D-Day, carried out many operations behind enemy lines.

Men of an LRDG patrol 'somewhere in the desert', observing enemy positions and vehicle movements. (IWM – EA 12434)

Commandos on D-Day. Heavily laden commandos making their way off the beach after arriving near Ouistreham and fighting their way forward against stiff opposition. (IWM — B 5071)

Commando (Cdo) Great Britain was the first nation to form commando units. In 1940 ten independent companies were raised for the Norway campaign, but only five were employed. They then formed the basis of battalion-sized units to carry out hit and run raids in Europe. By March 1941 there were twelve batalions (No. 10 being a special commando made up of anti-Nazi German personnel), each of 500 men. In 1942 the first Royal Marine Commando was formed (later battalions were numbered from 40 to 48). They were also reorganized within battalions into troops rather than companies,

each being three officers and sixty men. They were still lightly armed and equipped, with the minimum of wheeled transport and a battalion strength was approximately 24 officers and 440 ORs. The army commando battalions were all disbanded in 1946 and the Royal Marines took over entirely.

INTELLIGENCE

Although the collection, collation, interpretation and dissemination of intelligence material was the primary task of IOs and

After the battle. A member of 270 Field Security Section, 7th Armd Div, interrogates captured German soldiers after a desert battle. (Author's Collection)

Intelligence staffs at all levels, there was also the Intelligence Corps, which came into being in 1940 (AO 165) and was made up of officers and men with special qualifications and training. At a low level, these specialists included Field Security Sections (FSS), whose interpreters would assist intelligence staff with the interrogation of captured enemy. They were also responsible for the security of their own troops – men, information, materials, operations, training, etc., testing the security-mindedness of units and individuals, looking for weaknesses and advising accordingly.

Battlefield broadcasts to the enemy. An officer broadcasts offers of surrender to the Japanese over a portable amplifier. He was a member of the Psychological Warfare Division of SEAC. (IWM — IND 3984)

ANNEX 'A': STANDARD CODE NAMES

To avoid disclosing the nature of a headquarters by referring to specific appointments, such as BGS, staff captain, brigadier, CRA, etc., the following standard code names were used throughout the field force from 1943 onwards:

Commander	SUNRAY[1]
'G' Staff	SEAGULL[2]
'AQ' Staff	MOLAR
'I' Staff	ACORN
Signals adviser	PRONTO
RA	SHELLDRAKE
RE	HOLDFAST
ST	PLAYTIME
Med	STARLIGHT
Ord	RICKSHAW
REME	BLUEBELL

1. The commander of any formation, unit or subdivision of a unit was a 'SUNRAY', irrespective of rank and his second-in-command was called 'SUNRAY MINOR'. Who he was should have been evident to the recipient of the message without the need for further explanation. So, 'SUNRAY CALLSIGN VDF' would be the OC of the squadron/company with that callsign, while 'SUNRAY CALLSIGN VDF1' was the troop/platoon command of 1 Tp/1Pl, etc.

2. In a unit 'SEAGULL' would be the adjutant, 'MOLAR' the QM and 'ACORN' the IO, etc.

CHAPTER 6

THE SERVICES

RASC EARLY DAYS

The Royal Army Service Corps (RASC) had its roots in the supply and transport service that had worked under the Commissary General and Board of Ordnance, such as the Corps of Waggoners raised in 1794. When the BEF went to France in 1939 each division plus the corps and army troops had a slice of the logistic transport. It was the first time that the RASC had *ever* taken to the battlefield as a completely mechanized corps. However, in order to do so some 14,000 civilian vehicles had been impressed, because all RASC units held only a minimal number in peacetime and there were very few new vehicles available. In addition, four Indian mule companies of the RIASC had to be used to support the overstretched RASC companies in France. All the RASC vehicles were lost when the BEF was evacuated and once again had to be replaced by continuing

A fuel dump near Alexandria. The problem with the British petrol cans was that they were so flimsy that much of the fuel leaked out in transit. They were not a patch on the robust German 'Jerrican', which held 4½ gals and which everyone tried to acquire. Egyptian labourers are unloading this flatbed trailerload of cans. (IWM — E 11252)

There were always masses of stores to be moved, trains to be unloaded, etc. These boxes contained tinned sausages and the bulk would soon be broken down to form a welcome addition to unit rations. (Author's Collection)

the impressment scheme with a further 21,000 civilian vehicles being obtained. After that it was a matter of waiting while the motor manufacturers struggled to make up deficiences. With the help of imports from the USA, especially for the troops in the Middle East and India, the situation was eventually rectifed. Many new, improved models came into service. MT drivers were also in short supply so many RASC drivers in the UK were replaced by ATS, so that they could be posted abroad. Thereafter, some UK-based units remained mixed, while others were entirely ATS manned, most

of the officers coming from the FANYs.[1] Transportation was, however, only one of the aspects of RASC responsibility.

1. The FANYs (First Aid Nursing Yeomanry) was originally an unofficial organization formed before the First World War to provide medical aid for mounted troops. Many of the volunteers served as ambulance drivers and nurses during the Great War and, in 1927, they were officially recognized – although still not funded! In 1937 they became part of the Women's Transport Service and served in India and Kenya as well as the UK.

FUNCTIONS OF THE RASC

The RASC was responsible for the storage and issue of supplies, for certain phases of transporting them and also for the administration of barracks and quarters. Thus, they were the service that supplied the daily needs of the army – the food (including animal fodder when necessary), POL, hospital supplies, fuel for cooking and heating, etc. They were also responsible for the transportation of ammunition, anti-gas clothing and other miscellaneous items such as blankets. The major breakdown of the RASC was thus into the two branches of Supply and Transport. As far as the actual RASC soldiers were concerned, those in the Supply branch were tradesmen, such as butchers, bakers, clerks and issuers, who served in the Supply Companies responsible for baking the bread, butchering the meat, etc. In the Transport branch they were drivers, technical tradesmen (for example, coppersmiths), MT storekeepers and MT clerks, serving in units comprising an HQ and a number of officer-led Operating Sections, divided into sub-sections each of five vehicles under an NCO. RASC vehicles represented about one-fifth of the total number of mechanical vehicles in the Army.

SUPPLIES AND TRANSPORT

STORES AND SUPPLIES
In the British Army these terms covered:

Stores
(a). *Ordnance Stores* Personal and unit equipment, armament and small arms, ammunition and explosives, engineer and signal stores, AFVs, tractors, clothing, personal accessories, camp equipment, office supplies, materials for workshops and all MT vehicles apart from those that were the direct responsibility of the RASC.

(b). *Engineer Stores* Material and equipment needed for all types of engineer work, whether carried out by the RE or other arms, including permanent line signal stores, but not explosives, which were Ordnance Stores.

(c). *MT Stores* These included all material and equipment needed for all branches of MT not provided by other services.

(d). *RASC Stores* RASC MT vehicles, spare parts and the material and equipment needed for repairs to RASC vehicles.

(e). *Medical & Veterinary Stores* These included drugs, medicines, dressings, instruments and appliances.

Supplies This term covered expendable items such as food, animal forage, POL hospital supplies, disinfectants, fuel for cooking and heating, illuminants.

TRANSPORT[2]
There were five types of transport in the Army:

(a). *First Line* Organic unit (for example, infantry battalion, armoured regiment) transport, normally divided into A and B echelons, A being sub-divided into A1 and A2. A1 provided immediate resupply (for example, company/squadron POL[3] and Ammo trucks), A2 daily/nightly resupply. B was the back-up, more static echelon, where bulk was broken into company/squadron-sized packets and where the unit clerks etc. worked.

2. Vehicles were normally classified as 'A', 'B' or 'C'. 'A' were Armoured Fighting Vehicles (e.g. tanks, SP guns, armd cars); 'B' were 'soft-skinned' (e.g. lorries, trucks, Jeeps, etc.); 'C' were static engines and plant.
3. Petrol resupply was always difficult due to the flimsy nature of the British petrol can, losses being as high as 30 per cent across bad going. Whenever possible therefore, the more robust German 'Jerrican' was used which held 20 litres (4½ gal).

(b). *Second Line* This was the transport that the RASC operated and ran between the refilling points (RPs) – normally located to the rear of the divisional administrative area (DAA) or within the corps admin area (usually selected by divisional HQ) – and Delivery Points (DPs) – normally nearer the front of the DAA, which were selected by unit commands.

(c). *Third Line* Also normally operated by the RASC between railheads and major supply dumps, and the RPs. Both second and third line transport was known as 'Field Transport'.

(d). *Reserve* Not only provided a reserve but also undertook general transport duties.

(e). *Technical* These were specially equipped vehicles, such as mobile workshop lorries and ambulance car companies.

In 1942 the REME was formed (see later) and although the RASC retained their unit vehicle workshops, the personnel who ran them all became REME. In addition, the RAOC (see later) took over responsibility for the storage and issue of RASC vehicles.

Operating During the desert campaign in North Africa the tank transporter (for example, the famous Diamond 'T') made its first appearance. Although primarily designed for the out-of-battle movement of tanks, they were also used for the recovery of damaged/broken-down AFVs from the battlefield. Another new vehicle that came into prominence during the assaults on Sicily and Italy in 1943 was the American amphibious DUKW which could carry 2½ tons both on land or in the water. Four amphibious companies of

Left: Desert Recovery. Fitters attaching tow ropes onto a broken-down American-built M3 Medium tank in the Western Desert, before winching it onto their trailer. (IWM – E 27400) *Right:* An RAOC fitter at work in the Western Desert, before the formation of REME. (Author's Collection)

RASC, for example, equipped with DUKWs, successfully maintained one British and one Canadian division across the Straits of Messina during the invasion of Italy. The mountainous nature of much of Italy also meant a successful return of animal transport (for example, some 45,000 pack mules and horses were eventually used in forward areas), while local railway lines were repaired and supply trains used in rear areas, just as they had done in North Africa, where the Western Desert Railway had played an important part in logistic support and troop movement from the Canal Zone.

In the NW European campaign the volume of transportation was greater than anything that had gone before, but the logistic arrangements were now based on five years of wartime experience. Some 200 RASC transport companies, equipped with every type of vehicle – tank transporters, 3 ton trucks, ubiquitous US Jeeps, ambulances, etc. – were formed and allocated to formations to back up the companies already in the divisional columns. The problems that occurred supplying the massive Allied army across the Normandy beaches had to be overcome, over 5,000 ships and craft having been involved in

An Indian fitter works on an engine in a workshop in Italy. (IWM – NYF 19066)

Heavy tank transporters were driven by the RASC. This Scammell Pioneer, loaded with a cruiser tank, is snapped in Le Neubourg on its way to Le Havre. 'SNOW- WHITE' was lucky enough to escape from France and had a second 'life' in the Western Desert. (Tank Museum)

the assault alone, carrying more than 287,000 troops and 37,000 vehicles (all of which had to be waterproofed). By way of example, in the twenty-four hours that ended at 1800hrs on 11 June 1944, the RASC DUKWs carried 10,850 tons of stores from off-lying ships to the beaches, while in the first two weeks Rhino Ferries discharged 10,882 vehicles. Air transport was also successfully used to its limits, some 180 air despatch crews RASC being provided to the RAF, who dealt with the despatch of 360 tons daily from aircraft.

By the end of the war in Europe every type of load had been carried and delivered successfully, using every type of transport on land, sea and air to its limits. For example, over 1,000 British-built railway engines were sent to Europe and used; PLUTO (a 'pipeline under the ocean') brought petrol direct from England to Normandy and then on up through France.

Mention must also be made here of the difficulties and triumphs of supply in the Far East, where, for example, in 1943,

Recovery in Belgium. This light tank, belonging to one of the divisional cavalry regiments, is being backloaded by its regimental LAD. (IWM – F 4388)

Supply convoys on the Burma Road. This great highway was hacked out of the jungle and used, whenever possible, by British and Indian supply vehicles and troops. (IWM – IB 214)

Mountbatten ordered that everyone would '...march, fight and fly through the monsoon'. Transport aircraft (C47 Dakotas) were used to great effect with air despatch crews carrying a wide variety of cargoes including animals. On occasions they supported such operations as Wingate's Chindits. Ultimate victory was achieved in this theatre as well, thanks to improvization, co-operation and flexibilty.

Air Despatch Companies The primary units of these wartime organizations were the air despatch companies, who were responsible for delivering all stores required by the army, military missions and resistance groups, whether landed, dropped by parachute or free dropped. This meant they had four main tasks. First, they were responsible for loading all aircraft engaged in resupply sorties (loads had to be within the aircraft weight limits, properly positioned within its centre of gravity limits and securely lashed – so loading took a great deal of expertise and care). Secondly, they were responsible for packing and storing the containers used for dropping supplies (for example, airborne panniers – 500 lb wicker baskets; bombcell containers designed for free-fall but usually fitted with a parachute; the light canvas SEAC pack that could hold 200 lb). Next they had to provide the air despatch crews who flew with the aircraft and despatched the loads over the dropping zones. Finally, they were responsible for packing the parachutes used for supply dropping.

Air Despatchers at work sending Christmas dinners down to the troops in Burma, December 1944. (IWM – CF 227 XC)

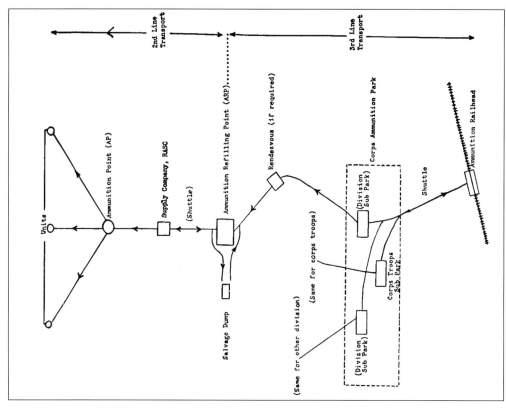

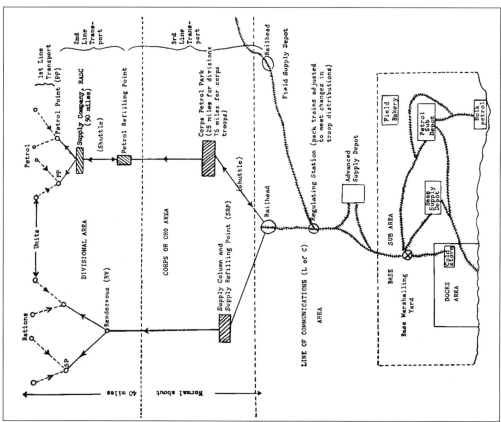

Resupply in the field. Left: the supply system; right: ammunition resupply.

Stretcher bearers arriving at a Regimental Aid Post at Casa Godenzo in the Santerno Valley in Italy. Note the mailed fist insignia (6th Armd Div) and the figures '63', which means that it was one of the three infantry battalions. (IWM – NA 19876)

MEDICAL

RAMC RESPONSIBILITIES

The medical services in the British Army during the Second World War were provided by the Royal Army Medical Corps (RAMC), which had been formed in 1898, prior to the Boer War. Under its jurisdiction also came the various nursing services of which the principal one was the Queen Alexandra's Imperial Nursing Service (QAIMNS). The QAIMNS are dealt with in detail in Chapter 12. The RAMC's main responsibilities were:

(a). The evacuation, care and treatment of all sick and injured troops in all situations.[4]

(b). Initiation and advice on matters affecting the health of all troops.

(c). Supply and resupply of medical equipment and supplies.

(d). Assisting commands at all levels to locate medical units appropriately,

4. This included gas casualties, although it was a unit responsibility to 'cleanse' contaminated soldiers, provided they were still fit to fight.

always bearing in mind that medical units in the field needed time to get established and, once open, could not move quickly because of the sick and wounded, who had first to be evacuated, and all the tentage and stores that had to be carefully packed up.

DEALING WITH THE WOUNDED

In any plan, the command and his 'G' Staff had to give a forecast of anticipated casualties to the 'A' Staff, who in consulation with the medical staff would plan what was needed in medical facilities and transport to deal with the anticipated dead and wounded (dealt with under the types of 'lying', 'sitting' or 'walking' wounded). The evidence from the First World War was that some 5–20 per cent of all those troops involved in an action

would be wounded, while the probable ratio of killed to wounded was 1 to 4. Also, in addition to battle casualties, the probable number of personnel reporting sick daily would normally be about 0.3 per cent. Most of these casualties and sick had to be dealt with by the 'Chain of Evacuation' (see opposite). When more transport, etc., was needed, then this had to be obtained via the 'Q' Staff, including a suitable reserve to meet with unexpectedly heavy losses. Once the plan was approved it would be put into effect – in a divisional operation, for example – by the ADMS (Assistant-Director of Medical Services). Any Operation or Adminstrative Order (see Appendix 3, page 341) had to contain a paragraph giving the opening and closing times for the forward evacuation points (known as Collecting Points (CP)).

Bringing in the wounded on the Arakan front in Burma, where they had to be carried back from the jungle to the nearest road/river transport. (IWM – IB 283)

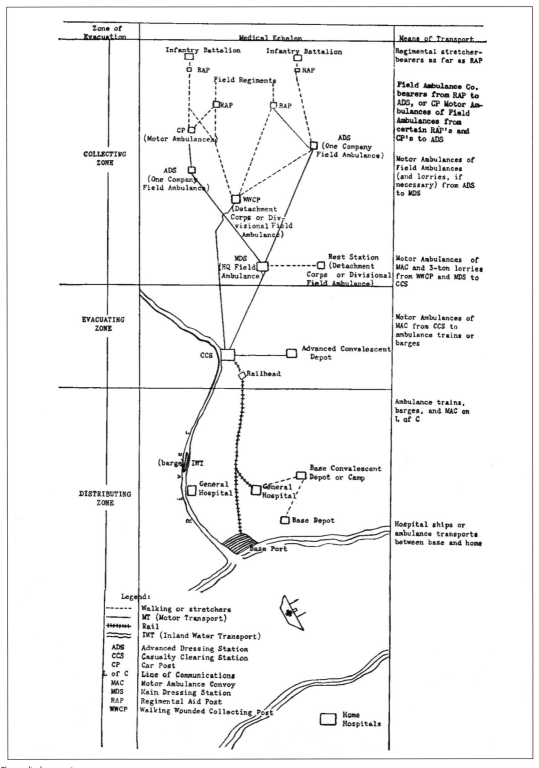

The medical evacuation system.

As will be seen from the diagram, RAMC units were present at all levels, every infantry battalion, for example, having a Medical Officer (MO), a medical orderly, a 15 cwt truck in which to carry their equipment, plus an NCO and some twenty infantrymen, who were trained as stretcher bearers (normally a task undertaken by the Regimental Band if one existed). Their task was to collect casualties and bring them back to the Regimental Air Post (RAP) where the MO and his orderly would deal with them. All soldiers carried a First Field Dressing for immediate use; all were trained in simple first aid, including the use of morphine. On tanks, most other AFVs and many 'B' vehicles a simple, boxed medical kit was carried. Little more than immediate attention could be given at the RAP, from where the field ambulance company was responsible for evacuating the casualties. The HQ of this company formed the Main Dressing Station (MDS), where records of patients were taken and urgent treatment performed. Superimposed, as the diagram shows, was the Field Ambulance Battalion, which was made up of divisional troops comprising an HQ and two companies. Each company could establish an Advanced Dressing Station (ADS), while the HQ could furnish an MDS (with a 100–150 casualty capacity). Each company also had thirty-six stretcher bearers and eight motor ambulances to collect casualties from RAPs and take them to the ADS and then to the MDS. When the action was more mobile then Casualty Clearing Posts (CCP) – also called Casualty Clearing Stations (CCS) – were

Stretcher bearers, clearly marked with the Red Cross symbol, pass Eighth Army tanks (M4 Shermans) in Portomaggiore. (IWM – BNA 24246)

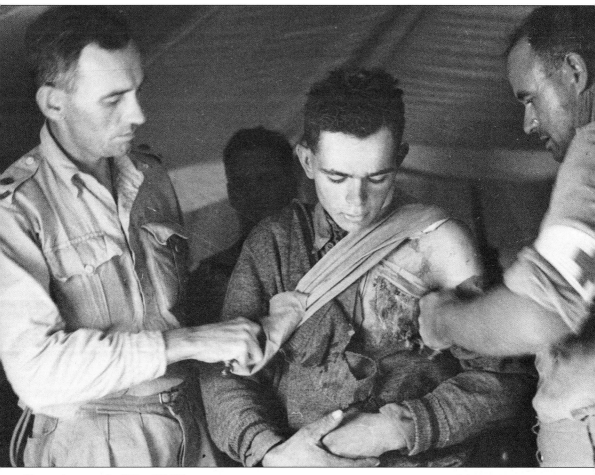

MOs at work on a casualty. (IWM – E 18491)

established between the RAPs and ADS/MDS, equipped with light ambulances or trucks to speed up the system. Even then evacuation could take a long time – for example, in the Western Desert in the winter of 1941/2 a soldier who had been wounded at Agheila had to travel 125 miles before he reached a CCS at Tobruk.

Beyond the MDS the next higher RAMC unit (corps troops) was responsible for the evacuation chain. For most of the war, evacuation was mainly by wheeled ambulance of one type or another (including the ad hoc use of any vehicle available), but gradually aircraft also began to be used, especially where the ground conditions were very difficult (for example, in jungle terrain). In Burma during the fighting retreat in 1942 the problems of evacuation grew until the system was virtually overwhelmed. In the later advance, evacuation still remained one of the most exacting and baffling difficulties. Although never easy, beachhead removal of casualties by naval craft was carried out when operations were near the coast, while further inland every kind of floating transport (even primitive rafts) was used. The ideal was of course air evacuation, but until early 1944 only small aircraft were in use. However, later in 1944 there was a great increase in the number and size of aircraft available so that, by the end of hostilities, some 200,000 sick and wounded had been evacuated by air, with the loss of only one aircraft. This was only possible because of the Allies' complete air superiority. Helicopters were not used until after the Second World War had ended.

First-class Treatment By 1944, at all levels and across the whole field of medicine, every soldier had access to the best treatment possible. There were specialists, and in some areas special centres, for chest surgery, neurosurgery, dermatology, ENT surgery, ophthalmology, orthopaedics, and venereology, as well as the normal more basic work of general surgeons and physicians.

DENTAL

Acute toothache, like bad sea-sickness, can rapidly demoralize even the toughest fighting man, so the Dental Corps made an invaluable contribution in all the campaigns of the Second World War. The Army Dental Corps, which was formed in 1921, was responsible for the state of the army's teeth. While this

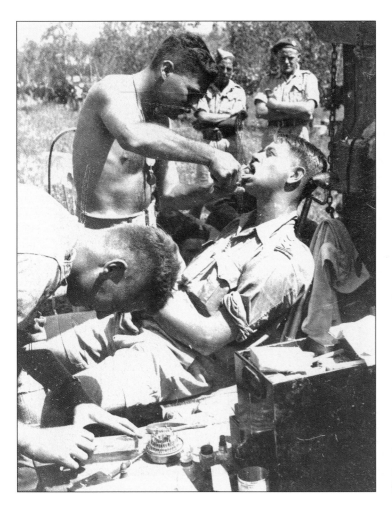

'You won't feel a thing!' A South African dentist of 6th Armd Div, pulling a tooth in the field, in Italy. (Author's Collection)

was relatively easy to achieve in the UK, for example, at PTCs, once the army was on operations then matters obviously became somewhat more complicated. Nevertheless, the Dental Corps was still able to operate, with mobile dental teams visiting units to give many forms of treatment, varying from quick relief of acute pain to the provision or replacement of false teeth (many men had poor teeth in the 1930s). In particular, they co-operated with the specially trained maxillo-facial (known as 'Max Factor') teams, in whose mobile trailers it was possible to perform emergency operations on facial wounds before casualties were evacuated, working with their plastic surgeon colleagues on the urgent treatment of such injuries as shattered jaws.

ORDNANCE

The Royal Army Ordnance Corps (RAOC) was established in 1918, but its history stretches back to the fifteenth-century Office of Ordnance and the Board of Ordnance of 1683. In the Second World War it was responsible for the procurement and issue of all ordnance stores (as already detailed in the RASC section above). At the start of the war and until the formation of the REME (see below) it was also responsible for the maintenance or repair of such stores, including

A mobile dental surgery as used in the Western Desert. (Author's Collection).

Bathnight tonight! Mobile Bath & Laundry Units provided hot water even in Burma! (IWM – SEU 1558)

vehicles of all types, manning ordnance workshops at all levels to effect these repairs. The RAOC was additionally responsible for laundries (MBLU – Mobile Bath & Laundry Units), officers' clothing depots, decontamination of clothing and for the protection of its own installations from enemy attack.

Ordnance Stores To recap, these cover all types of armament and ammunition (including RAF bombs); AFVs and unit transport; radios, electrical and optical equipment; clothing including footwear; barrack stores (tables, buckets, brooms, etc.). What is not included are consumables – rations, POL and expendable medical stores. Because of the unpredictable nature of ammunition resupply – simply because it was not always easy to estimate usage in a given period – the aim was to keep the flow of ammunition going

A barrack room laid out for inspection. The RAOC had to provide all barrack stores – such as those seen here. (Author's Collection)

from rear to front, so as to maintain stocks in forward areas. 'G' Staff decided on quantities of ammunition needed in the field on a ratio of 'rounds per gun' for all types of weapon.

Ordnance units were to be found at all levels from the bases forwards – for example, Base Ordnance Depot (BOD) and Base Ammunition Depot (BAD), where various classes of tradesmen were found, including storemen, clerks, artisans, technicans and technical experts (such as ammunition examiners). At every level of HQ above units (army, corps, division and brigade), there were ordnance experts ready to advise the command and his staff – thus at divisional level there was an ADOS (Assistant Director of Ordnance Services), while brigades had a BOWO (Brigade Ordnance Warrant Officer).

Vehicle Repair RAOC Repair units existed until mid-1942 when REME was formed, so repair and recovery is dealt with under REME below.

By the end of the war the RAOC had grown into a highly efficient organization of some 8,000 officers and 130,000 men. They had suffered over 5,000 casualties. The main features of the logistic support that they had provided were:

(a). A controlling HQ at the War Office, the Ordnance Directorate, which dealt with policy, organization of the corps worldwide and the provision of stores, vehicles and ammunition.

(b). The creation of a UK base for the supply of all items of Ordnance to all theatres, which comprised:

(i) Covered storage accommodation of approx 48 million square feet.

(ii) Open storage of about 50 million square feet.

(iii) Vehicle accommodation for 250,000 vehicles.

(iv) Open accommodation for ammunition covering 1,600 square miles.

(v) Covered ammunition accommodation of 10 million square feet.

(c). A similar though smaller base in the Middle East, making full use of local resources.

(d). The creation of a comprehensive field force organization that provided a reliable and flexible system for the maintenance of a field army. The units were: Ordnance Field Parks, Forward Maintenance Ammunition Sections, Forward Maintenance Stores Sections, Mobile Laundry Units, Mobile Bath Units, Mobile Ammunition Repair Units, Ordnance Beach Detachments, Industrial Gas Units.

(e). The formation of essential base and LofC units in theatres of operation, for example, Base Ordnance Depots, Base Ammunition Depots, Vehicle Depots, Base and Hospital Laundries, Base Industrial Gas Units, Port Ordnance and Ammunition Detachments.

(f). The creation of a workshops organization for the repair, recovery and manufacture of equipment at the base and in the field. This organization was the basis for the creation of REME, as explained.

(g). The creation of a system of packing, preservation and identification of stores which would ensure that they survived the hazards of wartime transport and handling and storage conditions in all climates, and that they would reach the unit in a condition fit for immediate use.

(h). The formation of a highly trained technical ammunition branch that inspected, conditioned and repaired our own ammunition and dealt with captured and unexploded enemy ammunition. The branch also undertook the manufacture

of certain natures of ammunition such as a tk mines. This activity saved lives, helped give our troops confidence in their ammunition and, through the salvage and repair work undertaken, saved the country considerable sums of money.

REME

FORMATION OF REME

As we have seen, vehicle repair and recovery was initially divided between the RASC and RAOC, but this was considered to be extremely wasteful in technical manpower. Therefore, the Beveridge Committee was established to look into the demand for skilled vehicle artificers in the three Services and it was found that a scale of one vehicle mechanic for every 100 vehicles was the most economical and that all should belong to the same corps. However, the RAOC would remain responsible for the provision of vehicles and spare parts. Accordingly the committee recommended the formation of a new corps to repair all vehicles, and Army Order 70 of May 1942 authorized the formation of the Royal Electrical and Mechanical Engineers as a regular and permanent corps of the army and the necessary transfers of men to the new corps were completed by 1 October 1942. All RAOC units with a workshop role were transferred, as were all RASC Heavy Repair Workshops (RASC retained command of its own units' workshops until 1951). To give some idea of the situation, between 1939 and 1942 the engineering service of the RAOC had grown from 400 officers and 4,000 soldier-tradesmen to over 5,000 officers and 80,000 soldier-tradesmen. Both the RE and RASC were also affected, in fact the latter provided the first Director of Mechanical Engineering. Many RASC officers and men with the appropriate qualifications were transferred. Some 100 static RAOC base workshops in the UK also had to be taken over by the new corps. In addition, within the now enormous AA Command there was a mass of technical equipment, especially radar, which had led to an unprecedented demand by the army on civilian sources for engineers and technicians to maintain and repair these new devices. This was initially done by RAOC(E) personnel, but was automatically passed over to REME on its formation, thus, as *Craftsmen of the Army* says:

'REME came into being with a recognized responsibility for what in some eyes was the most important task of all – the care of the equipment that protected the homeland from destruction from the air.'

Repair and Recovery The REME units now formed carried on the vital repair and recovery work all over the battlefield. There were four echelons of vehicle maintenance for the army in battle:

(a). *First echelon maintenance*: unit operators and technical personnel in the unit Light Aid Detachment (LAD).
(b). *Second echelon maintenance*: brigade or armoured brigade workshops working under a divisional CREME; corps troops and/or army troops under a CREME corps or army troops.
(c). *Third echelon maintenance*: infantry and armoured troops workshops on a scale of one for each infantry or armoured division, working normally under corps control and helping out with second echelon maintenance whenever possible.
(d). *Fourth echelon maintenance*: advanced base workshops and base workshops under GHQ control, sited normally in the LofC or the GHQ area.

Skilled technicians had to be able to repair not just the basic armoured and unarmoured vehicles, but also a wide range of other equipments such as static engines and plant, armament and fire control systems of all types, radios and telecommunications equipment, radar, sound ranging and survey equipment, and even specialized medical items including x-ray, physiotherapy and surgical equipment. A variety of different workshops were therefore needed, and all would require specifically trained technicians – for example, an armoured workshop would have to deal with very different items from an airborne workshop, or one with LAA, HAA, SL and observation units. Add to this the diversity of

A field workshop detachment dismantling a tank engine in training somewhere in England in April 1942. Where possible repairs would always be done in situ by forward repair teams. (Author's Collection)

operational theatres in which technicians had to work, and the wide range of skills required by members of the new corps, the REME, can be readily imagined. (The humidity in the Far East could play havoc with delicate equipment, while the sand and grit in the desert affected all mechanical equipment.)

PROVOST

The Corps of Military Police (CMP) was formed in 1926, although it could trace its ancestry back as far as the fifteenth century, and in the 1930s it underwent some major changes:

(a). The formation of provost companies and sections with fixed establishments took place in 1935.

(b). In May 1937 the Field Security Wing was formed (but later, in 1940, was transferred to the Intelligence Corps).

(c). In 1938 direct enlistment into the corps became possible.

(d). In 1939 Provost companies were alloted to TA divisions. Guards reservists with civil police experience were earmarked for posting to the CMP on mobilization.

All these measures meant that, when war was declared, the CMP was able to deploy some 3,500 men from all sources. All non LofC field formation units were completely mechanized, companies had a number of motor cars, 15 cwt and 30 cwt lorries and motorcycle combinations, while all LCpls were mounted on solo motorcycles. Although there were considerable modifications to

This immaculate MP has parked his motorcycle below a number of directional signboards – but how could you miss the Western Desert?! (Author's Collection)

establishments during the war, the CMP did at least go to war in reasonable shape. When the BEF went to France, the CMP played a key role signing routes and controlling traffic, then once the BEF was in position they began normal policing duties and the maintenance of discipline. The Special Investigations Branch (SIB) was reborn in 1940, composed of just nineteen detectives, all volunteers, from the Metropolitan Police. The CMP were a 'visible symbol of British presence' in both the debacle in Norway and again in France. 'As the last troops pulled out a corporal maintained his usual post, resplendent in red cap and white sleeves.'[5] Back in the UK, another part of the Provost – the Military Provost Staff Corps (MPSC) – looked after the jails and 'glasshouses' (Corrective Centres) where soldiers under punishment (that is, having been tried by Courts Martial and found guilty) served their sentences.

Thereafter, the 'Redcaps' played an important part in every theatre of war, both on and off the battlefield. An example from the Western Desert: at El Alamein, there was so much traffic trying to get forward that six additional main tracks had to be provided to supplement the coast road. Each track was marked with cairns of white-painted stones, two provost sections policed each track, with sections deployed and a 24-hour Straggler Post constantly manned. In the words of one desert veteran, 'it was the sappers, signals and military police who led the armour into battle'. The 'Redcaps' were needed everywhere to meet new tasks, for instance in the Normandy landings four beach provost companies laid out and controlled the beach maintenance and assembly areas, while the movement of 21 Army Group to the embarkation ports on the south coast was a 'triumph of administration', One traffic post alone, for

An RMP checks a vehicle work ticket. (Author's Collection).

example, handled nearly 30,000 vehicles by the end of July 1944. 6th Airborne Division Provost Company was the 'spearhead' of the CMP during Operation Overlord.

Provost duties of all types continued in all theatres, the problems of lack of trained men and equipment being most pressing in the Far East where much had to be improvized – the only traffic control equipment received by one unit being hurricane lamps, red and green flags and stencil brushes! A good example of the increased load on the CMP concerns the looking after of POWs: as the war progressed and more and more enemy were taken prisoner and the task of looking after them fell to the CMP. For example, in Tunisia in May 1943 some 275,000 German

5. *The Redcaps* by G.D. Sheffield (Brassey's (UK), 1994).

An MP on traffic duty tries to repair a battered German road signpost. (IWM – B 8934)

and Italian personnel surrendered. When Germany eventually surrendered, the problem was greatly magnified – some 7.7 million military prisoners were held by the Western Allies, while there were 3,750,000 former slave workers now categorized as displaced persons to deal with as well. The CMP played an important role in producing order from chaos – the 5th Division Provost Company, for example, received 11,000 prisoners into the company cage in just one day! Of course, their other duties had grown enormously as well; for example, at the end of the war I Corps had six field provost companies, five traffic control companies, two VP companies and three SIB sections.

CHAPLAINS

'IN THIS SIGN CONQUER'
The Royal Army Chaplains' Department (RAChD) goes back to a Royal Warrant of 1796, and of course there were regimental chaplains even earlier. When the war started the RAChD contained 169 chaplains, of whom 121 were Church of England and the remainder drawn from the Church of Scotland, the Methodist, Presbyterian, Baptist and Congregational churches. There were twenty Roman Catholic priests, about 100 TA chaplains and a few in the Reserve Forces. At the peak period of the war these numbers had expanded to 3,052 chaplains and 640 RC priests. The Chaplain-General remained at his HQ in London and appointed Deputies (DCGs) in the different theatres of war. The senior chaplain with an army was an Assistant Chaplain-General (ACG) with the rank of Chaplain 1st Class. The senior chaplain with a corps was a Deputy Assistant Chaplain-General, with the rank of Chaplain 2nd Class, while the senior chaplain of a division was called the Senior Chaplain (SCF), with the rank of Chaplain 3rd Class. The battalion/regiment

padre normally based himself on or near the RAP, where he could be on hand to comfort the wounded and the dying. Many such chaplains performed heroic deeds and received the highest bravery awards for rescuing wounded under fire, staying with the wounded when a position was overrun and continuing to minister in POW camps. Out of action, the chaplain would be one of the prime movers in setting up unit clubs/ canteens, wherever possible, and especially when NAAFI could not provide anything. Ninety-six chaplains of all denominations gave their lives in the Second World War and their memorial is in the chapel of the RAChD Centre at Bagshot Park.

PAY

Soldiers' pay is always a tricky subject, dear to the heart of every 'squaddie'. However, in wartime, especially when National Service is in operation, it assumes even greater importance because of the requirement to pay hundreds of thousands of dependants as well as the soldiers themselves. The corps in the army which had replaced the regimental paymasters of the nineteenth century became the Royal Army Pay Corps (RAPC) in 1920. At the start of the Second World War they were undoubtedly adept at handling all matters of pay and allowances, maintaining personnel records and occurrences and advising everyone, as necessary, about accounting procedures, living up to their motto *Fide et Fiducia* (In Faith and Trust). However, their strength was a mere 239 officers, 1,147 ORs and 580 civilian clerks. By the end of the war, the Pay Services comprised 2,166 officers and 18,543 ORs RAPC; 28 officers and 13,088 ORs ATS; and 6,756 civilians. Meanwhile pay establishments included, in addition to all the theatres of operations and LofCs, twenty-three fixed centre regimental pay offices in the UK – a mammoth undertaking.

A padre conducting an open-air drumhead
service for a Gunner regiment in France, 1940.
(IWM – F 4083)

Above and left: Ditto – one is in the Western Desert,
the other in Burma.
(Both Author's Collection)

'When you go home, tell them of us, and say, for your tomorrow we gave our today.' (IWM – NA 10126)

Pay Accounting On mobilization, the Loose Leaf Accounts (AF N3085 for the soldier; AF N3086 for his dependants) were re-introduced. Units embarking for active service took into use AB64 (Part II) and used Acquittance Rolls. Officers' pay was still dealt with by army agents (and would be so until 1969). However, the added complications, which included the introduction of family allowance for married officers, necessitated the opening of the Army Pay Office (Officers' Accounts) in Manchester in May 1940. Towards 1943/4 machine processing was introduced, which certainly speeded up the posting of entries, while even earlier the use of microgram photography had overcome the problem of getting post to the Mediterranean, which was virtually closed to shipping. As the war progressed and the number of servicemen increased, the General Post Office was rapidly overwhelmed by the number of PO Savings Bank accounts being opened and this had to be taken over by the RAPC. Field and area cash officers in all theatres of operations, who had all the responsibilities of bank managers but none of their safeguards, dealt in millions. Some £20 million in cash was conveyed to Normandy for the initial stages of the invasion, while the cashier in Cairo had to deal with over fifty different currencies!

When the war ended, demobilization put another heavy burden on the pay services. release wings were set up in all Regimental pay offices, whose task it was to close down the soldiers' army account (AFN 3085B) and open a new account sheet (AFN 3085X) for all those entitled to release benefits, payment being made by means of a special army allowance order book.[6]

VETERINARY

Although the British Army had whole-heartedly embraced mechanization, animal transport was still used in some areas, so the need for veterinary expertise continued to be an essential requirement. The Royal Army Veterinary Corps (RAVC) was immediately able to recall its regular reservists and to call upon its TA personnel, so from just 85 officers (59 of whom were stationed in India) and 105 soldiers, the corps increased dramatically to 519 officers and 3,939 ORs. The RAVC Depot moved from Woolwich to Aldershot for a few months at the start of the war, then to Doncaster racecourse where it remained for the duration. The RAVC's first major task was to provide veterinary and remount support to the 1st Cavalry Division, which was sent to Palestine in 1939 with 8,000 horses. In 1941, when the division was mechanized, the horses were retained for other tasks – such as draught

and pack transport roles. By the end of 1942 the strength of military animals in thc arca was 6,500 horses, 10,000 mules and 1,700 camels. RAVC personnel were also involved in Greece, Eritrea and Syria and in the local provision of livestock for slaughter, meat inspection and the rearing of livestock.

Mules were used extensively in Italy during 1943–45, some 11,000 being purchased in Sicily and Southern Italy to supplement those shipped in from North Africa and the Middle East. In India, the Indian Army Veterinary Corps (IAVC) grew during the war to 481 officers (230 were RAVC), 329 veterinary asstistant surgeons and 6,385 Indian ORs, there being a continually rising demand for animal transport, military farms and meat inspection. Mules, horses and bullocks were used on operations, as by Gen Wingate's Chindits during their two

In the Far East mule transport helped to maintain supplies. Here men of the RIASC follow the course of a river – their only path forward. (IWM – IND 1885)

6. As one might expect, many of those being demobilized did not feel satisfied with the total amount of money paid to them, so it became necessary to form a 'Release Aftermath Wing' to deal with the volume of letters of complaint!

expeditions into Japanese occupied Burma – no fewer than 5,500 mules and horses were 'de-voiced' for the second and larger scale Chindit operation, so that they did not give away troop positions to the enemy! Immediately postwar, the RAVC was involved with all aspects of vet-erinary in the many war devastated countries worldwide.

EDUCATION

In 1920 the Corps of Army Schoolmasters was disbanded and the Army Education Corps (AEC) formed. In 1938, at the moment when intensive rearmament began, the AEC consisted of just 106 officers (of whom 55 were overseas) and 449 instructors (185 overseas); but the establishment had been increasing as the Army Technical Schools expanded – the annual intake rising to nearly 3,000 – while it soon became clear that the danger of war would bring in National Service and that would produce an army composed of all scholastic levels. However, the planning to meet the new situation was impeded by an extra wartime role for the AEC (from 1930s onwards), namely taking over the responsibility for ciphers so as to leave the R Sigs free to expand its new radio communications. Cipher training began at once, but the duties, although a break from classroom routine, were extremely monoto-nous. Later, as already mentioned in the previous chapter, the R Sigs took over all cipher duties.

With the first Militia Intake in July 1939 an 'educational revival' began, with a con-ference in December 1939 that approved the founding of a Central Advisory Council for Adult Education in the HM forces (CAC) with twenty-three regional committees being set up. A Director of Education was also appointed at the War Office, with civil servants from the Board of Education being seconded to assist him.

From 1940 onwards, in the UK, under the 'Haining Scheme' educational activity was envisaged in three groups: Humanities (history, geography, and economics and inter-national affairs); utilities (vocational subjects, much done via the post with the technical colleges; 'Postal Study Courses'); and arts and crafts. Participation was voluntary and carried out during free time. The scheme was adapted as the war progressed, and had to deal with problems such as how to arrange for men in the more distant theatres, or aboard submarines, to take part in postal schemes initially. However, with the efficient help of the Army Postal Services, the AEC dealt with a staggering 222,745 enrolled students during the war, of which 117,423 were from the army.

Another important move was the establish-ment of an Army Bureau of Current Affairs (ABCA) in the War Office, which produced much important literature – for example, there were 118 issues of *Current Affairs* covering home and foreign affairs; another highly effective pamphlet was *Map Review*, printed fortnightly.

In the field, educational studies were con-tinued and an important second duty for the AEC was to provide quiet places where the soldier might read (and there were mobile libraries in some theatres), or write to his family or friends, or join others in study. As the end of the war approached, the AEC was heavily involved in the 'Release Period', running resettlement courses in a wide variety of subjects for servicemen and servicewomen.

PIONEERS

Under Army Order 200 of 1939, the Auxiliary Military Pioneer Corps (AMPC) came into existence as a combatant corps and was later redesignated as the Pioneer Corps (P Corps) in 1940. The cap badge of a rifle, shovel and pick 'piled' and their motto

The Pioneer Corps in action. These 25 pdrs belonging to 94 Fd Regt RA are being moved up towards the Rhine along trackway laid by the Pioneer Corps, the unsung heroes of many tough battlefields. (IWM – BU 2716)

Labor Omnia Vincit (Work conquers all) both explain their duties more than adequately. Initially they were undoubtedly the 'Cinderella Corps of the Army', as they were composed of reservists from a mixture of infantry and cavalry regiments, elderly volunteers of First World War vintage, and militiamen who were below the physical standard required by front line troops. In addition, they were at first indifferently administered. The growth and development of the corps into a fighting force that could provide a disciplined body of highly skilled labour, also able to share in the fighting when the need arose – as happened on a number of occasions, the first being at Boulogne in 1940 – was truly remarkable. At its peak strength in 1944–45, the P Corps reached a total of 444,591 all ranks, who then recruited and controlled a further

1 million foreign civil labour personnel. Not all the P Corps companies were entirely British, even as early as 1940 there were numerous non-British companies, including fifteen of mixed German-Austrian nationality, one Spanish, two Czech, and one Indian. They suffered nearly 10,000 deaths (including 3,500 on the British P Corps establishment) on active service worldwide.

As has already been mentioned, together with the RE the P Corps played an important role in the Battle of Britain, dealing with unexploded bombs. In addition, they also worked non-stop throughout the London Blitz, clearing rubble, rescuing trapped civilians, and so on, all as part of 'Special Force London'. To give an entirely different example of the work of the Pioneers, in Italy, during the desperate battles to capture

Cassino and Rome, the much-cratered Highway 6 was constantly repaired by a special task force, which not only included RE mechanical equipment, road construction and quarrying companies but also a good number of P Corps who did much of the basic 'spade-work' with pick and shovel.

On 1 June 1944 the P Corps consisted of 106 Group HQs and 376 companies, with 65 Group HQs and 376 companies in UK, ready for D-Day, while the rest were scattered along the vast military Lines of Command which encircled the world. On D-Day, within each beach group, there was a force of Pioneers whose task it was to clear mines and underwater obstacles, to unload landing craft, to build ammunition and other dumps,

to help construct beach tracks for vehicles to to firm ground, to help collect and evacuate the wounded, to collect and bury the dead, to guard POWs and, when necessary, to fight. Once these tasks were completed there were (cf the REs) always many more awaiting them – truly *Labor Omnia Vincit*!

CATERING

Prewar, a Chief Inspector of Catering Services (RASC) had been appointed in the rank of colonel, while all cooks were normal regimental personnel receiving an additional sixpence a day 'extra duty pay' for cooking. A new School of Army Cookery was built in Aldershot in 1939, but it was not until 1941

Very satisfactory white loaves were produced by the field bakeries in Libya, using a double-decker oil fired oven. (Author's Collection)

that real progress was made towards the formation of a new corps. The Army Catering Corps (ACC) – motto 'We Sustain' – came into existence on 22 March 1941 (Special AO 35 of 1941) with the task of providing catering services and advice throughout the army. All regimental cooks were supposedly transferred to the new corps, although its formation did not see a complete end to regimental cooks, who continued to supplement the ACC cooks in many units. In addition, the longer the war progressed then the more common it was for vehicle-borne troops to cook for themselves when in action (tank crews invariably did so). This was because rations became much more palatable, easier to divide and cook (i.e. dried, tinned and packeted in suitable sizes), as opposed to fresh food that had to be cooked centrally and then kept hot and palatable while being distributed. Nevertheless, the staple 'Field Service Rations' generally had to be cooked centrally within the vast majority of units/sub-units.

There were also reserve rations of course, held permanently by units, which consisted of hard tack biscuits, preserved meat (corned beef), preserved vegetables and other dry goods like tea, coffee, sugar and tinned milk. However, they were spartan fare, as were the 'Iron Rations' kept for the most dire emergencies. It was the arrival of the palatable tinned rations from the US Army pack ration system during the Second World War that revolutionized field rations. This was explained in some detail in the *US Army Handbook* in this series, so it is not repeated here. However, to give some examples of the amount of work involved in feeding just one division: during the 1944–45 operations in NW Europe the 53rd (Welsh) Infantry Division consumed over 6 million rations – 4.3 million field service rations and 1.7 million compo rations. That meant transporting 14,363 tons of food from the corps maintenance area to the divisional admin area for

that one division alone, every man in the division eating 17 cwt of food (roughly fourteen times his own body weight!) during the period of operations. In the same period, 1,030 portable cookers were issued for use by the ACC – all that adding up to a great deal of effort by the cooks, which of course did not end immediately the firing ceased.

During the war and the subsequent period of operations to 31 March 1946, the ACC suffered 1,316 casualties, including 659 deaths. They had fed the army throughout the world, in every climate and under extremely varied conditions, providing a good catering and cookery service and ensuring that a satisfactory and uniform standard of messing was maintained in all units because, as one official report commented, 'one of the main factors affecting the morale of the soldier is the food he eats'.

Troops get a cuppa in a jungle cookhouse in Burma. (IWM – IND 1852)

'Come to the cookhouse door boys!' Men of the BEF line up for breakfast at the unit cookhouse in their billets area somewhere in France. (IWM – F 3692)

Cold Comfort Farm. BEF soldiers make the best of their barnyard billets, somewhere in France in mid-December 1939, but at least they have their dartboard! (IWM – O 2228)

PHYSICAL TRAINING

On the outbreak of war the Army Physical Training Staff (APTS) numbered just 280. By the time the war ended there were some 3,000 in the APTC, the APTS having changed its name to the Army Physical Training Corps in 1940. Initially, the APTS had been built up by incorporating all peacetime Regt Asst PT instructors from regular units, calling up some 150 reservists who were in civilian PT appointments and a similar number of PT graduates, and incorporating some 100 selected football, cricket and boxing coaches (including Tommy Lawton, Joe Mercer, Len Hutton and Jack Peterson). Thirty-one staff instructors were posted into the BEF (twelve to field formations and nineteen to convalescent depots). After Dunkirk, it was decided that the staff should be formed into a combatant corps, with its HQ at Aldershot, all Staff instructors firing a musketery course and learning how to handle weapons efficiently, the link between war and physical fitness thus being made apparent to all. Thereafter, they more than lived up to their adopted motto 'Fighting fit and fit to fight'. Montgomery once emphasized their importance thus:

An APTC 'Tough Tactics' team with Maj (later Lt Col) Jerry Hedley, who was the instigator of this training in the Middle East. (Author's Collection)

'There is only one standard of fitness, the standard for Total War. We have got to make ourselves tougher than the Germans and they are pretty tough. Besides, no man's brain is at its best unless he is physically fit.'

APTC instructors served in all theatres of war, supervising PT and other forms of fitness training and giving advice on all types of sporting activities. They were naturally much in evidence in PTCs and the like in the UK. The APTC were also present in all theatres of war; for example, in the Middle East, in order to toughen up the soldiers for the rigours of desert war, the APTC designed and put into effect 'Tough Tactics Training'. After Alamein, Tough Tactics Mobile Teams were formed. Each team was self-contained, with its own transport and apparatus, and they visited all Eighth Army units to give demonstrations of 'Tough Tactics'. In the Far East special training was adapted for jungle warfare, while a new *Manual of Basic & Battle Physical Training* appeared in December 1944 to incorporate this novel training. The APTC's role in assisting with the training of airborne forces was considerable and as the units of the 1st Airborne Division were built up, APTC instructors who were also trained parachutists were incorporated into their establishment. Twenty-six members of the APTC dropped with the parachutists they had trained at Arnhem and fought shoulder to shoulder with them.

POSTAL

Letters from home were of course one of the most important features of life for every soldier, no matter where he was serving, so an efficient mail service was a very important factor in sustaining high morale. The Royal

A NAAFI/EFI mobile canteen bringing 'char and wads' to troops in the Western Desert. (HQ NAAFI via Author's Collection)

A morale booster. Plenty of regular mail from home was vital for troops in all areas, such as these happy receivers of parcels and letters somewhere in NW Europe. (IWM – B 12804)

Well-known war reporter and broadcaster Frank Gillard making a Christmas broadcast on 25 December 1944. Sadly, Cpl Bob Pass of 1/6 Queens, who is being interviewed here, was killed just before the war ended. (IWM – B 13074)

Engineers, who ran the Army Postal Service, did their level best to keep the mail flowing as smoothly as possible. They were not, however, responsible for performing the unenviable task of censorship that had to be imposed on all outgoing mail, this being done by unit officers.

WELFARE

The Navy, Army & Air Force Institute (NAAFI) was, and still is, a non-profit making corporation, developed from the sutlers of the seventeenth to nineteenth century and really coming into its own during the Second World War. It provided basic comforts and canteen facilities everywhere, living up to its motto of 'Service to the Services' with mobile canteens often serving tea and buns just behind the battle line! Small wonder that it grew during the war from a staff of 5,000 with a trade of some £10 million, into a 'canteen colossus' with a staff of 120,000, a trade of £200 million and 10,000 establishments in over forty countries serving 5 million-plus customers! The policy of NAAFI was to sell goods at retail prices, the profits accrued being returned to units in the form of rebates and other services, such as entertainments and sports goods. The other name used for the NAAFI when serving abroad was the 'Expeditionary Force Institutes' (EFI), all NAAFI employees being incorporated into the armed forces when in theatres of war.

WVS ladies teaching soldiers, who are due for overseas postings soon, how to darn their socks! (Author's Collection)

The NAAFI Entertainment Branch provided an ENSA chorus line to rival the Tiller Girls in the shade of the Pyramids. (NAAFI via Author's Collection)

'Sally, Sally, Pride of our Alley'. Well-known actress and singer Gracie Fields enjoys a teabreak at a YMCA mobile canteen, with men of GHQ Liaison Regiment (Phantom Signals), whose insignia was a white 'P' on a black square. (IWM – F 4073)

These views taken inside a NAAFI canteen will bring back many memories to old soldiers. (NAAFI via Author's Collection)

CHAPTER 7

DIVISIONAL ORGANIZATIONS

THE DIVISION

The division is without doubt the ideal sized field formation to use so as to explain the basic make-up of the operational British Army of the Second World War, the brigade and below being too small and unrepresentative, the corps and above being too large as they could contain a far more diverse mix of units. There were really only three different lasting types of division – Armoured, Infantry and Airborne – although three other types – Cavalry, Motor and Mixed – did make brief appearances, as will be explained. All divisional organizations were laid down in War Establishment tables, issued from time to time by the War Office, to incorporate the changes demanded by operational experience, changing conditions and, in some cases, by theatres of war. Therefore, in order to obtain a clear picture of their make-up, one must look at all the variations in establishment that occurred to the basic types of division during the war and which are set out in this chapter.

ARMOURED DIVISION

There were nine changes to the basic organization of armoured divisions between 1939–45, as follows:

I – May 1939	VI – Aug 1942
II – Apr 1940	(Middle East)
III – Oct 1940	VII – Apr 1943
IV – Feb 1942 (Middle East)	VIII – Mar 1944
V – May 1942 (UK)	IX – May 1945

Space does not permit the organization to be shown in full every time, so this has been done for the 1944 division only, the others being shown in outline.

I. 1939 Establishment

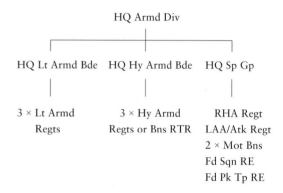

The tank establishment of the armoured division was:

HQ Armd Div	3 × Lt cruisers		
	5 × Hy cruisers	=	8 tanks
HQ Armd Bde	6 × Lt cruisers		
	4 × Hy cruisers	=	20 tanks
Lt Armd Regt (3)	36 × Lt tanks		
	22 × Lt cruisers	=	174 tanks
Hy Armd Regt (3)	26 × Lt cruisers		
	8 × CS cruisers		
	15 × Hy cruisers	=	147 tanks
	TOTAL		349 tanks

(CS = Close Support)

Cromwell cruiser tanks on training in England prior to D-Day. In NW Europe it was one of the main British tanks used, but the crews of 7th Armd Div were unhappy when they had to give up their Shermans to re-equip with Cromwells. This column is led by a Mk VI, which mounted a 95 mm howitzer. (Tank Museum)

Matilda Mk IIs advancing in close formation at Tobruk, 1941. (IWM – E 5558)

II. April 1940 Establishment

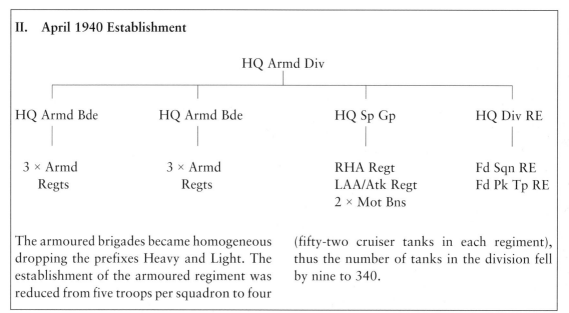

The armoured brigades became homogeneous dropping the prefixes Heavy and Light. The establishment of the armoured regiment was reduced from five troops per squadron to four (fifty-two cruiser tanks in each regiment), thus the number of tanks in the division fell by nine to 340.

III. October 1940 Establishment

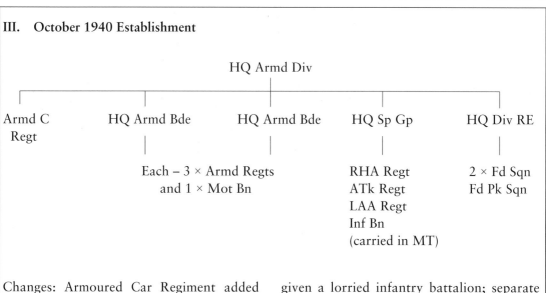

Changes: Armoured Car Regiment added (not in Middle East); the two motor battalions were given (one each) to the armoured brigades; Support Group was given a lorried infantry battalion; separate a tk and LAA regiments; Field Pk Troop became a squadron. Tank establishment remained at 340.

IV. February 1942 Establishment

For tactical reasons the brigade group became the basic battle formation in the Middle East. One of the two armoured brigades was replaced by a motor brigade (of three motor battalions) and the two brigades were reorganized into brigade groups by the addition of artillery units from the Support Group (now abolished), and of engineer and

Tanks of 11th Armd Div (note the black bull on the yellow rectangle), led by an A30 Challenger, mounting a 17 pdr. (Tank Museum)

A line of British Comets pounding away at targets somewhere in Germany. (Tank Museum)

admin services from Divisional Troops. A tk regiments were broken up and each RHA/Field Regiment was allotted an a tk battery of sixteen (2 pdr/6 pdr) guns in addition to its three 25 pdr batteries. LAA regiments were also broken up and batteries allocated to each brigade group. Divisional HQ was allotted a staff and a signals organization sufficiently large to control all elements – brigade groups, HQ Div RA, HQ Div RE, plus workshops and supply echelons. The tank establishment of the armoured regiment varied as armoured regiments were re-equipped with a proportion of American tanks.

V.   May 1942 Establishment

Here also one of the two armoured brigades was replaced, this time with an infantry brigade. The Support Group was abolished and the artillery – which now included another RHA/Field Regiment – placed under HQ Div RA. Div HQ received two AA tanks, while the armoured regiment received eight AA tanks, while the fifth troop per squadron, which had been taken away in 1940, was restored. These changes put up the armoured regiment tank establishment to 61, while the tank establishment of the armoured division was now 227:

HQ Armd Div	8 × cruisers		
	2 × AA	=	10 tanks
HQ Armd Bde	10 × cruisers	=	10 tanks
Armd Regt (3)	55 × cruisers		
	6 × CS		
	8 × AA	=	207 tanks
	TOTAL		227 tanks

VI.   August 1942 Establishment

The changes from Serial IV were: the armoured division once again became the basic battle formation in the Middle East instead of the Brigade Group. With just a few exceptions armoured brigade groups were redesignated and reorganized as armoured brigades. The artillery returned to under HQ Div RA, this including a third RHA/Field Regiment being added, while the A tk and LAA regiments were reformed. RE from the brigade groups was turned to HQ Div RE and a second field squadron was added. AA tanks were also added (see below), while during the autumn of 1942 all armoured regiments in the Middle East began to be equipped with American Sherman M4 medium tanks. The tank establishment was now:

HQ Armd Div	8 × cruisers		
	2 × AA	=	10 tanks
HQ Armd Bde	8 × Shermans	=	8 tanks
Armd Regt (3)	52 × Shermans		
	4 × AA	=	168 tanks
	TOTAL	=	186 tanks

Towards the end of 1942 one MG battalion was split up into three in brigade support companies (later called support groups) between 1st, 7th and 10 Armoured Divisions.

British riflemen advance cautiously through the rubble of bombed buildings in Italy, November 1943. (IWM – NA 8440)

7th Armd Div on parade. Winston Churchill, accompanied by Montgomery, Brooke and Maj Gen 'Lou' Lyne (GOC), inspects his 'Dear Desert Rats' in Berlin. (IWM – BU 9078)

VII.   April 1943 Establishment

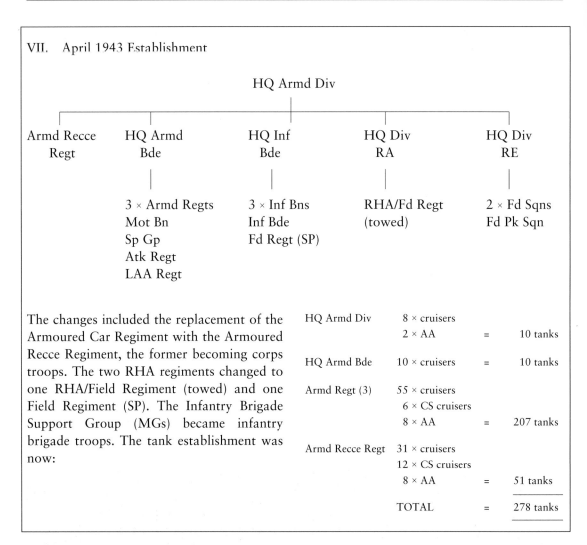

The changes included the replacement of the Armoured Car Regiment with the Armoured Recce Regiment, the former becoming corps troops. The two RHA regiments changed to one RHA/Field Regiment (towed) and one Field Regiment (SP). The Infantry Brigade Support Group (MGs) became infantry brigade troops. The tank establishment was now:

HQ Armd Div	8 × cruisers		
	2 × AA	=	10 tanks
HQ Armd Bde	10 × cruisers	=	10 tanks
Armd Regt (3)	55 × cruisers		
	6 × CS cruisers		
	8 × AA	=	207 tanks
Armd Recce Regt	31 × cruisers		
	12 × CS cruisers		
	8 × AA	=	51 tanks
	TOTAL	=	278 tanks

VIII.   **March 1944 Establishment** (continued on page 153)

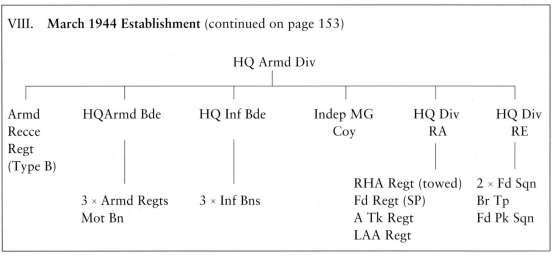

See detailed establishment for the 1944 armoured division as at Annex 'A' to this chapter. The tank establishment was now:

HQ Armd Div	8 × cruisers		
	2 × AA	=	10 tanks
HQ Armd Bde	10 × cruisers		
	8 × OP	=	18 tanks
Armd Regt (3)	55 × cruisers		
	6 × CS cruisers		
	11 × lights		
	6 × AA	=	234 tanks
Armd Recce Regt (Type B)	40 × cruisers		
	6 × CS cruisers		
	30 × lights		
	5 × AA	=	81 tanks
	TOTAL		343 tanks

In addition to the armoured division organization see also the detailed organization of the armoured brigade, armoured regiment and armoured division artillery.

IX. May 1945 Establishment

This establishment was the result of changes approved in February 1945, but not implemented until the end of the campaign in NW Europe. The Armoured Recce Regiment became a fourth armoured regiment in the division. The tank establishment was now:

HQ Armd Div	7 × cruiser/infantry		
	2 × AA	=	9 tanks
HQ Armd Bde	7 × cruiser/infantry		
	8 × OP		
	2 × AA	=	17 tanks
Armd Regt (4)	55 × cruiser/infantry		
	6 × CS		
	11 × lights		
	6 × AA	=	312 tanks
	TOTAL		338 tanks

Riflemen of the BEF, in a defensive position on the Somme, wait to engage the enemy from a hedgerow position. (IWM – F 4529)

INFANTRY DIVISIONS

Like the armoured divisions there were constant changes to the War Establishment (WE) of infantry divisions during the war. However, there was never any major change to the number of infantry battalions (three per brigade). The most important WE are shown below. The strength of the infantry division at the start of the war was 13,863 all ranks and rose to 18,347 by the end of the war. There was of course a fair difference in the types of weapons and vehicles, as is evidenced by the comparison below.

I. **1939 War Establishment**

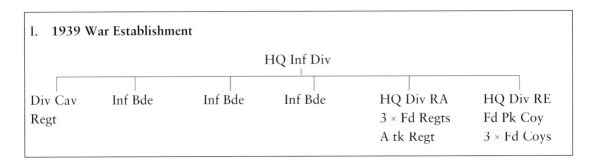

II. **1941 War Establishment**

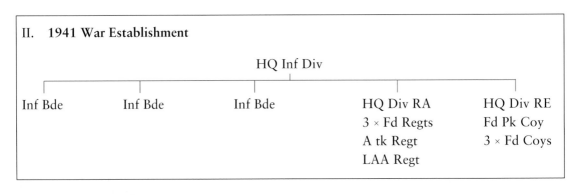

III. **1944/45 War Establishment**

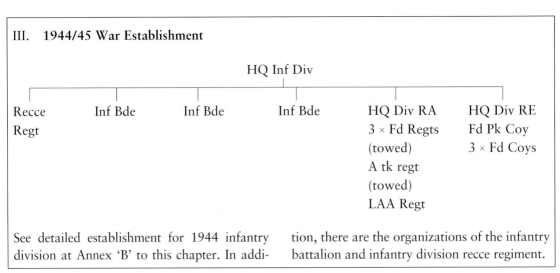

See detailed establishment for 1944 infantry division at Annex 'B' to this chapter. In addition, there are the organizations of the infantry battalion and infantry division recce regiment.

Normal Grouping for Mobile Operations

Irrespective of attached armour, the infantry divison mobilized operations grouping was as follows:

Bde Gps (each)	Div Tps	Admin units & 'B' Ech (in DAA)
Bde HQ	Div HQ incl	Comd Admin Gp
3 × Bns	HQ RA, HQ RE	3 × Bde 'B' Echs
MG Coy	HQ RASC, HQ REME	Div Tps 'B' Ech
Hy Mor Pl	Fd Security Sec	Fd Pk Coy RE*
Fd Regt	Postal Unit	4 × RASC Coys*
A Tk Bty	HQ MG Bn	Fd Hyg Sec
Fd Coy RASC	Recce Regt	3 × Wksp REME*
Fd Amb	HQ A Tk Regt (-)	+ unit LADs
Tp LAA	(+ A Tk Bty)	(- those in Bdes
	HQ LAA Regt (-)	and Div Tps)
	(+ LAA Bty)	OFP*
	Fd Pk Coy RE*	
	Div Sigs (-)	
	4 × RASC Coys*	
	2 × FDS	
	3 × Wksp REME*	
	Pro Coy	
	OFP*	

* These can be in either Divisional Troops or DAA

AIRBORNE

I. Establishment 1944/45

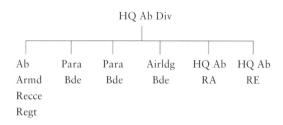

See detailed establishment for the 1944 airborne division at Annex 'C' to this chapter.

British patrol from 2nd Inf Div guarding a wing position on the banks of the Irrawaddy, 16 March 1945. (IWM – SE 3115)

A jungle patrol attacks a 'basha' (native hut) in a banana grove. (IWM – SE 198)

Men of 1/6 Queens marching into Tobruk as it was recaptured for the final time in November 1942. (Author's Collection)

Paratroopers in action at
Arnhem with their
3 in mortar firing at enemy
positions across the Rhine.
(IWM — BU 1099 via Bruce
Robertson)

British paratroopers on the second
airborne landing moving forward
into Arnhem with their A tk gun,
September 1944.
(IWM— BM 1091)

CAVALRY, MOTOR AND MIXED

The best way of explaining the organization of these three formations is to compare them in tabulated form:

Arm/Svc	Cav Div	Mot Div	Mixed Div
HQ	HQ Cav Div	HQ Mot Div	HQ Div
Bdes	3 × Cav Bdes (each 3 × Cav Regts)	2 × Inf Bdes (each 3 × Inf Bns & 2 × A tk Coys)	2 × Inf Bdes (each 3 × Inf Bns) 1 × Tank Bde (3 × Tk Bns)
RA	3 × Regts RHA	2 × Fd Regts 1 × A tk Regt	3 × Fd Regts 1 × A tk Regt 1 × LAA Regt
RE	1 × Fd Sqn 1 × Fd Pk Sqn	2 × Fd Coys 1 × Fd Pk Coy	3 × Fd Coys 1 × Fd Pk Coy
R Sigs	Cav Div Sigs	Div Sigs	Div Sigs
Inf		Div Mot Cycle Bn	Recce Regt
ST	Cav Div Amn & Pet Coy Cav Div Sup Coy	Div Amn Coy Div Pet Coy Div Sup Coy	Tk Bde Coy 2 × Inf Bde Coys Div Tps Coy
Med	3 × Cav Fd Ambs Cav Div Hygiene Sec	2 × Fd Ambs Fd Hygiene Sec	2 × Fd Ambs 2 × FDS Fd Hygiene Sec
Vet	3 × Mobile Vet Secs		
Ord			Tk Bde Ord Coy 2 × Inf Bde Ord Coys
Pro	Cav Div Pro Coy	Div Pro Coy	Div Pro Coy
Post	Cav Div Postal Unit	Div Postal Unit	Div Postal Unit
Misc		Mobile Bath Unit	

PERSONNEL AND ANIMALS

All Ranks	11,097	10,136	16,119
Horses	6,081		

Arm/Svc	Cav Div	Mot Div	Mixed Div
WEAPONS BY TYPE			
Machine Carbine	–	–	1,196
Pistols	1,358	1,111	2,933
Rifles	7,808	7,449	9,916
Rifles A tk			
.303	81	–	–
.55	166	241	380
LMGs	203	466	Bren 886
			Twin Bren 121
			MG Besa 156
MG Vickers	36	–	–
Pistols Sig	12	184	347
Mortars 2 in	–	81	114
3 in	–	12	42
Guns 18/25 pdr	48	48	72
" 2 pdr A tk	–	81	48
" 25 mm A tk	–	18	–
" 6 pdr A tk	–	–	160
" 3 in How	–	–	18
" 40 mm AA	–	–	54
" 20 mm AA	–	–	48
VEHICLES			
Bicycles	5	220	221
Motor cycles	574	531	999
combination	–	99	37
Cars misc	93	103	284
Cars Scout	–	–	100
Cars Armd	–	–	18
Carriers Scout	6	26	–
Bren	–	60	–
Misc	–	–	241
Ambulances	39	16	36
Trucks 8 cwt	192	237	40
	195	420	874
Vans 12 cwt	23	17	–
Lorries 1 ton	14	16	2
30 cwt	325	289	99
3 ton	277	184	1,023
Dragons	72	–	–
Tractors Fd Arty	–	108	–
Armd Comd Vehs	–	–	1
Arms OPs	–	–	27
Carriages 40 mm AA	–	–	54
Tractors Misc	–	–	180
Trailers	119	161	191
Tanks Cruiser			4
Inf			156
CS			18
AA			24
Scissors Br			3

Men of the Eighth Army on their way to Rome. (IWM – NA 11322)

Mixed Division This new organization was tried in 1942, the third infantry brigade being replaced by a tank brigade to endeavour to produce a better balanced formation. The five UK-based 'mixed' divisions returned to the normal Infantry Division organization in 1943.

Armoured Division HQ Staff To give an example of the size of a divisional head-quarters, here is the breakdown of the HQ of an armoured division:

Command:	Comd	– 1
	ADC	– 1
'G' Staff:	GSO 1	– 1
	GSO 2	– 1
	GSO 3	– 4
	LOs	– 3
'AQ' Staff:	AA & QMG	– 1
	DAAG	– 1

	DAQMG	– 1
	Staff Capts	– 2
		Total = 16
Attached	Engr – CRE	– 1
	staff	– 4
	Int – IO	– 1
Services	RAChD – SCF	– 1
	Chaplains	– 3
	RAMC – ADMS	– 1
	DADMS	– 1
	Ord – ADOS	– 1
	Ord Offr	– 1
Pro		– 1
		Total = 15
HQ Sqn	Offrs	– 5
	ORs	– 244
		Total = 249

TOTAL HQ Armoured Division = 36 Officers, 244 ORs = 280 All Ranks

Annex 'A': Organization of an Armoured Division, 1944

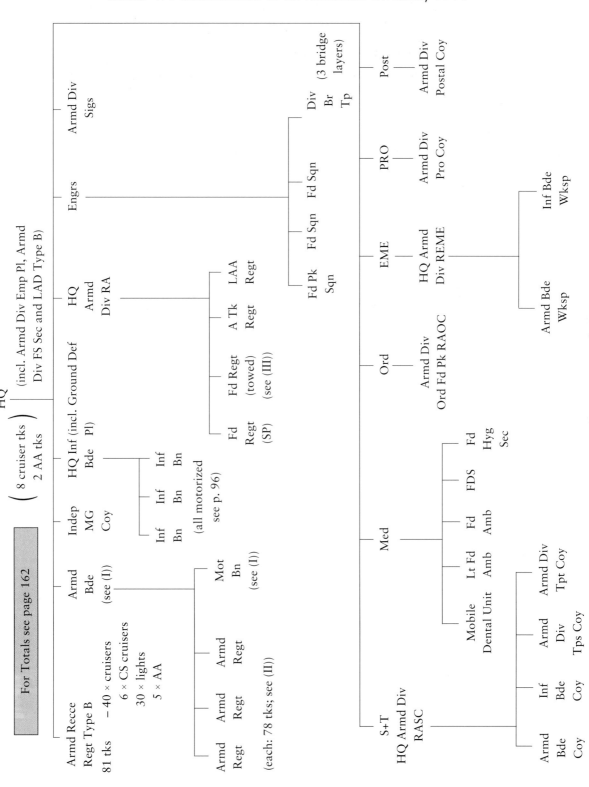

TOTALS – ARMOURED DIVISION

Manpower:

724 Officers, 14, 240 ORs = 14,964 All Ranks

Vehicles: 3,414 vehicles including:
cruiser tanks – 246
light tanks – 44
tracked carriers (armoured) – 261
scout cars (armoured) – 100
trucks and lorries – 2,098

Weapons:

rifles and pistols – 9,013
machine carbines – 6,204
LMGs – 1,376
mortars (2 in, 3 in and 4.2 in) – 160
PIATs – 302
field guns 25 pdr – 48
a tk guns (6 pdr and 17 pdr) – 78
AA guns – (20 mm and 40 mm) – 141

(I) ARMOURED BRIGADE 1944

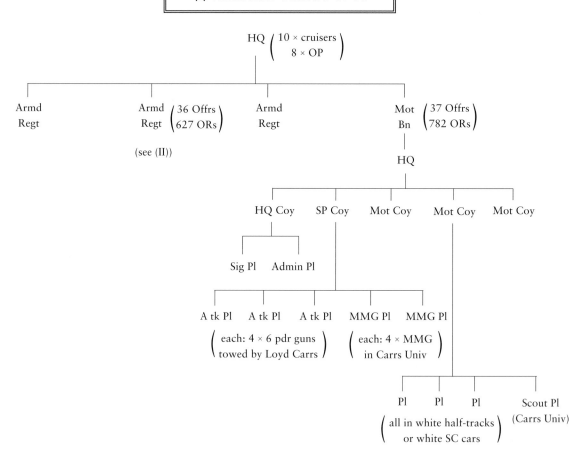

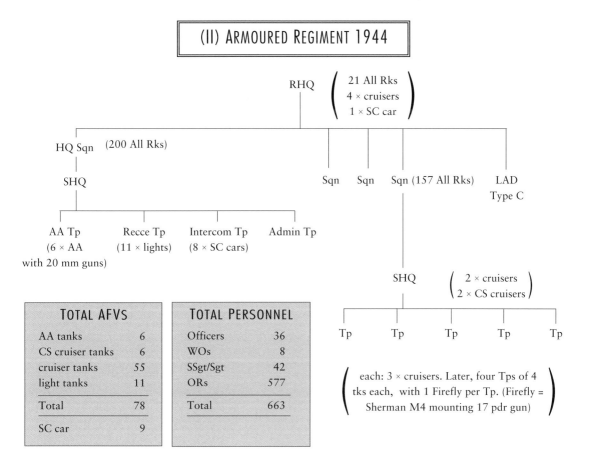

(II) ARMOURED REGIMENT 1944

RHQ (21 All Rks / 4 × cruisers / 1 × SC car)

HQ Sqn (200 All Rks)

SHQ

Sqn   Sqn   Sqn (157 All Rks)   LAD Type C

AA Tp (6 × AA with 20 mm guns)   Recce Tp (11 × lights)   Intercom Tp (8 × SC cars)   Admin Tp

SHQ (2 × cruisers / 2 × CS cruisers)

Tp   Tp   Tp   Tp   Tp

(each: 3 × cruisers. Later, four Tps of 4 tks each, with 1 Firefly per Tp. (Firefly = Sherman M4 mounting 17 pdr gun))

TOTAL AFVS	
AA tanks	6
CS cruiser tanks	6
cruiser tanks	55
light tanks	11
Total	78
SC car	9

TOTAL PERSONNEL	
Officers	36
WOs	8
SSgt/Sgt	42
ORs	577
Total	663

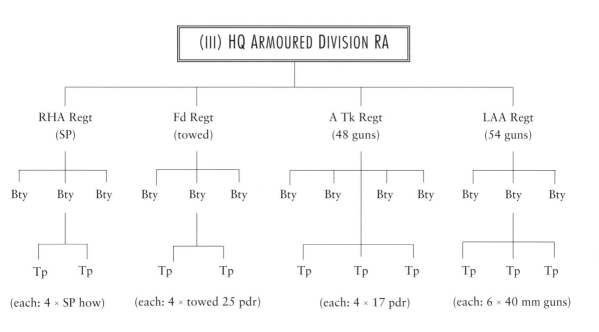

(III) HQ ARMOURED DIVISION RA

RHA Regt (SP)   Fd Regt (towed)   A Tk Regt (48 guns)   LAA Regt (54 guns)

Bty Bty Bty   Bty Bty Bty   Bty Bty Bty Bty   Bty Bty Bty

Tp Tp   Tp Tp   Tp Tp Tp   Tp Tp Tp

(each: 4 × SP how)   (each: 4 × towed 25 pdr)   (each: 4 × 17 pdr)   (each: 6 × 40 mm guns)

ANNEX 'B': ORGANIZATION OF AN INFANTRY DIVISION, 1944

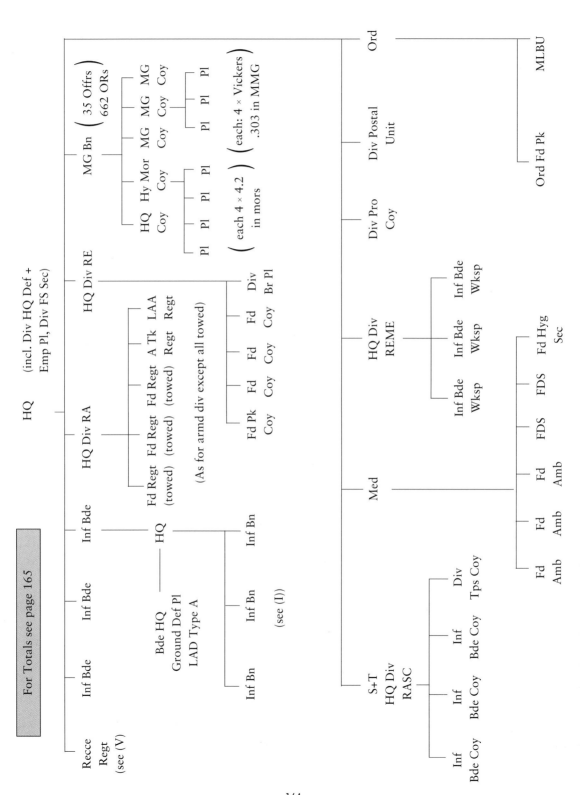

For Totals see page 165

TOTALS — INFANTRY DIVISION

Manpower:
870 Officers, 17,477 ORs = 18,347 All Ranks

Vehicles: 3,347 vehicles including:
tracked carriers (armoured) – 595
armoured cars – 63
trucks and lorries 1,937

Weapons:
rifles and pistols – 12,265
machine carbines – 6,525
LMGs – 1,262
MMGs – 40
mortars (2 in, 3 in and 4.2 in) – 359
PIATs – 436
field guns 25 pdr – 72
a tk guns (6 pdr and 17 pdr) 110
AA guns (20 mm and 40 mm) – 125

(I) ORGANIZATION OF INFANTRY BATTALION

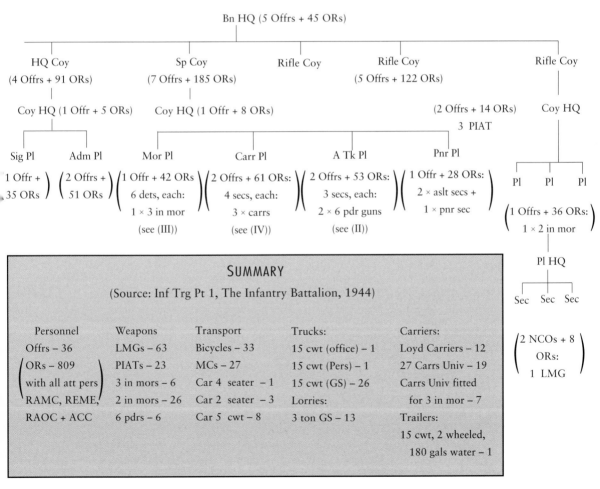

Bn HQ (5 Offrs + 45 ORs)

HQ Coy (4 Offrs + 91 ORs)
Sp Coy (7 Offrs + 185 ORs)
Rifle Coy
Rifle Coy (5 Offrs + 122 ORs)
Rifle Coy

Coy HQ (1 Offr + 5 ORs)
Coy HQ (1 Offr + 8 ORs)
(2 Offrs + 14 ORs)
3 PIAT
Coy HQ

Sig Pl — 1 Offr + 35 ORs
Adm Pl — 2 Offrs + 51 ORs
Mor Pl — 1 Offr + 42 ORs: 6 dets, each: 1 × 3 in mor (see (III))
Carr Pl — 2 Offrs + 61 ORs: 4 secs, each: 3 × carrs (see (IV))
A Tk Pl — 2 Offrs + 53 ORs: 3 secs, each: 2 × 6 pdr guns (see (II))
Pnr Pl — 1 Offr + 28 ORs: 2 × aslt secs + 1 × pnr sec

Pl Pl Pl

(1 Offrs + 36 ORs: 1 × 2 in mor)

Pl HQ

Sec Sec Sec

(2 NCOs + 8 ORs: 1 LMG)

SUMMARY

(Source: Inf Trg Pt 1, The Infantry Battalion, 1944)

Personnel	Weapons	Transport	Trucks:	Carriers:
Offrs – 36	LMGs – 63	Bicycles – 33	15 cwt (office) – 1	Loyd Carriers – 12
ORs – 809	PIATs – 23	MCs – 27	15 cwt (Pers) – 1	27 Carrs Univ – 19
with all att pers	3 in mors – 6	Car 4 seater – 1	15 cwt (GS) – 26	Carrs Univ fitted
RAMC, REME,	2 in mors – 26	Car 2 seater – 3	Lorries:	for 3 in mor – 7
RAOC + ACC	6 pdrs – 6	Car 5 cwt – 8	3 ton GS – 13	Trailers:
				15 cwt, 2 wheeled,
				180 gals water – 1

(II) Organization of Infantry A Tk Platoon

HQ		
Carr Univ	Pl Comd (Capt)	– Pistol
	Dvr Mech	– Rifle
MC1	2IC (Sub)	– Pistol
MC2	Orderly	– Sten
Truck:		
15 cwt	Pl Sgt	– Rifle
4 × 2 GS (1)	Storeman	– Rifle
(6 pdr amn)	Dvr batman	– Sten
Truck:		
15 cwt	Fitter REME	– Rifle
4 × 2 GS (2)	Fitter gun REME	– Rifle
(6 pdr amn +	Dvr batman	
fitter's stores)		

Three Sects (each)		
MC	Orderly	– Sten
No. 1 Det		
Loyd Carr (1)	Sgt (Sec Comd)	– Rifle
6 pdr gun,	3 gun numbers	– 3 Rifles
6 pdr amn,	Dvr Mech	– Rifle
2 in mor		
Loyd Carr (2)	1 Cpl	– Rifle
6 pdr amn,	Dvr Mech	– Rifle
LMG side shields		
No. 2 Cooker		
No. 2 Det		
As per No. 1 except comd is L/Sgt.		

(III) Mortar Platoon

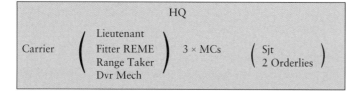

HQ				
Carrier	Lieutenant / Fitter REME / Range Taker / Dvr Mech	3 × MCs	Sjt / 2 Orderlies	

Summary			
Offr	– 1	Rifles	– 42
ORs	– 45	3 in mor	– 6
Pistols	– 4	A tk rifle	– 3

No. 1 Det	No. 2 Det	No. 3 Det	No. 4 Det	No. 5 Det	No. 6 Det
Carr	Carr	As No. 1	As No. 2	As No. 1	As No. 2
Sjt	L/Sgt				
3 Ptes	3 Ptes				
Dvr Mech	Dvr Mech				
3 in mor	3 in mor				
66 rounds of amn	66 rounds of amn				
No. 1 Truck	No. 2 Truck	No. 3 Truck			
15 cwt	15 cwt	15 cwt	3 ton lorry		
Cpl	Cpl				
Batman	Pte				
Dvr i/c	Dvr i/c		Dvr i/c		
A Tk rifles 200 rounds	as No. 1	as No. 2	324 rounds of		
72 rounds 3 in mor amn			mor amn		

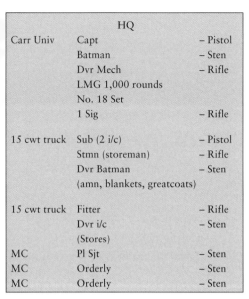

HQ

Carr Univ	Capt	– Pistol
	Batman	– Sten
	Dvr Mech	– Rifle
	LMG 1,000 rounds	
	No. 18 Set	
	1 Sig	– Rifle
15 cwt truck	Sub (2 i/c)	– Pistol
	Stmn (storeman)	– Rifle
	Dvr Batman	– Sten
	(amn, blankets, greatcoats)	
15 cwt truck	Fitter	– Rifle
	Dvr i/c	– Sten
	(Stores)	
MC	Pl Sjt	– Sten
MC	Orderly	– Sten
MC	Orderly	– Sten

(IV) CARRIER PLATOON

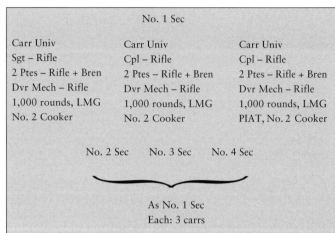

No. 1 Sec

Carr Univ	Carr Univ	Carr Univ
Sgt – Rifle	Cpl – Rifle	Cpl – Rifle
2 Ptes – Rifle + Bren	2 Ptes – Rifle + Bren	2 Ptes – Rifle + Bren
Dvr Mech – Rifle	Dvr Mech – Rifle	Dvr Mech – Rifle
1,000 rounds, LMG	1,000 rounds, LMG	1,000 rounds, LMG
No. 2 Cooker	No. 2 Cooker	PIAT, No. 2 Cooker

No. 2 Sec   No. 3 Sec   No. 4 Sec

As No. 1 Sec
Each: 3 carrs

(V) INFANTRY DIVISION RECCE REGIMENT [1]

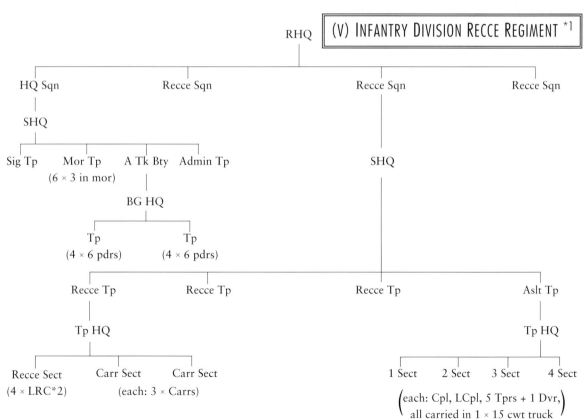

*1   Prior to June 1942 infantry terminology was used (Bn/Coy/Pl).

*2   Towards the end of the Tunisian Campaign Recce Tps were issued with armoured
      cars and then deployed 2 × Armd Cs and 3 × LRCs.

Source: R. Doherty, *Only the Enemy in Front.*

ANNEX 'C': ORGANIZATION OF AN AIRBORNE DIVISION, AUGUST 1944

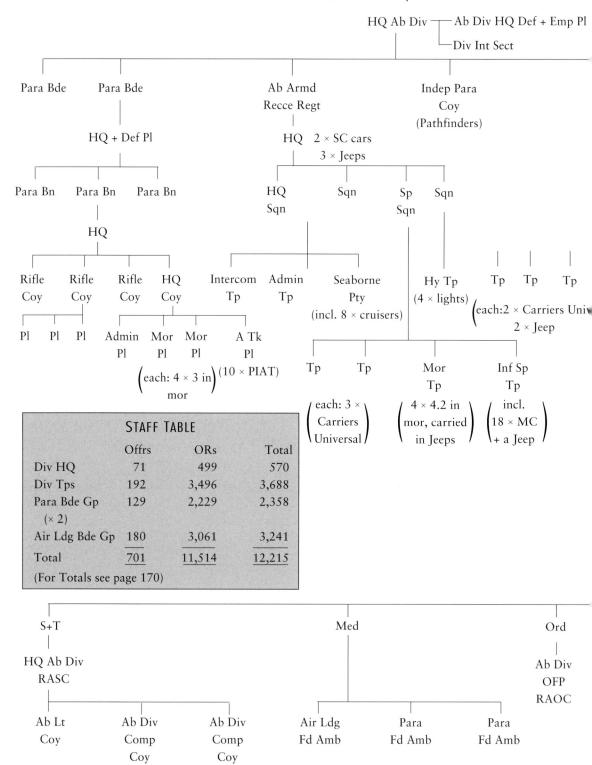

HQ Ab Div — Ab Div HQ Def + Emp Pl
— Div Int Sect

Para Bde · Para Bde · Ab Armd Recce Regt · Indep Para Coy (Pathfinders)

HQ + Def Pl

HQ   2 × SC cars
3 × Jeeps

Para Bn · Para Bn · Para Bn

HQ Sqn · Sqn · Sp Sqn · Sqn

HQ

Rifle Coy · Rifle Coy · Rifle Coy · HQ Coy · Intercom Tp · Admin Tp · Seaborne Pty (incl. 8 × cruisers) · Hy Tp (4 × lights) · Tp · Tp · Tp

Pl · Pl · Pl · Admin Pl · Mor Pl · Mor Pl · A Tk Pl

(each: 4 × 3 in) mor · (10 × PIAT)

(each:2 × Carriers Univ
2 × Jeep)

Tp · Tp · Mor Tp · Inf Sp Tp

(each: 3 × Carriers Universal) · (4 × 4.2 in mor, carried in Jeeps) · (incl. 18 × MC + a Jeep)

STAFF TABLE

	Offrs	ORs	Total
Div HQ	71	499	570
Div Tps	192	3,496	3,688
Para Bde Gp	129	2,229	2,358
(× 2)			
Air Ldg Bde Gp	180	3,061	3,241
Total	701	11,514	12,215

(For Totals see page 170)

S+T · Med · Ord

HQ Ab Div RASC · Ab Div OFP RAOC

Ab Lt Coy · Ab Div Comp Coy · Ab Div Comp Coy · Air Ldg Fd Amb · Para Fd Amb · Para Fd Amb

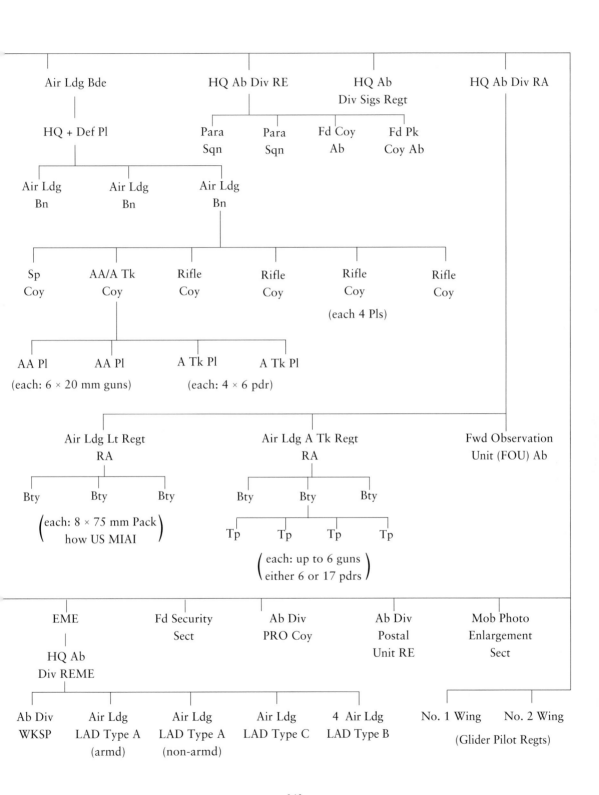

Air Ldg Bde

HQ Ab Div RE

HQ Ab
Div Sigs Regt

HQ Ab Div RA

HQ + Def Pl

Para
Sqn

Para
Sqn

Fd Coy
Ab

Fd Pk
Coy Ab

Air Ldg
Bn

Air Ldg
Bn

Air Ldg
Bn

Sp
Coy

AA/A Tk
Coy

Rifle
Coy

Rifle
Coy

Rifle
Coy

Rifle
Coy

(each 4 Pls)

AA Pl

AA Pl

A Tk Pl

A Tk Pl

(each: 6 × 20 mm guns)

(each: 4 × 6 pdr)

Air Ldg Lt Regt
RA

Air Ldg A Tk Regt
RA

Fwd Observation
Unit (FOU) Ab

Bty

Bty

Bty

Bty

Bty

Bty

$\left(\begin{array}{c}\text{each: 8 × 75 mm Pack}\\ \text{how US MIAI}\end{array}\right)$

Tp

Tp

Tp

Tp

$\left(\begin{array}{c}\text{each: up to 6 guns}\\ \text{either 6 or 17 pdrs}\end{array}\right)$

EME

Fd Security
Sect

Ab Div
PRO Coy

Ab Div
Postal
Unit RE

Mob Photo
Enlargement
Sect

HQ Ab
Div REME

Ab Div
WKSP

Air Ldg
LAD Type A
(armd)

Air Ldg
LAD Type A
(non-armd)

Air Ldg
LAD Type C

4 Air Ldg
LAD Type B

No. 1 Wing

No. 2 Wing

(Glider Pilot Regts)

TOTALS — AIRBORNE DIVISION

Manpower:
701 Officers, 11,514 ORs = 12,215 All Ranks

Vehicles: 1,708 vehicles including:
light tanks – 16
Jeeps – 904
trucks and lorries –567
In addition, they had 4,502 bicycles and
motorcycles

Weapons:
pistols – 2,942
rifles –7,171
carbines (sten) ab – 6,504
LMGs – 996
MMGs – 46
mortars:
  2 in – 46; 3 in –56; 4.2 in – 5
PIATs – 392
LAA 20 mm (ab) – 23
flame throwers port – 38
guns:
  75 mm pack How – 27; 6 pdr a tk (ab) – 84;
  17 pdr a tk – 16

CHAPTER 8

THE SOLDIER

UNIFORMS

Soldiers have always worn some form of uniform/badge, etc., so that they could be easily distinguished on and off the battlefield, but it was not until the twentieth century that any effort was made to replace parade uniforms with clothing suitable for wear in combat. Khaki was the chosen colour and combat uniforms became more and more simple and robust, as did all the various items of personal equipment that were issued to every soldier. Personal weapons are dealt with in the next chapter, so here we shall look briefly at the British Army uniform and equipment, enlarging on various topics in the annexures – 'A' being badges of rank and proficiency and 'B' being decorations and medals.

TEMPERATE CLIMATE UNIFORMS

Battledress When war was declared the introduction of the new 'battledress' (BD) and the new range of webbing equipment, which was similar to, but less bulky than, that worn in the First World War, was still in progress. Issues of the new khaki-serge BD were not completed until the end of 1940, although most of the BEF was so equipped. The short-waisted blouse was worn fastened to the neck with a series of buttons and two concealed hooks and eyes at the collar, except for officers, who wore it open at the neck with a matching khaki collar and tie. The jacket had buttoned epaulettes, fastened down the front with five buttons, normally hidden by a fly front (although on later 'economy' versions the buttons and pocket buttons

were uncovered), while the two breast patch pockets usually had box pleats and concealed buttons. The integral half-belt did up from left to right and fastened on the right hip with a built-in buckle of dull metal. The straight trousers had a capacious map pocket on the front of the left thigh, conventional slashed side pockets, a single right hip pocket with a pointed flap and concealed button, and four, spaced belt loops for use with the web belt when in shirt-sleeve order. The trousers were normally worn with boots and webbing gaiters, rather than puttees. The ORs' shirt was collarless. Some officers had their BD tailored, so that the folded-back portions of the collar, which normally showed the sandy-coloured lining, were covered with pieces of khaki serge.

Service Dress While all the peacetime dress uniforms, blue patrols, etc., had generally been put away for the wartime years, officers were still permitted to wear Service Dress (SD) for office duty or 'walking out'. This uniform resembled the officers' uniform of the First World War and was made of good quality barathea, the tunic being single-breasted, with shoulder straps, patched pockets, open (tailored) at the neck to show the matching shirt, collar and tie. Trousers were of the same material, although some officers were entitled to wear riding breeches of cavalry twill, kilts or trews (Scottish regiments only). Normal headgear was the khaki SD cap, although some regiments would wear their own particular form of headdress such as the RTR's black beret.

What an infantryman carries with him into battle, *c.* June 1944. 4911986 Fusilier Tom Payne, 11 Platoon, B Company, 6th Royal Welch Fusiliers, together with his kit and equipment, is seen in the following set of photographs:

Front and rear views of Fus Payne. Note that as well his No. 4 rifle, jack-knife, bayonet and ammunition pouches, Fus Payne also carries a verey pistol (the butt and lanyard are just visible under his pouch). On his back he carries his small pack, the new smaller respirator in its haversack carrier (on his left hip), shovel (under the small pack), entrenching tool in its carrier (across his lower back) and old-pattern water bottle in its container (on right hip). (IWM – B 9005 & B 9006)

The contents of Tom Payne's small pack. Left to right, from the top: gas cape, spare socks, mess tins, shaving gear, tin of emergency rations, cigarettes and chocolate, face net, toothbrush and washing kit, water sterilising outfit, balaclava, spare boot laces, hairbrush, cutlery. Kit is spread on his towel. (IWM – B 9010)

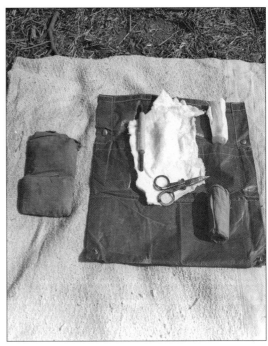

Field dressing and additional medical kit (found useful from experience) carried in a gas wallet: elastoplast bound around a pencil, bandage, lint and scissors. (IWM – B 9011)

Contents of entrenching tool carrier. Head and handle of entrenching tool, 4×2 for rifle cleaning (lying on head of entrenching tool), oil bottle, pull through, rifle cleaning brush, dubbin, brush and gauze. (IWM – B 9008)

Tom's personal belongings including photographs of his family, AB 64, writing pad, etc. (IWM – B 90012)

An excellent photograph showing a selection of officers' battledress, some of which have been tailored, others not, web belts of various colours (none for Monty), an assortment of headgear, boots, gaiters, puttees and shoes. Monty as always wears his famous double-badged beret, with its RTR badge and general's badge side by side. (IWM – B 15688)

An immaculate RTR officer in his Service Dress and Sam Browne belt. He should be immaculate of course, because he was attending an investiture at Buckingham Palace. Capt (later Maj) E.D. 'Gin' Hollands was receiving the DSO to add to the DCM he had already won in France in 1940. (Author's Collection)

Headgear Initially, the OR wore a sidecap of khaki serge, also known as a forage cap or a 'fore-and-aft' for obvious reasons. It had been designed so that it could be undone to protect the ears and part of the face, buttoning over the chin, but this was only partly successful and most soldiers did not like wearing it in this way, preferring to wear the stocking-type 'balaclava' instead. The stiff OR SD-type cap was seldom worn, except by CMP, whose caps had red tops, and some drill instructors in training establishments, who sometimes 'broke' the peak so that it was close to the eyes. By far the greatest headwear 'revolution' came when the RTR-type beret was adopted by

Kilts and Tam-o-Shanters (Balmoral Bonnets) are worn by the Scottish pipers, seen here as they try to teach some French soldiers how to play the bagpipes! (IWM – F 3500)

everyone, although only the RAC wore black berets. Paratroops wore red berets, and most of the infantry pale khaki berets (into most units by 1943) Scottish regiments still retained 'Balmoral' Tam-o-Shanters or 'Glengarry' bonnets, even in action.

The most universal headgear worn in action was of course the Mk I steel helmet, whose bowl-shaped appearance dated back to the First World War. It was worn uncovered, with a string net in which to put natural or artificial camouflage, or with a hessian cover. The new M1944 helmets, shaped more like a tortoise shell, were issued in time for D-Day

and widely used thereafter. Only the RAC and the airborne forces wore other types of steel helmet, which were more close fitting.

Protective clothing A new khaki greatcoat had been issued in 1937 and continued to be used throughout the war. It was mid-calf in length, double-breasted and had four pairs of buttons (bronze or plastic). Officers also wore the greatcoat, a privately-purchased superior model, or a light khaki raincoat, or the beige 'British Warm', the latter being privately manufactured. Another favourite cold weather wear was the old First World

This Chin warrior, Havildar Raldon of the Lushai Brigade, carries a number of spare magazines for his Sten Machine Carbine in his ammunition pouches. He is wearing light denims, ideal for rough use on the battlefield, and carries a pair of WD binoculars. (IWM – IND 4265)

Hospital Blues (see text page 181) being worn at a tea party for wounded soldiers in Cairo in May 1940. Most are not wearing the royal blue single-breasted jackets, just the white shirts, red ties and serge trousers. (IWM – E 105)

War leather trench waistcoat – collarless and sleeveless. The normal rainwear was the rubberized waterproof groundsheet, although despatch riders and the like had sturdy protective clothing. Finally, for armoured soldiers a tank oversuit (usually called a tank suit) was introduced from the summer of 1943 – it was warm, waterproof and comfortable, although the rain always collected in the crotch when in the sitting position (for example, when driving a tank!). Also with such clothing warm khaki pullovers, scarves, gloves/mittens were all worn.

Denims were considered as protective clothing to be worn by those doing dirty jobs, although, two-piece and one-piece denims were often worn in combat, especially by tank crews in the summer.

Specialist Clothing The airborne forces in particular needed specialist clothing, such as jump jackets and denison smocks, which were made of extra-strong, camouflaged material and incorporated zips or heavy duty snap-fasteners. Both were windproof and showerproof, but the latter quickly became waterlogged in heavy rain. Nevertheless, they were highly prized. A third overgarment – the Airborne Forces (sleeveless) oversmock – was issued later in the war but was not in general service until just before D-Day.

A convoy arrives safely in Malta and the troops disembark. Many are wearing the OR pattern greatcoat – double-breasted – which replaced the single-breasted prewar coat. The men are in 'Full Service Marching Order' (FSMO), with big packs, kitbags and the rest. (IWM – BM 8436)

Two good examples of the double-breasted British Warm, which was made of angola cloth of a light drab colour, with leather covered buttons. It could be worn by generals (like the 'Auk' seen here talking to Crown Prince Olaf of Norway), brigadiers and colonels, while other officers could only wear it when not parading with troops. (IWM – BH 8406)

Monty, when he was commanding V Corps in March 1941, wears one of the alternative style officers' greatcoats, which was modelled on the style of the RAF officers' coats. He is with a group of War Correspondents in a variety of military gear – trench coats and greatcoats. Note also their special capbadge. (IWM – H 8492)

Another cold weather garment was the leather jerkin, which had its beginnings during the First Wolrd War. It was made of strong, brown leather and had four large, flat brown buttons. These armoured car crews belong to 4th South African Armd Car Regt and are having Christmas dinner near Benghazi Cathedral. (IWM – E 1394)

The standard garment for protecting the average soldier against the rain was the groundsheet, although in the Far East nothing could really protect against the monsoon. (Author's Collection)

The oversuit for tank crews was an excellent garment, except that if worn while driving in an open cab (for example, in a scout car), the water, which inevitably found its way inside the suit, ran down and collected in a pool around your crotch and couldn't then escape – most uncomfortable! (Author's Collection)

A good selection of officers' khaki drill uniforms can be seen in this group photograph. Everyone is wearing something different and Gen Sir Claude Auchinleck, the CinC, looks as though he is wearing 'Bombay Bloomers'! (IWM – AUS 745)

Things look very different here, when the 'Auk' visited a New Zealand unit in the Western Desert to present awards for bravery in Crete. Every man on parade is wearing khaki drill shorts and shirts, boots and short puttees, forage caps, normal webbing, etc. (IWM – BM 6568)

Hospital Clothing 'Hospital Blues' were issued to in-patients at military hospitals and comprised a royal blue serge jacket and matching trousers, plus a white shirt and red tie. All were made of inferior material and badly tailored. Some similar coloured tropical hospital clothing was also issued.

KHAKI DRILL AND JUNGLE GREEN

BD was clearly too hot for normal wear[1] in both the Middle East and the Far East, so suitable 'Khaki Drill' and 'Jungle Green' uniforms were worn. These comprised tunics, shirts, long trousers and shorts, being worn with boots or shoes. One of the most unpopular of the tropical items were KD shorts with extra deep turnups, worn either buttoned up or let down to be bound around the ankles with special threaded white tapes, thus eliminating the need to wear KD trousers. They were a disaster when issued (early on in the Middle East) and did not last long, being known by all as 'Bombay Bloomers'! Headgear such as slouch hats were issued for jungle wear, but in the Middle East most soldiers wore their normal regimental hats/berets or, in action, steel helmets. Other necessary clothing items such as long stockings, hose tops, thin vests and pants, etc., were issued to all ranks as necessary.

PECULIAR DRESS ITEMS

In the desert many officers wore hard-wearing corduroy trousers, desert boots (suede with crepe rubber soles and universally known as 'brothel creepers'), coloured silk scarves, etc. This continued in some formations even when they left North Africa (for example, in the 7th Armd Div).

---

1. Desert nights were often bitterly cold once the sun had set, as were the mountainous areas of Tunisia. Thus, BD was worn on occasions and greatcoats, sheepskin coats and the like were widely used.

PERSONAL EQUIPMENT

WEBBING

The 1937-pattern webbing had been developed from the 1908 pattern but was far lighter and had been designed to suit all arms and not just the infantry. Apart from the bayonet, no articles were suspended below the wearer's waist-line so as not to impede movement. However, it was still designed to accept blanco and its brass fittings were polished for parades. From 1944 onwards an even lighter weight webbing was issued, using alloy metal and incorporating such items as the excellent US-type water-bottle and cup. The new webbing was dyed Jungle Green with dulled metal fittings so was definitely not to be blancoed or have its metal parts 'bulled-up'. The basic harness was

Monty was always an individual dresser – witness his corduroy trousers and a sheepskin flying jacket, worn on a Normandy beach as he talks to a properly battledressed but somewhat dishevelled beachmaster. (IWM – B 5175)

'Get your knees brown!' Newly arrived British soldiers wear their Solar topees (soon discarded in the desert), and carry their kit including kitbags, respirators, etc., as they disembark at Alexandria. (IWM – E 473)

Jungle Green blended into the jungle scene, especially when it got muddy. This patrol, wearing light webbing, slouch hats, etc., were probably Gurkhas. (IWM – IND 3803)

Alexander, wearing an even more extravagant sheepskin coat, somewhere in Italy. Note also the good close-up of an American-made Thompson submachine gun. (IWM – TA 14766)

as follows: a belt (approximately 2½ in wide) joined by a patent buckle; two web pouches 'universal', to be fixed on the front of the belt, each of which could accommodate Bren magazines, rifle ammunition clips, or No. 36 grenades; two braces that went up and under the BD shoulder straps to cross at the back and be attached to buckles on the rear of the belt. A bayonet frog, an entrenching tool (from 1942) that had a head and separate handle, both conveyed in a carrier, and a water-bottle/canteen were other items carried.

Tank soldiers normally wore the minimum of webbing because it hindered movement within the confined spaces of the tank and could be hazardous – all tank crewmen had an understandable horror of being trapped inside a burning AFV after snagging some item of equipment. Therefore they usually wore just a belt, holster and cartridge pouch. These were all normal issue items, except for the holster, which had the special long RAC legstrap and was open-topped, with six cartridge loops on the outer face.

Two packs, termed Large and Small, were issued, both being simple webbing bags with flap tops fastened by two narrow webbing straps and buckles. Other items issued included anti-gas equipment as explained in detail on page 185; simple cotton bandoliers in which the pockets could take five-round clips of rifle ammo; and the roll-type kitbag into which a soldier stowed all the kit he could not carry in his packs.

Uniforms had to be tough because on many occasions the only laundering they got was when the wearer came across a jungle stream – but watch out for the leeches! (IWM – SE 4346)

Or they were 'laundered' while fording the rivers! (Author's Collection)

Kit inspection. Getting ready to be shipped to France, these REs of the BEF have a hurried kit check. The Sappers wear old-prewar type uniforms, while the officers are in battledress. Note the inspecting officer's immaculate brand-new webbing, including pistol holster, ammunition pouch, binocular case and compass case above it. (Tank Museum)

Anti-gas equipment The service respirator was carried in a waterproof canvas haversack, the main part of which was divided into two – one part for the container, the other for the facepiece and anti-dimming outfit. The haversack had a canvas carrying sling and a length of stout cord attached, which was used when the respirator was being worn in the alert position (that is, on the chest), being tied around the upper part of the waist. In 1943 a new respirator was issued, known as 'Respirator, Anti-Gas, Light' as it was

about half the weight and bulk of the earlier model and was carried in a much smaller carrier. Other items of general issue anti-gas equipment included eye shields and anti-gas capes, whilst more specialized items included hoods, overboots and gloves.

MISCELLANEOUS ITEMS

Identity Discs All serving soldiers were issued with a set of fibre identity discs – a green disc (No. 1), a red disc (No. 2) – and

Anti-gas clothing. These British soldiers are demonstrating to various newly arrived Indian Army units in France in 1939/40 that it is possible to carry out heavy manual labour such as digging even when wearing respirators and anti-gas clothing, including overboots. (IWM – F 3808)

a 3 ft length of thin cord. Both were worn around the neck under the shirt, with the red disc on a separate extension piece of the cord so that it could be removed. There was a second red disc issued separately that was attached to the soldier's service respirator. The discs worn by the soldier showed his army number, initials, surname in full and his religious denomination (CE = Church of England, RC = Roman Catholic, etc.). The red disc was removed before burial – to assist in identification – but the green disc was

never to be removed. Unfortunately, it was found that the fibre discs lost their markings, especially in the intense heat of an AFV 'brew up', while the cord burnt away. Therefore, for jungle use stainless steel ID discs and nylon cord were issued, but were still not as good as the US Army equivalents.

'Housewife' Holdalls As the name implies this was a small sewing/darning kit carried by all soldiers so that they could repair minor tears, sew on buttons, darn holes in socks, etc.

Gen Sir Claud Auchinleck, CinC India, resplendent in full dress uniform, about to receive the Star of Nepal First Class. (IWM – IND 4890)

First Field Dressings Carried in battle by every soldier, this consisted of a small khaki bag containing waterproof gauze, cotton wool, bandage and two safety pins. In the UK the issue was restricted (for example, to NCOs, MT drivers, those attending battle schools or major exercises) and held in bulk in company/battalion stores, to be issued as and when ordered.

Eating Utensils, etc. Water-bottles have already been mentioned, in addition each man was issued with a pair of rectangular mess tins with folding carrying handles, one slightly smaller than the other so that they could be stowed together (prewar ones were made of tinplate, wartime manufacture was in aluminium alloy). Brown enamelled drinking mugs (1 or ½ pint) were issued during the war to replace the prewar white enamel ones. Finally, there was an all-metal set of knife, fork and spoon – most soldiers stamped their number on the handles.

ANNEX 'A': RANKS OF THE BRITISH ARMY

COMMISSIONED OFFICERS

(Badges of rank were normally worn on shoulder straps/epaulettes.)

Rank	Abbreviation	Symbol	Remarks
Second Lieutenant	2nd Lt or 2Lt	one star (also called a 'pip')	Also called a 'subaltern' and addressed as 'Mr'.
Lieutenant	Lt	two stars	ditto

A 2Lt or Lt was normally a platoon/troop level commander.

Captain	Capt	three stars	

A Captain was normally second in command (2IC) of a company/squadron.

Major	Maj	one crown	

A Major was normally the Officer Commanding (OC) of a company/squadron, while the Senior Major in a unit would be the unit 2IC.

Lieutenant Colonel	Lieut Col or Lt Col	a crown with one star below	

A Lieutenant Colonel normally commanded a battalion/regiment and was known as the Commanding Officer (CO).

Colonel	Col	a crown with two stars below	
Brigadier	Brig	a crown with three stars below (one on top of the other two)	

A Brigadier normally commanded a brigade and was known as the Brigade Commander.

Major General	Maj Gen	a star, with a crossed sabre and baton below	

A Major General normally commanded a division and was known as the General Officer Commanding (GOC).

Lieutenant General	Lt Gen	a crown, with a crossed sabre & baton below	

A Lieutenant General normally commanded a corps and was known as the Corps Commander.

General	Gen	a crown and a star, with crossed sabre & baton below	

A General normally commanded an army and was known as the Commander-in-Chief (CinC).

Field Marshal	FM	crossed batons surrounded by a wreath and surmounted by a crown	

The highest rank in the British Army, they were presented with a baton by the Sovereign as a symbol of their rank.

(See also notes opposite)

ARMY OFFICERS BADGES OF RANK

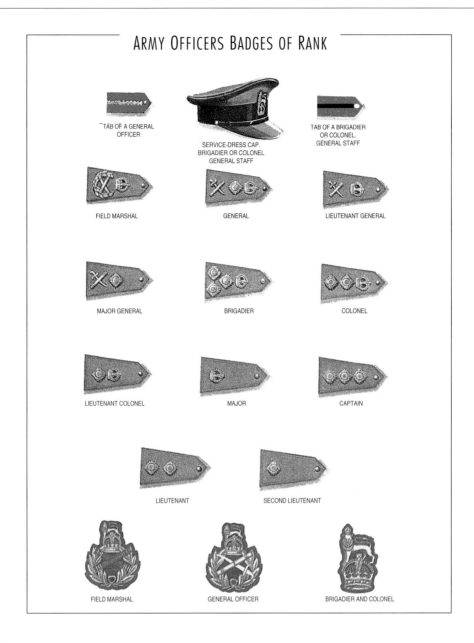

Notes:

1. **Appointments** The appointments shown are just some of the normal ones and no doubt circumstances would have altered in individual cases, especially on operations. For example, there were many other jobs in units and on the staff to be filled by officers of various ranks (Chapter 4, for instance, explains the ranks of staff officers at various levels). Within a unit appointments such as the Adjutant (Adjt), Assistant Adjutant/Intelligence Officer (IO), Regimental Technical Adjutant (Tech Adjt), Quartermaster (QM), Squadron Second Captain, etc., were normally filled by Captains or senior Lieutenants.

2. **Temporary Rank** Acting (paid after twenty-one days) and/or Local (unpaid and temporary) rank was sometimes given in special circumstances and for short periods. The prewar system of awarding 'brevet' rank was discontinued during the war. An officer holding temporary rank who, for any reasons – other than while recuperating from wounds – was unable to perform his duties for a period of twenty-one days reverted to one grade lower in rank (known as his 'war substantive' rank), but would not go lower during the war.

OTHER RANKS (OR)

This term covered warrant officers (WO), non-commissioned officers (NCOs), all of whom wore badges of rank, and privates, who were also known as trooper (Tpr), gunner (Gnr), sapper (Spr), signalman (Sgm), fusilier (Fus), rifleman (Rfn), guardsman (Gdsm), driver (Dvr), craftsman (Cfn), etc., depending upon their regiment, arm or Service.) ORs were also known by the old term 'Rank and File'. They wore their badges of rank on both arms.

OTHER RANKS BADGES OF RANK AND EXAMPLES OF PROFICIENCY BADGES

REGIMENTAL SERGEANT-MAJOR (WARRANT OFFICER, CLASS I)

REGIMENTAL QUARTER-MASTER-SERGEANT AND COMPANY SERGEANT-MAJOR (WARRANT OFFICERS, CLASS II)

COMPANY QUARTER-MASTER SERGEANT AND STAFF-SERGEANT

SERFEANT AND LANCE-SERGEANT

CORPORAL

LANCE-CORPORAL

GUNNERY INSTRUCTOR

BANDSMAN

SIGNALLER

ARMOURER

PIONEER

BOMB DISPOSAL SQUAD

GOOD CONDUCT CHEVRON

Rank	Abbreviation	Symbol	Remarks
Private	Pte	no badge of rank, but could be awarded proficiency badges (see later) which were then worn on the sleeve	
Lance Corporal	LCpl	one chevron (also called a 'stripe') on both upper arms	
Corporal	Cpl	two chevrons	In the RA known as a 'Bombardier'

Infantry section commanders were normally Corporals.

Rank	Abbreviation	Symbol	Remarks
Sergeant	Sgt	three chevrons	In the Household Cavalry known as a 'Corporal of Horse'

Infantry platoons had Pl Sergeants as 2IC to the platoon commander.

Rank	Abbreviation	Symbol	Remarks
Staff Sergeant	SSgt	three chevrons with crown above	Also known in the infantry as the Company Quartermaster Sergeant (CQMS), or SQMS in a tank sqn, he normally looked after the 'Q' matters at coy/sqn/bty level.
Warrant Officer Class II	WOII	Crown surrounded by a laurel wreath worn on lower arm	In the inf he was as the Company Sergeant Major (CSM) – SSM in a tank sqn, BSM in a field battery, etc.

This badge of rank was also worn by the Regimental Quartermaster Sergeant (RQMS), who was the Quartermaster's 'right-hand man'.

Note: At the beginning of the war there was a rank, Warrant Officer Class III, but this went out in 1941.

Rank	Abbreviation	Symbol	Remarks
Warrant Officer Class I	WOI	The Royal Arms on the lower arm	In a unit the WOI was the Regimental Sergeant Major (RSM), who was responsible for all aspects of discipline and duty of the Other Ranks

TRADESMEN'S, INSTRUCTORS' AND SKILL AT ARMS BADGES

(a). **Tradesmen's Badges** A wide range of these badges were worn, made both of metal (prewar) or worsted material. Examples are:

Hammer & Pincers	–	Armament artificers, armourers, fitters, and smiths
Wireless signals	–	wireless mechanics
'S' in a wreath	–	surveyor

(b). **Instructors' Badges** Again, a wide range in metal (prewar) and worsted material. Examples are:

Crossed guns	–	instructor, School of Artillery
Grenade	–	instructor, RE
Crossed rifles	–	musketry instructor
Crossed swords	–	PT instructors
Crossed flags	–	signalling instructors

(c). **Skill at Arms Badges** Authorized by units and awarded annually (prewar). They were not worn by WOIs. There were both competition badges and qualification badges, which featured rifles, swords, lances, ships and spurs, steering wheels, etc., some with stars.

DISTINGUISHING MARKS ON BATTLE DRESS

Arm of service	Colour of backing to officers' insignia of rank	Distinguishing marks on sleeves for all ranks
Staff Corps of Military Police	Red	Red
Royal Armoured Corps	Yellow	Yellow–Red
Royal Regiment of Artillery	Red	Red–Blue
Royal Corps of Engineers	Blue	Blue–Red
Royal Corps of Signals	Blue	Blue–White
Infantry (except rifle regiments) and general list	Scarlet	Scarlet
Infantry (rifle regiment)	Rifle Green	Rifle Green
Reconnaissance Corps	Green	Green–Yellow
Royal Army Chaplains' Department	Purple	Purple
Royal Army Service Corps	Yellow	Yellow–Blue
Royal Army Medical Corps	Dull cherry	Dull Cherry
Royal Army Ordnance Corps	Dark Blue	Dark Blue
Royal Army Pay Corps	Yellow	Yellow
Royal Army Veterinary Corps	Maroon	Marroon
Army Educational Corps	Cambridge blue	Cambridge Blue
The Army Dental Corps	Green	Green–White
Pioneer Corps	Red	Red–Green
Intelligence Corps	Green	Green
Army Catering Corps	Grey	Grey–Yellow
Army Physical Training Corps	Black	Black–Red–Black

Annex 'B': Principal Army Decorationa and Medals of the Second World War

EXAMPLES OF GALLANTRY DECORATIONS

GEORGE CROSS

VICTORIA CROSS

DISTINGUISHED SERVICE
ORDER

MILITARY MEDAL
(REVERSE)

MILITARY CROSS

DISTINGUISHED CONDUCT MEDAL

DECORATIONS

Victoria Cross (VC) The VC is Great Britain's highest decoration for 'conspicuous bravery or devotion to the country in the presence of the enemy'. It is open to all ranks. The medal was instituted by Royal Warrant towards the end of the Crimean War, on 29 January 1856, and is one of the most coveted decorations in the world. The simple bronze crosses were – and still are – made of the metal of Russian guns taken at Sevastopol and consist of a maltese cross bearing the royal crown surmounted by a lion upon a scroll inscribed FOR VALOUR. On the reverse side of the cross is the date of the act for which the decoration has been bestowed, together with the name, rank and unit of the recipient. The ribbon is crimson, although it is described as being 'Red' in the Warrant. During the Second World War, 106 VCs were awarded to members of the British Armed Forces, of which the army was awarded sixty-one.

George Cross (GC) Instituted on 24 September 1940 to replace the Medal for Gallantry of the Order of the British Empire, it ranks next to the VC and both decorations precede all others. It is a simple silver cross at the centre of which the words FOR GALLANTRY surround the horsed figure of St George slaying the dragon. On the reverse is the name, rank and Service of the holder. It was intended mainly for civilians, but was also open to the military and numerous soldiers did win it, for example, for acts of bravery in connection with bomb disposal. The ribbon is blue (1½ in wide – initially 1¼ in).

George Medal (GM) Instituted on 24 September 1940, the GM was to be awarded in circumstances similar to those required for the GC but of lesser merit (the wording of the initial Royal Warrant said, 'for acts of great bravery during the present war'). The silver medal hangs from the ribbon by means of a ring. It bears a crowned effigy of HM King George VI, while on the reverse is the same horsed figure of St George slaying the dragon encompassed by the words THE GEORGE MEDAL. The ribbon is red (1¼ in wide) with five equidistant narrow, vertical blue stripes.

Distinguished Service Order (DSO) The DSO was established in 1886 to reward distinguished service by officers who have been specially recommended in Despatches for service in the field. It was a cross in silver-gilt and enamel, with a central crown inside a wreath (on the reverse there is the royal cipher). To distinguish those who have gained additional awards a bar is attached to the ribbon, up to a maximum of three, thus representing four DSOs.

Distinguished Conduct Medal (DCM) The DCM was instituted by Royal Warrant in 1854 in order to provide a gallantry medal for ORs in the army (and later open to naval and air force personnel as a result of ground action). It is open to WOs, NCOs and men for 'distinguished service in the field'. The ribbon is crimson, 1¼ in wide with a ⅜ in central blue stripe. The medal bears the crowned head of the Sovereign, whilst on the reverse are the words FOR DISTINGHISHED CONDUCT IN THE FIELD.

Military Cross (MC) The MC was instituted by Royal Warrant on 28 December 1914, 'in recognition of distinguished, gallant and meritorious services'. It was open to commissioned officers of the rank of captain and below, and to WOs of 'Our Army, Our Indian or Colonial Military Forces and to foreign officers of equivalent rank who have been associated with our Army'. Its ribbon is white with a central purple stripe.[1]

Military Medal (MM) The MM is a gallantry award instituted by Royal Warrant on 26 March 1916, for 'Bravery in the Field' by NCOs and men of the army. Subsequent Warrants made it available to ORs of 'Any of Our Military Forces', also to equivalent ranks of allied or 'associated' armies and to women. The medal ribbon is dark blue, with three white and two crimson stripes down the centre. During the Second World War it was only won three times by one NCO in all three of the Armed Services; he was Sgt Frederick W. Kite, a tank commander serving with 3 RTR.[2]

1. In 1995 it was decided to drop the awarding of the MM and to open the award of the MC to all ranks.
2. A silver rose on gallantry ribbons (e.g. on MC and MM) identified a second award.

CAMPAIGN MEDALS [3]

Eight six-pointed stars, all identical in design, with the crowned cipher of King George VI in the centre were produced. However, to distinguish between the various medals the central cipher was surrounded by the name of the appropriate campaign and all had different ribbons. They were created to reward active service in the Second World War. Discounting those normally awarded to RN or RAF personnel, there were five campaign medals that were usually awarded for army service – and five was the *maximum* number that any one person could be awarded. However, this is not to say that army personnel could never be eligible for the other three (provided, in doing so, they did not exceed the mandatory limit of five) – for example, soldiers who took part in the Battle of the Atlantic, crewing guns on merchant ships, would be awarded the Atlantic Star. However, the more usual ones for army service were:

1939–45 Star Awarded for a determinate period of service between 3 September 1939 and 15 August 1945. The ribbon was dark blue, red and light blue (representing the three Services: RN, Army and RAF).

Africa Star Awarded for service in North or East Africa from 10 June 1940 to 12 May 1943. The metal numbers '1' and '8' on the ribbon identified the wearer as serving with the First or Eighth Army respectively. The ribbon was sand coloured with a wide red stripe in the centre and thin dark blue and light blue stripes on either side.

Italy Star Awarded for service in Italy, the ribbon was red, white and green stripes – red at the edges, then white, with green in the centre.

France and Germany Star Awarded for service from 6 June 1944 in Normandy until the end of the war. The ribbon was red, white and blue stripes (blue at edges, then white, with red in the centre).

Burma Star Awarded for service from 11 December 1941 until the end of the war. The ribbon was red in the centre, then dark blue, with a thinner orange stripe in the centre.

There were two other medals:

Defence Medal This was basically awarded for three years of service in the UK or one year overseas. However, in certain conditions the necessary qualifying period could be reduced to six months – or even to three months for mine and bomb disposal personnel. The round cupro-nickel medal showed an uncrowned effigy of HM King George VI with the usual legend, while on the reverse was the Royal Crown resting on the stump of an oak tree flanked by two lions, with 1939–1945 at the top and THE DEFENCE MEDAL at the bottom. The ribbon was said to symbolize air attacks on England during the blackout (a flame-coloured wide central stripe with green edges containing two thin black stripes).

War Medal 1939–45 (sometimes known as the Victory Medal) Also a round cupro-nickel medal with the crowned head of King George VI and the usual legend around it. On the reverse was a lion standing on a dragon that was lying on its back. It required the qualification of twenty-eight days of operational or non-operational service. The ribbon was red, white and blue, with a thin red central stripe inside narrow white stripes which in turn were in slightly wider blue stripes, with wider still red stripes on the outside.

---

3. A brass oak leaf on campaign ribbons signified a 'Mention in Despatches'.

CHAPTER 9

WEAPONS, VEHICLES AND EQUIPMENT

'MADE IN ENGLAND'

The weapons, vehicles and equipment described in this chapter are all 'Made in England'. Of course, the British Army also used a vast amount of American weapons (such as the Thompson sub-machine gun), 'B' vehicles (the Jeep and the DUKW), tanks (the M4 Sherman and the M3 Grant and Lee) and numerous items of equipment, rations

and other supplies from the middle of the war onwards, but these have already been covered in the *US Army Handbook of World War II*, so descriptions are not included here.

WEAPONS

PERSONAL WEAPONS

Pistols During the First World War, the standard officer's pistol was the Webley .455

These young tank crewmen of 4 RTR practise with their .38 in pistols in a farmyard in France. Also note the long, knee-strapped pistol holster, the two piece black denims, RTR black berets and RTR beret badges, bearing the King's Crown. (IWM – F 49)

in revolver, but this had proved to be difficult to handle accurately and the round was unnecessarily large. Therefore, it was decided to opt for a smaller calibre and in 1926–27 the Royal Small Arms Factory (RSAF) at Enfield modified the Webley design to produce the .38 in calibre six-shot Pistol, Revolver No. 2 Mk I (taken into service in 1932), to be followed by the Mk I*, which had a lighter trigger pull. It was carried by all officers, despatch riders (DRs), most tank crewmen and some NCOs (sergeant and above). However, it has to be said that many of these preferred to carry a Sten gun or other weapon (often a rifle). The six-shot pistol weighed 1.68 lb and had a muzzle velocity of 600 ft/sec.

Rifles Various types of rifle were in service during the Second World War, all being of .303 in calibre, viz, Rifle No. 1 Mk III, Short Magazine Lee-Enfield (SMLE) as used in the First World War (one of the finest rifles *ever* produced, it remained the standard rifle of the Australian and other Commonwealth armies (large numbers were produced in India at Ishapore and at Lithgow in Australia)); Rifle No. 3 Mk I, P 14 (produced in the USA (also in .30 calibre), some 785,000 were sold to the UK in 1940 but only a few were used by front-line units and then mostly by snipers); Rifle No. 4 Mk I (the replacement for the SMLE), which went into mass production in 1940. By 1944 a new pattern aperture backsight was fitted that included a battle-sight to use up to 400 yd; Rifle No. 5 Mk I (a cutdown version of the No. 4 (5 in shorter and 2 lb lighter)). Details of the SMLE and No. 4, which were the most numerous, were:

A good close-up of a rifle – a No. 3 Mk I – the P 14 as issued to the Home Guard and others. This man was a member of the Observer Corps. The service respirator and binoculars can also be seen clearly in this view. (Author's Collection)

Another good close-up, this time of the Short Magazine Lee-Enfield (SMLE) No. 1 Mk III, one of the best rifles in the world in its day. These tired squaddies of 3rd Inf Div (note divisional insignia) were on an exercise in Dorset, and were snapped having a quick siesta on the roadside in the village of Bere Regis. (IWM – H 8499)

This tough group from HQ 81st West African Div hold their No. 4 Mk I rifles ready for action in the Burmese jungle. (IWM – SE 205)

	SMLE	No. 4 Mk I
Length	3 ft 8.6 in	3 ft 8.4 in
Weight	8.66 lb	9.13 lb
Muzzle velocity	2,080 ft/sec	2,465 ft/sec
Magazine capacity	10 rounds	10 rounds

Both weapons could be fitted with a cup discharger for projecting grenades – see below.

Bayonets Both rifles could also be fitted with a bayonet. The SMLE had a long 'sword' type bayonet, which clipped onto a boss below the end of the barrel, while the No. 4 had a shorter 'dagger' type bayonet with a ring, which clipped around the end of the protruding rifle barrel. The former was 18 in long – almost half as long as the rifle itself –

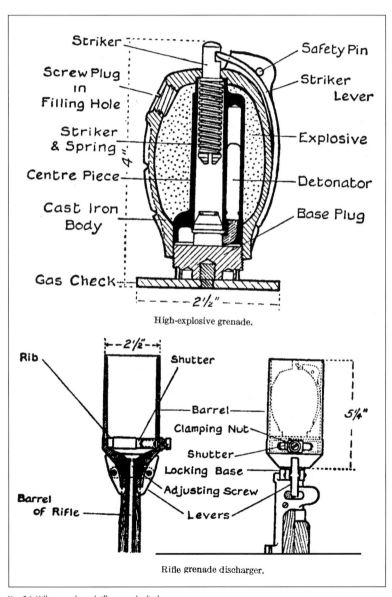

High-explosive grenade.

Rifle grenade discharger.

No. 36 Mills grenade and rifle grenade discharger.

while the latter was only some 9 in long, of cruciform section with a tapering point and weighed only ½ lb (its scabbard weighed a further ¼ lb).

Machine Carbines The Machine Carbine Sten Mk 1, Mk 1*, Mk 2, Mk 2 (Silencer), Mk 5 and Mk 6 (silenced version of Mk 5).

The 9 mm Sten was a cheap, simply designed weapon that could be mass-produced by relatively unskilled labour as it required minimal machining. It was introduced from late 1941 onwards. More Mk 2s were produced than any other type – over 2 million (also produced in Canada and New Zealand). The 'silencer' version was designed for special

Shaving in his foxhole in the jungle, Pte Maycox of Salford has his Sten Machine Carbine, with 32-round magazine, lying at the ready in front of him together with other kit (note: pouches, water-bottle, mess tin), while his main weapon, the platoon's 2 in mortar, is on the right of the trench. (IWM – SE 3764)

forces and used extensively by commando units, while the Mk 5 was a much-improved version and probably one of the best sub-machine guns of the war. Details of the Mk 2 and Mk 5 are:

	Mk 2	Mk 5
Length	2 ft 6 in	2 ft 6 in
Weight	6.625 lb	8.6 lb
Muzzle velocity	1,200 ft/sec	1,200 ft/sec
Magazine capacity	32 rounds	32 rounds
Cyclic rate of fire	540 rpm	540 rpm

Hand Grenades There were various types ranging in weight between 1¼ and 4 lb, including High Explosive – the No. 36M Mills fragmentation grenade, 1.7 lb in weight and 2.165 in in diameter, with a variable length fuse 4 to 7 sec; the No. 69 Mk I bakelite blast grenade, 0.683 lb in weight and

2.36 in diameter with an impact fuse. Both could be thrown 25–35 yd (depending on the dexterity and strength of the thrower) or fired from a cup discharger (fitted to a rifle), which increased the range to some 200 yd. There were also smoke, signal and a tk grenades used in small numbers, three examples of the last of these being the No. 73 'Thermos' bomb (ineffective and used more for demolition work); the No. 74 'Sticky' grenade (its fuse often broke off, or the bomb got stuck to the thrower!) and the No. 75 'Hawkins' grenade, which was really a hand thrown/surface laid anti-tank mine and only effective against lighter AFVs.

MACHINE GUNS (MG)
The Bren Gun It had its origins in the Czech ZB 26 MG and was developed by the RSAF at

A Bren gun being used on its AA mounting somewhere in Italy. (Tank Museum)

An excellent shot of a Bren LMG using the tripod developed for long-range firing, but not much used (see the normal bipod hanging free). (IWM – F 4128)

Enfield Lock in 1937. The Mk 1 had a drum rearsight, butt handle and adjustable bipod, but all these refinements were dropped in the wartime production model. The Mk 3 and 4 were produced in 1944 and were lighter, shorter and cheaper. For AA work various mounts were employed both single and twin. Gun details were:

Weight (c/w bipod)	23 lb
Calibre	.303 in
Length	3 ft 9¼ in
Muzzle velocity	2,440 ft/sec
Magazine capacity	29 round overhead box magazine (there was also a 200 round drum magazine which was little used)
Cyclic rate of fire	500 rpm (normally fired in single shots or in short bursts)
Effective range	1,000 yd

Vickers 'K' LMG This .303 in MG was really an RAF/Fleet Air Arm weapon for use with old-type open-cockpit aircraft, but a number of spare guns found a use in the Western Desert mounted on vehicles, such as the Jeeps of the LRDG. It was also often employed as an LMG on the Humber scout car (see later). It weighed 19½ lb and had an overhead drum containing ninety-six rounds.

Besa 7.92mm Tank MG Another modified Czech designed MG that became the main MG for all British tanks during the war. There were three marks and several sub-variants, also a 15 mm version, which was not much used. Gun details were:

Length	3 ft 7.7 in
Weight	47 lb
Muzzle velocity	2,700 ft/sec
Rate of fire	700–750 rpm
Type of feed	220 round link or metal and fabric belt

The Vickers 'K' LMG in single and twin mountings was a favoured weapon of the Long Range Desert Group on their Jeeps. Note also the German Jerricans of spare fuel and water stowed in every conceivable location! (Tank Museum)

The 7.92 mm Besa machine gun became the main coaxial machine gun for use in British armoured fighting vehicles and went on in service well after the end of the war. (Author's Collection)

The Lewis Gun   Mention must also be made of the Lewis gun, which was produced internationally in .30 and .303 calibres during and after the First World War. A fair number were purchased from the USA to replace guns lost at Dunkirk. The Home Guard used them, also the Merchant Service. The feed was from a drum magazine containing either forty-seven or ninety-seven rounds.

SUPPORT WEAPONS

MEDIUM MACHINE GUNS

Vickers .303 Mk 1   This magnificent belt-fed, .303 in water-cooled MG first entered service in 1912, yet was still in use worldwide over sixty years later. It could be used on a variety of mounts, but its ground tripod was the norm. There was also a variation for use in tanks. It was used to provide medium MG support. Gun details were:

Length	3 ft 9½ in
Weight, complete with tripod and water	88½ lb (gun alone 40 lb)
Muzzle velocity	2,440 ft/sec
Cyclic rate of fire	400/500 rpm (normal rate – 250 rounds in 2 min; rapid – one belt in 1 min)
Type of feed	250 round fabric belt

There was also a .5 version which was used on some early tanks.

Home Guard weapons. A selection of the weaponry with which the Home Guard was armed, including small arms and a tk weapons, is laid out on public display on this War Savings stall at Swanage Railway Station. (Author's Collection)

The First World War Lewis gun was bought in considerable numbers from the USA to make up for BEF losses after Dunkirk. This one is being used on an AA mounting on top of an armoured car. (Author's Collection)

The Vickers medium machine gun, seen here in action in Italy, was used extensively in the supporting fire role during the Second World War by both British and Commonwealth forces. (IWM – NA 8670)

MORTARS

2 in Mortar   The smallest British mortar was first designed during the trench warfare of the First World War, then declared obsolete in 1919. However, during the mid-1930s the need for a platoon mortar was recognized and the best one (based on a Spanish design) was put into production in 1938. During the Second World War there were many variations of this excellent little weapon, adapting it to tank, airborne, carrier, etc., use as well as three basic infantry forms that used a small baseplate. It could fire HE, smoke or illuminating ammunition. It was a smooth-bore, muzzle-loading, high-angle of fire weapon (although it could be fired horizontally for street fighting), lanyard trigger fired mortar, which was still in service 25 years after the end of the war.

Weight in action	18.96 lb
Bomb weight	2.25 lb
Range	100–500 yd
Rate of fire	5 rpm

It could be carried into action by one man (plus some ammunition) or carried in/ mounted on a vehicle.

The Ordnance ML 2 in mortar being demonstrated early in 1939, just prewar. It had gone into production the year before. (IWM – I 15)

While crossing the Irrawaddy River, this cheerful Gurkha keeps his 2 in mortar dry, neatly folded, bombs in the pouches. (IWM – IND 4516)

3 in Mortar   The first 3 in mortar entered service during the First World War, development continuing between the wars, thus it was the Mk 2 version that was in service at the start of the war. Improvements followed: new propellants increased its range by over 1,100 yd; the Mk 4 had a heavier baseplate and a new sight; the Mk 5 (specially designed for use in the Far East) was lighter but only some 5,000 were produced. It was usually vehicle/ animal borne although there was a man-harness so that it could be carried by its crew of three men. The ammunition (HE or smoke) was carried in three-round bomb carriers. It was a smooth-bore, muzzle-loading, high-angle of fire weapon, which was popular despite its initial short range as compared with similar weapons (US 81 mm mortar = 3,300 yd: German 80 mm = 2,625 yd).

Weight in action	126 lb (mortar 43 lb, mounting 45 lb, baseplate 38 lb)
Weight of bomb	10 lb
Range	charge I – 500–1,500 yd
	charge II – 950–2,800 yd
Rate of fire	5 rpm

A 3 in mortar in action in the Western Desert. (IWM – E 13833)

An immaculate 3 in mortar crew demonstrates its weapon just prewar (note the old uniforms). (IWM – I 6A)

4.2 in Mortar Its origins, like the US equivalent, were because of a stated requirement for a chemical mortar, made in the spring of 1941. This soon changed when its HE capability was recognized, although its initial range was poor, mainly because of the poorly shaped cast-iron bombs, which could only reach some 3,500 yd. These were hastily improved and a range of 4,100 yd achieved. Originally designed for RE use, it was soon taken over by the RA as a most effective supporting fire weapon.

Weight in action	1,320 lb
Weight of bomb	20 lb
Range	charge I – 1,050–2,800 yd
	charge II – 1,550–4,100 yd

A 4.2 in mortar crew of the 5/5 Royal Mahratta MG Bn in Italy. (IWM – NA 20071)

The Blacker Bombard Towards the end of 1941 the Home Guard was also armed with a somewhat 'Heath Robinson' 29 mm spigot mortar, which had been designed by a TA artillery officer, Lt Col LVS Blacker, hence its name. This weighed about 345 lb and could fire a 20 lb bomb some 900 yd and had a rate of fire of 12 rpm.

INFANTRY ANTI-TANK WEAPONS

Boys Mk 1 This heavy (36 lb), cumbersome (5 ft 4 in long), .55 in calibre, ineffective weapon, which had a kick like a mule, was the standard infantry platoon anti-tank weapon when war began (and also the main armament of some light AFVs). As it could only penetrate 21 mm of armour at 300 yd

it was virtually useless after 1940, being not much better than a large calibre infantry rifle. A shorter airborne version was produced but fortunately did not see service!

Northover Projector Another post-Dunkirk 'ad hoc' weapon (cf the Blacker Bombard) eventually inflicted on the Home Guard was this pipe-gun bottle thrower, which hurled grenades/Molotov cocktails (petrol-filled bottle bombs) out to some 300 yd, although the accurate effective range was under 100 yd. It was not very popular as the bottles tended to break inside the bore!

PIAT Here at last was an a tk weapon that worked, although it was nowhere near as good as the American bazooka or the German panzerfaust. It fired hollow-charge

The .55 in Boys a tk rifle could only penetrate 21 mm of armour at 300 yd and was obsolescent soon after the war began. (IWM – 2/19)

The Projector Infantry Anti-Tank (PIAT) fired a 3 lb hollow-charge grenade that could penetrate most enemy tanks at close range (100 yd). (IWM – B 8913)

a tk grenades out to a combat range of about 100 yd but, because it worked on a spigot principle, it could also toss HE or smoke shells to a far greater range (750 yd). Not a popular weapon because it took the combined strength of two men to cock it, it was nevertheless widely used and virtually replaced the Boys a tk rifle.

Weight	23.5 lb
Bomb weight	2.5 lb
Max effective range v tanks	115 yd
Max effective range v buildings	350 yd

ANTI-TANK ARTILLERY

Hotchkiss 25 mm SA 34 A tk gun Although not a British-made weapon, mention must be made of this virtually useless small calibre a

tk gun, which was the standard light infantry a tk gun in the French Army. Some were issued to the British Army in a misguided attempt at standardization. The problem was that the 1 in calibre weapon was incapable of penetrating anything but the lightest AFVs. It found its way into many infantry brigade a tk companies.

Ordnance QF 2 pdr A tk gun Entering service in 1938, this was the standard British a tk gun at the start of the war and did well in France in 1940. However, large numbers were left behind after Dunkirk (and used thereafter by the Germans as the 4 cm PaK 192(e)). It was a heavy gun, mainly because of its 360 degree tripod carriage, so had to be towed behind a lorry or carried 'portee' in the back. Although several different marks were designed for mounting on Universal

In 1939 some of the almost useless French 25 mm Hotchkiss 34 SA infantry a tk guns were issued to the British Army in an attempt at standardization. Its anti-armour capability was minimal. (IWM – F 4117)

and Loyd Carriers, none of them saw action. Difficult to conceal, with a relatively poor performance – it could only penetrate 53 mm of armour at 500 yd – it was withdrawn from RA service in mid-1942 and handed over to the infantry.

Weight complete	1,850 lb
Calibre	1.575 in
Muzzle velocity	2,615 ft/sec
Max effective range	600 yd
Max rate of fire	20–22 rpm

Ordnance QF 6 pdr A tk Gun Entering service in September 1941, the Mk 1 was quickly replaced by the Mk 2 (shorter barrel), later replaced itself by the longer barrelled Mk 4 (the Mk 3 was lighter and intended for airborne use). However, by 1943 its anti-armour capability – 2.7 in at 1,000 yd – was not good enough to penetrate the frontal armour of German heavy tanks (Tigers for example), so it was gradually replaced in RA service by the 17 pdr and given to the infantry who used it for the rest of the war.

This 2 pdr A tk gun belonged to the Mobile Division, the predecessor of 7th Armd Div and was photographed at Matruh just before the war began. Even then it was an obsolescent weapon, but adequate enough against Italian AFVs. (Author's Collection)

Askaris of 11th East African Div load their 6 pdr A tk gun, during the Khabaw Valley campaign in Burma. (IWM – K 10–72(WA))

Both the 2 pdr and 6 pdr (seen here) A tk guns could be carried 'portee' and fired from the back of a lorry – note the loading/unloading rails at the rear. (IWM – E 12643)

This 6 pdr A tk gun was commanded by Sjt Crangles DCM, 1/7 Queens, on 6 March 1943, when it accounted for ten German tanks during the Battle of Medenine. Some of the German panzers can be seen still smoking in front of the gun position. (Author's Collection)

Weight complete	2,471 lb
Calibre	2.245 in
Muzzle velocity	2,700 ft/sec
Max effective range	5,500 yd
Rate of fire	10 rpm

Ordnance QF 17 pdr The need for a really effective a tk gun was appreciated early in the war (1941), and 3 in was the chosen calibre. The resulting weapon – the Ordnance QF 17 pdr – was designed and produced in double-quick time, the first deliveries being made in August 1942. These were 100 'guns only' as the carriages had not been completed in time, so they were mounted on 25 pdr carriages, this ad hoc gun and mount being known as the 17 pdr Mk 2. Once the complete gun was issued (Mk 1) the Mk 2 was phased out.

Soon there were more carriages than guns, so some old 3 in AA guns were mounted for UK use. The 17 pdr was a very effective a tk gun, which could penetrate 130 mm of armour plate at 1,000 yd, while its HE shell was also very useful.

Weight complete	2.9 ton
Calibre	3 in
Muzzle velocity	2,900 ft/sec
Max effective range	10,000 yd
Rate of fire	10 rpm

ANTI-AIRCRAFT ARTILLERY

LAA Guns As already mentioned, MGs were widely used on various types of AA mounts, while the 20 mm Polsten cannon,

Twin Brens on an AA mounting using the 200-round high-speed drum magazines. (IWM – IND 3268)

An excellent photograph of a 17 pdr a tk gun and its crew in a somewhat exposed temporary position. Note in the foreground that as well as the Bren gun, there is a French Hotchkiss MMG, which must have been in use by the German close bridge garrison before the British arrived. (IWM – B 1071)

Two 17 pdr a tk guns being towed through the narrow back streets of Scafati, Italy. The photo provides an excellent view of the massive gunshields. (IWM – NA 7455)

This 17 pdr a tk gun and its crew have collected quite a crowd of onlookers; one hopes they will disperse before the gun has to be fired! (IWM – B 10020)

20 mm Hispano-Suiza gun and Vickers 40 mm gun were all used on AA mountings. The Polsten had a rate of fire of 450–480 rpm and the Hispano-Suiza 650 rpm. Both had 60-round magazines (a round weighed approx. ½ lb). Effective ceiling was 3,000 ft and its horizontal range 1,000 yd.

However, by far the most numerous LAA weapon was the Swedish-designed 40 mm Bofors, which was used worldwide by both Allied and Axis armies. By 1945 the British had produced three main marks of gun, six specialized mountings, two lightweight mountings and five different types of firing platform for land use alone! The Bofors was undoubtedly a world beater and is still in service all over the world.

Weight in action	1.9 ton
Weight of shell	2 lb
Calibre	40 mm
Muzzle velocity	2,800 ft/sec
Effective ceiling	5,000 ft (ground range 10,800 yd)
Max ceiling	23,000 ft
Rate of fire	120 rpm (cyclic) 60–90 rpm (single shot)

This Bofors 40 mm LAA gun was photographed in the snows of Italy. Note how the loader stands over the gun ready to feed in the next four-round clip.
(IWM – BNA 10605)

Best and most widely used of all LAA guns during the Second World War was the Swedish 40 mm Bofors, which was made under licence in the UK. Seven other countries received licences while the Swedes exported their version to eighteen other countries. (IWM – 4/44)

Winnie watches the guns fire. Prime Minister Winston Churchill, with his familiar large cigar, watching 3.7 in AA guns engaging enemy aircraft. His wife, Clementine, plugs her ears, while daughter Mary points out targets. (IWM – H 39500)

HAA Guns There were four main types of HAA gun: the Ordnance QF 3 in; Ordnance QF 3.7 in Mks 1, 2, 3 and 6; Ordnance QF 4.5 in Mk 2; Ordnance QF 5.25 in Mk 2. The first of the four was the oldest and phased out gradually during the war. The 3.7 in was probably the most widely used, Vickers producing the pilot model in 1936 with production beginning in January 1938. There were both static and mobile mountings. The Germans were most impressed with the 3.7 in and used any captured ones, indeed they even manufactured ammunition for them. The Mk 6 was produced to meet a requirement to produce an AA gun that could fire a shell to 50,000 ft in half a minute and was a 4.5 in gun lined down to 3.7 in. The 4.5 in and 5.25 in began life as naval guns and both were excellent weapons, in static mounts (single and twins). Comparing the three calibres:

Despite the night raid a YMCA tea car goes on serving 'cuppas', while the 3.7 in emplaced AA guns blast away at the enemy. (Author's Collection)

At one of the HAA gunsites in wartime Dorset, gun crews rush to man their guns when the alarm is given. (IWM – H 2548)

This 3.7 in AA gun towed by a carrier was used in the desert war and had just escaped from the Knightsbridge 'Box' before it was overrun. (Author's Collection)

Type	3.7 in		4.5 in	5.25 in
	mobile	static	static	static
Weight in action (tons)	9.2	17.1	14.7	49.5
Muzzle velocity (ft/sec)	2,600	3,425	2,400	2,800
Ground range (yd)	20,600	25,600	22,800	27,000
Effective ceiling (ft)	32,000	45,000	34,500	43,000
Rate of fire (rpm)	25	19	8	10

FIELD ARTILLERY

Ordnance QF 18 pdr In widespread service prewar, with either pneumatic wheels (British Army) or old wooden spoked wheels (Commonwealth armies), they were left behind in large numbers in France after Dunkirk. Replaced thereafter in active units by the 25 pdr, the 18 pdr was used for training and home defence. There were few in service by the end of the war.

Weight in action	3,228 lb
Shell weight	18½ lb
Muzzle velocity	1,653 ft/sec
Max range	11,100 yd
Traverse	9 degrees (25 degrees with Mk 5 carriage)

Ordnance QF 25 pdr Mk 1 and Mk 2 In the mid-1930s it was decided to produce a combined gun-howitzer to fire a 25 pdr shell. Initially, this was achieved by reboring existing 18 pdr barrels to take the 25 pdr shell; this was known as the 25 pdr Mark 1 (or 18/25 pdr) and was mounted on a modified 18 pdr carriage. Over 1,000 had

been converted and issued, so that the 25 pdr Mk I was the main equipment in Gunner field regiments when war began. Many were lost in France and later used by the Germans. Some were left in the UK to be used (as was the 18 pdr) for training and coastal defence, while others saw action in the Western Desert. By 1944 the majority had been replaced by the Mk 2.

In 1936, when the RA asked for an increase in range, a new design was necessary so the Mk 2 was produced. It did away with the split trail and the first guns were used in action in Norway in 1940. Rugged and dependable, over 12,000 had been issued by the end of the war. It served worldwide and on occasions (for example, in the desert) was used in the anti-tank role.

	Mk 1	Mk 2
Weight in action	3,570 lb	3,968 lb
Shell weight	25 lb	25 lb
Muzzle velocity	1,706 ft/sec	1,745 ft/sec
Max range	12,000 yd	13,400 yd
Traverse	9 degrees	360 degrees
Rate of fire	3 rpm normal	

This 25 pdr Mk I was photographed in action at St Maxent during the German assault on the West. The Mk I was at the time the main equipment of British field artillery. (IWM – F 4610)

A 25 pdr plus ammunition limber being towed by a 'Quad' in the Western Desert, where they were also used in the anti-tank role. The 25 pdr rapidly became a legend in its own time because of its rugged dependability. (Author's Collection)

A 25 pdr Mk II in action in NW Europe. Note that it has been fitted with a muzzle brake (and telescopic sights) so as to be able to perform even better in the anti-tank role. (Tank Museum)

The Field Artillery Tractor 4×4 Both the 18 pdr and the 25 pdr were normally towed into action using a fully enclosed artillery tractor, the first being the Guy 'Quad' Ant, which towed the 18 pdr. This was followed by the Morris C 8 'Quad' (also produced by Ford of Canada and Chevrolet), which towed the 25 pdr. Both had an excellent cross-country performance and seating accommodation for the entire six-man gun detachment, as well as space for ammunition and battery stores in the rear compartment. In addition to the gun, the tractor towed an ammunition limber that held additional HE, armour-piercing and smoke rounds.

MEDIUM AND HEAVY ARTILLERY

QF 4.5 in Howitzer Mk 2 Another elderly weapon, the Mk 1 was in service during the First World War and there were many Mk 2s in service throughout the British Army when the Second World War started. Nearly 100 were captured by the Germans in France and used for coastal defence, while they were used for training in the UK and saw action in the desert, Somalia and Eritrea early on. They were all withdrawn by 1944.

Weight in action	3,291 lb
Shell weight	34.5 lb
Muzzle velocity	1,000 ft/sec
Max range	6,600 yd
Traverse	6 degrees

4.5 in Gun Mk 1 on Carriage 60 pdr and BL 4.5 in Gun Mk 2 During the thirties the RA expressed an urgent need to update and re-equip their medium regiments but there was little money, so it was decided to convert

The crew of this medium artillery gun appear to be having quite a party. However, it was Christmas 1939, and the 'Phoney War' was in full swing – although at this stage there was no hint of the German onslaught to come the following summer. (IWM – O 2319)

some 60 pdr carriages to take the new 4.5 in barrels and the first of these guns was ready just before the war. The BL 4.5 in Gun Mk 2 was still on the drawing board, so the BEF took thirty-two of the seventy-six converted guns with them but none were brought back to the UK. There they were used for training, although some saw action in the Western Desert.

When it was realized that the 4.5 in/60 pdr conversion would not meet all the Gunners' needs, it was proposed that a new design of 4.5 in gun could use the same carriage as was being built for the 5.5 in howitzer (see below). There were design and production problems with the new carriage, so it was not until 1941 that the new gun reached operational units. It was a good, robust weapon but its HE projectile had a low HE filling, so the guns were withdrawn from service soon after war ended.

	Mk 1	Mk 2
Weight in action	15,985 lb	12,880 lb
Shell weight	55 lb	55 lb (3.875 lb of HE filling)
Muzzle velocity	2,250 ft/sec	2,250 ft/sec
Max range	21,000 yd	20,500 yd
Traverse	7 degrees	60 degrees

BL 5.5 in Mk 3 Gun This gun began life as a 5 in gun capable of firing a 100 lb shell

5.5 in field guns seen here in action near Derna. One of the best British field guns, the 5.5 in could fire an 82 lb shell over 18,000 yd. (IWM – E 1833)

Normandy, 15 August 1944. A 5.5 in gun shelling the enemy over the wooded slopes of the village of Vallee. (IWM – B 9174)

out to 16,000 yd. However, in 1939 this was changed to 5.5 in calibre. Although the gun was proofed in 1940 the proposed carriage was found to be not strong enough and had to be redesigned. The first guns entered service in 1941 and proved to be ideal and much more useful than the 4.5 in.

Weight in action	12,768 lb
Shell weight	100 lb (also a lighter 80 lb shell was available)
Muzzle velocity	1,675 ft/sec
Max range	16,200 yd
Traverse	60 degrees

BL 6 in Mk 9 Gun on Mk 8 or 8A travelling carriages This was the only 6 in long bombardment weapon in service in 1939,

although there were some older Mk 8 guns in coast artillery service with the US Army. The BEF had just a dozen of these guns in support (plus one in reserve). All were destroyed or captured. A few Mk 9s were used in the UK for home defence.

Weight in action	22,792 lb
Shell weight	100 lb
Muzzle velocity	2,405 ft/sec
Max range	18,750 yd
Traverse	8 degrees

BL 6 in 26 cwt Howitzer Mk 1 In 1939 this First World War designed howitzer was still the main weapon in service with British medium regiments, so over 200 were with the BEF, most of which were left behind and captured. As with other artillery pieces, those in the UK were used for home defence and training, while others fought in Africa. From 1941 they were gradually withdrawn and were declared obsolete in 1945.

BL 7.2 in Howitzer Mk 1 to 5 and Mk 6   At one point between the wars the use of heavy artillery was dismissed as it was felt that aircraft could do their job. However, this opinion changed in the mid-1930s. Various projects were started, but all were dropped, so that the British Army post-Dunkirk still had virtually no heavy field artillery, having left behind the BEF's only heavy regiment's guns

(8 in – see below). A stop-gap weapon was produced in the shape of the 7.2 in howitzer, by re-lining existing 8 in barrels. It proved useful despite the need for ramps behind the wheels to allow for run-up after firing. The weapon would often run over these wooden ramps and have to be man-handled back into position and re-layed after each firing. Marks 1 to 5 differed only as far as the source of the 7.2 in liners was concerned – some being relined American barrels. The Mk 6, however, was fitted on to an American carriage (155 mm/8 in Howitzer M1 carriage) and was much improved in stability, range and accuracy. It entered service in 1944.

Men of 134 Medium Regt, RA, bombarding Japanese positions at Fort Dufferin (in the heart of Mandalay), which was surrounded by a 30 ft rampart and a moat 70 yd wide. (IWM – IND 4537)

Lord Gort and French Gen Georges inspecting a British 8 in howitzer, which fired 200 lb shells over 12,400 yd. The BEF took one heavy regiment over to France; thereafter, it was mainly used for home defence and training. (IWM – F3971)

BL 8 in Howitzer Mk 8 Dating back to the First World War, the Mk 8 had been modernized with pneumatic tyres, etc. However, the loss of the twelve BEF Heavy Regiment guns left a few in the UK that were initially used for training and home defence. Then, when more and more 8 in barrels were converted to 7.2 in, the 8 in was withdrawn entirely although there were still a fair number of similar US weapons (8 in Howitzer M1917) spread around the USA and in American bases overseas.

EXAMPLES OF MEDIUM AND HEAVY ARTILLERY HOWITZERS

Type	6 in	7.2 in	7.2 in (Mk 6)	8 in
Weight in action (lb)	9849	22,900	29,120	20,048
Shell weight (lb)	100.2	202	202	200
Muzzle velocity (ft/sec)	1,409	1,700	1,630	1,500
Max range (yd)	11,400	16,900	19,667	12,400
Traverse (degrees)	8	8	60	8

The largest gun used by the BEF was this 12 in howitzer, located near Lille, which belonged to 2nd Super Heavy Regt, attached to II Corps. (IWM – F 4227)

Medium Artillery Tractor 4×4 AEC Matador   Used to haul the 4.5 in, 5.5 in and 6 in guns/howitzers was the Matador, which could tow up to 6½ tons. It had a top speed of 36 mph and was used in every theatre. A total of 8,612 were built for the British Army and a further 400 for the RAF.

RAIL-MOUNTED AND COAST ARTILLERY

There is insufficient space to cover these weapons in detail. However, as they were mainly employed in home defence and were thus part of our 'last line of defence', they do merit more than just a passing mention.

Railway artillery had mainly been built during the First World War, apart from the 18 in Howitzer Mk 1 of 1920, and it varied in calibre from 9.2 in up to 18 in. Rail mounting meant that the heavy guns (weighing anything up to nearly 500 tons) could be moved relatively easily and quickly over long distances. The 'HM Gun Scene-Shifter', a 14 in gun, had a firing position near Dover in 1940–41 and regularly bombarded German positions on the French coast. Coast artillery, on the other hand, varied from small calibre guns not in emplacements up to massive 15 in guns in concrete blockhouses. Examples of railway and larger calibre coast artillery were:

Coastal artillery. This 9.2 in gun is being installed in the East Weares Battery, Portland, Dorset.

'They shall not pass'. Looking through the gun embrasure of one of the 9.2 in coastal artillery guns. Note also the rolled gas cape on the sentry's back. (IWM – H 11316)

Type	Date of manufacture	Calibre (in)	Wt in action (tons)	Shell wt (lb)	Range (miles)
<u>Railway</u>					
Gun	1918	12	470	850	21
Gun	1916	14	250	1,585	20
How	1920	18	350	2,500	13
<u>Coast</u>					
Gun	1939	6	NK	100	12½
Gun	1942	8	NK	255	16½
Gun	1936	15	370	1,900	24

Airborne Artillery

QF 3.7 in Howitzer Mk 1 This 'pack' mountain howitzer came into service prewar and was used mostly by colonial forces; it was known as the 'screw gun' because of its barrel. It came back into British Army use in the Far East, in particular in Burma. It also became the initial artillery piece for airborne forces until replaced by more modern equipment (the QF 6 pdr Mk 2). In this role it had its spoked wheels replaced by pneumatic tyres.

Weight in action	1,669 lb
Muzzle velocity	973 ft/sec
Max range	6,000 yd
Shell weight (HE)	20 lb

QF 6 pdr Mk 2 The problem with the 6 pdr gun was that it was too wide for the Horsa glider fuselage, so a small number of carriages were modified to fit (Carriage Mk 3). Towed by a Jeep, it was used in action at Arnhem and at the Rhine crossings in March 1945. The gun could fire HE and AP – the APDS round (issued in 1945) could penetrate 146 mm of armour plate at 1,000 yd.

Armoured Fighting Vehicles

This section covers tanks, self-propelled guns, armoured cars and carriers.

TANKS
In the early stages of the war Britain continued much in the same way as they had done during the interwar years, producing obsolete designs, undergunned and lacking in armoured protection. Although these early models were adequate against the Italian and Japanese

A good close-up of an Auster of 654 Sqn, serving in Italy. The Auster was the British-built equivalent of the US Taylorcraft Model A, the Auster I entering service in August 1942. More than 1,000 Austers (I, III, IV and V) were built. Unarmed, it had a cruising speed of 112 mph and a range of 250 miles. (Museum of Army Flying)

tanks, which were of an even worse standard, they were markedly inferior to the German panzers. Hidebound both by the choice of the 2 pdr as the main tank gun and by building tanks with turret rings that were too small to accept anything larger, the resulting small calibre main armament was far too small to produce an effective HE round, although its AP performance was reasonable. Dual capability and larger calibre tank guns did not start to appear until the arrival of American Lend-Lease tanks such as the Grant and Sherman. Tank production during the war years was on a par with Germany, but because of its inadequacies the British still needed American tanks to equip many armoured formations from 1941–42 onwards.

BRITISH TANK PRODUCTION 1939–1945

Year	Total	Comments
1939	969	In addition there were the prewar models still in service.
1940	1,399	Nearly 700 tanks were lost in France by the BEF.
1941	4,841	From 1941, British armoured units were also increasingly equipped with American-built tanks.
1942	8,611	
1943	7,476	
1944	4,600	
1945	1,392	In the first six months only.

Total = 29,288

The Tetrarch Light Tank Mk VII was used by the airborne forces. Here one is being guided out of a Hamilcar glider at RAF Tarrant Rushton during training prior to D-Day. (Tank Museum)

Light Tanks Although some of the earlier interwar years models must have been in service the main light tank of the early war years was the Light Mk VIB. Light, fast and mechanically reliable, it had thin armour and poor armament. However, it saw active service in France, the Western Desert and in other areas of the Mediterranean (Greece, Crete, Malta (used for clearing airfield runways) and Syria). Two further light tanks were later produced, the first – another Vickers private venture – being the Light Mk VII (A 17), sometimes known by its code-name 'Purdah' or 'PR' tank, which, in 1943, became known as the Tetrarch. A total of 177 were built. Steering was achieved by flexing the tracks. Although designed as a 'cavalry' tank it was used by airborne forces in Normandy on 6 June 1944, being ferried over in Hamilcar gliders. (There was also the Tetrarch Mk 1 CS, which mounted a 3 in howitzer.) Secondly, there was the Light Tank Mk VIII (A 25), known as Harry Hopkins, which was a development of the Tetrarch, some ninety-two being built in the period up to 1944. They did not enter service as gun tanks, but some were converted into the Alecto SP (with either a 95 mm how or 6 pdr gun).

Type	Lt Mk VIB	Lt Mk VII	Lt Mk VIII
Weight	5 tons	7.5 tons	8.5
Length	12 ft 11.5 in	13 ft 6 in	14 ft
Height	7 ft 3.5 in	6 ft 11.5 in	6 ft 11 in
Width	6 ft 9 in	7 ft 7 in	8 ft 10.5 in
Speed	35 mph	40 mph	30 mph
Armour	up to 14 mm	up to 14 mm	up to 38 mm
Armament	1 × Vickers .5 MG	1 × 2pdr QFSA	1 × 2pdr OQF
	1 × Vickers .303 MG	1 × 7.92 Besa MG	1 × 7.92 Besa MG
Crew	3 (comd, gnr, dvr)	3	3

Two Light Mk VIBs belonging to 1 RTR in the Western Desert soon after the outbreak of war. The little 5 ton tanks were poorly armed and armoured, but were used extensively in the early part of the war. (Tank Museum)

Last of the Light Mk VI line was the VIC, which had a 15 mm Besa machine gun as its main armament, with a 7.92 mm Besa as coax. (Tank Museum)

The Light Tank Mk VIII was the last of the light tanks, but only saw action as the Alecto dozer. (Tank Museum)

The A9 Cruiser Tank Mk I was the first of the lightly armoured, fast cruiser tanks. The two 'dustbin-shaped' turrets on either side of the driver's position contained machine guns. This is a close support version, mounting a 3.7 in howitzer as its main armament. (Tank Museum)

Cruiser Tanks A bewildering array of cruiser tanks were built from the mid-1930s onwards, but they were a disappointing bunch, undergunned, under-armoured and with poor mechanical reliability despite their speed. The first was the Cruiser Tank Mk I (A9), designed by Sir John Carden of Vickers Armstrong in 1934. It was meant as a close support tank – mounting a 3.7 in mortar – to complement the Vickers Mediums, which were the mainstay of the RTC in the prewar years.[1] Its two side-mounted 'dustbin-

shaped' one-man MG turrets put the crew up to six men, but with little real advantage. It was powered by a 150 hp AEC A179 petrol engine. It did reasonably well against the Italians in the desert, but was outclassed when the DAK panzers arrived in 1941. It was followed by another Carden-designed cruiser – the Mk II (A10), which had thicker armour and no side turrets, then the Mk IIA. Both had single hull-mounted 7.92 BESA MGs as well as their turret-mounted 2 pdr and coax MG, but both were underpowered as they still had the same engine as the lighter A9. Next came the Cruiser Mk III (A13), which incorporated the revolutionary Christie suspension (large roadwheels) and was powered by a V-12 340 hp Nuffield 'Liberty' engine that gave the tank a top speed of 30 mph. It was followed by the Cruiser Mk IV (A13 Mk II), which was essentially

1. Some Vickers mediums were still in service at the start of the war, both in the UK and the Middle East, where they were dug in to the defences at Mersa Matruh – a few being unearthed later by enterprising Australian troops when there was a shortage of fighting tanks, although it is not on record as to whether they ever fired a shot in anger in either role!

an up-armoured version of the A13, then by the Cruiser Tank Mk V (A13 Mk III), the ill-starred Covenanter, which, despite its good looks, was mechanically unreliable, broke down and overheated constantly, so not one of the 1,700 built ever saw action (apart from a few fitted with a scissors type bridge and used by the Australians in the Far East). Their building also clogged the production lines preventing the manufacture of better tanks. Probably the most reasonable of the early wartime cruisers was the Cruiser Tank Mk VI (A15) Crusader, some 5,300 being built between 1940 and 1943. It first

saw action in the desert in June 1941 and a number were adapted for use as mobile AA guns, OPs, command vehicles, ARVs, dozers and gun tractors.

A new breed of Christie-type suspensioned cruiser tank then began to appear, starting with the Cruiser Tank Mk VII (A24) Cavalier, followed by the Mk VIII (A27L) Centaur, and finally the Mk VIII (A27M) Cromwell, the first British tank to be designed with an all-welded hull (later models) and a V-12 600 hp Rolls-Royce Meteor engine. In 1944–45 it became the main equipment in some British armoured divisions, replacing

The Cruiser Tank Mk VIII (A 27L) Centaur came after the Mk VII Cavalier; the version seen here – the Centaur IV – mounted a 95 mm howitzer. It belonged to H Tp, 2nd Bty, Royal Marine Support Regt and is moving inland off the Normandy beaches. (Tank Museum)

A line of Cruiser Tank Mk II (A 10)s exercising on Lulworth ranges. Second of the cruisers, it weighed 13.75 tons and saw service in France and the Western Desert. (IWM – H 6239)

Taking part in a War Savings drive is a Cruiser Tank Mk IVA (A 13 Mk II), the first cruiser to have the big wheel Christie suspension. (Tank Museum)

The ill-starred Cruiser Tank Mk V Covenanter (A13 Mk III) was used only for training, except for a few that were converted into bridgelayers. (Tank Museum)

The Cruiser Tank Mk VI, the Crusader was the best of the early cruisers, despite its initial poor armament (2 pdr), which was eventually upgunned to 6 pdr. (IWM – BM 19289)

There were various types of Crusader AA tanks; this is the AA Mk I, which mounted a 40 mm Bofors gun. (Tank Museum)

A line of Cromwells, Cruiser Tank Mk VIII (A 27M)s, which came after the Centaur and was used to re-equip British armoured divisions becoming, numerically, the most important British tank of 1944/5. (Tank Museum)

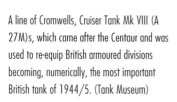

the Shermans in those units destined to fight in NW Europe – but many of the crews considered it to be inferior to the Sherman, principally because of its lack of firepower and armoured protection, although this latter problem was addressed by the addition of applique armour, increasing the thickness from 76 mm to 101 mm. Undoubtedly, it did not have the gunpower of the Sherman Firefly, which mounted the British 17 pdr, nevertheless, its speed and manoeuvrability meant it was able to deal with the large numbers of enemy towed anti-tank guns on which the Germans were forced to rely after their heavy tank losses in 1944. Next came the A30 Challenger, which mounted the newly developed 17 pdr gun in a large, rather ungainly looking turret (a foot higher than the

Cromwell) on top of a widened, lengthened Cromwell hull. It was adequate but only as a stop-gap. Finally came the pick of the bunch, the A34 Comet, which had firepower, protection and mobility comparable with the German Panther (which had been in service for two years when the Comet first appeared in late 1944 – a measure of how far behind the British were in tank design!). The Comet was undoubtedly the best British tank of the Second World War. Close on the Comet's heels was the first of the medium-gun tanks, the Centurion Mk 1 (A41), which would prove to be a world beater but did not enter service before the war ended, although six were delivered in May 1945 and rushed over to Germany for troop trials. However, they did not arrive until after VE-Day.

The Challenger A30 Cruiser Tank, mounting a 17 pdr gun in a rather tall, ungainly turret, was a worthwhile stopgap until the Sherman Firefly became more readily available. (Tank Museum)

The A34 Comet was the best British tank of the Second World War. However, as it did not enter service until late 1944, it had little impact. This 3 RTR Comet is driving through a ruined German street. (Tank Museum)

EXAMPLES OF CRUISER TANKS

Type	A9	A10	A13	A27M	A30	A34
Weight (tons)	12	13.75	14	19	32.5	35.2
Length	19 ft	18 ft 4 in	19 ft 9 in	20 ft 10 in	26 ft 9 in	25 ft 1 in
Height	8 ft 8.5 in	8 ft 8.5 in	8 ft 6 in	8 ft 2 in	9 ft 1 in	8 ft 9.5 in
Width	8 ft 2.5 in	8 ft 3.5 in	8 ft 4 in	9 ft 6.5 in	9 ft 6.5 in	10 ft
Armour (max)	14 mm	30 mm	14 mm	76 mm (101 mm)	101 mm	101 mm
Armament Main	1 × 2 pdr	1 × 2 pdr	1 × 2 pdr	1 × 6 pdr (or 75 mm)	1 × 17 pdr	1 × 77 mm
Secondary	3 × MG	2 × MG	1 × MG	2 × MG	1 × MG	2 × MG
Crew	6	5	4	5	5	5

The tiny Infantry Tank Mk I (A11) was very heavily armoured, so despite its small size it weighed 11 tons. It fought bravely against the German panzers in France, but was really obsolete before the war began. (Tank Museum)

Infantry tanks   The third type of tank to see service was the so-called infantry tank, designed to support infantry, with protection as its main characteristic, especially as regards spawl/splash-proofing[2]. Speed did not matter as the tank would be moving at the same

2. It had been found in the First World War that although heavy rifle/machine gun fire might not penetrate armour, it could cause flakes ('spawl') to come off the inside face of the armour plate and injure the crew. The same happened with fragments entering through gaps/joints in the plates (known as 'splash').

pace as the infantry walked. The first 'I' tank produced was the Infantry A11 in 1936, known as the Matilda after a cartoon duck of the period because it waddled like one! The successor to this small 11 ton tank was the Matilda II (A12), which was a vast improvement and earned itself the title 'Queen of the Desert' in 1940–41. Both types of Matilda had been used in France in 1940, being the only tanks to halt the all-conquering panzers in a battle near Arras, thus allowing time for the BEF to escape at Dunkirk. Once the Matilda I was withdrawn from service the

'Queen of the Desert', the Infantry Tank Mk II (A12) was far superior to anything the Italians could produce but found itself outgunned when the German panzers arrived. These Matildas belonged to 4 RTR. (Tank Museum)

A12 simply became known as the Matilda and, although outclassed by German heavy tanks it continued in service and was adapted to numerous roles (mine clearers, dozers, bridgelayers, etc.). The most interesting was the Matilda CDL, which entailed fitting a very powerful searchlight in place of the main armament to support night operations by temporarily blinding the enemy. This top secret weapon was never used in its proper role (on D-Day) although a few were used in 1945 to provide illumination for the Rhine crossing. The third of the early 'I' tanks was the private venture Infantry Tank Mk III, the Valentine, designed by Leslie Little of Vickers Armstrong Ltd, Engineers, Newcastle upon Tyne (hence its name). Despite being difficult to handle – because of the uncomfortable driving position – the Valentine was a reliable and well-liked tank.

This Australian-manned Matilda Mk II was equipped with an Australian flame-throwing device in place of its main gun and was known as a 'Matilda Frog'. (Tank Museum)

The Infantry Tank Mk III, the Valentine, was a private venture by Vickers. It was well liked by its crews and the later model (Mk IX) was armed with a 6 pdr gun. (Tank Museum)

The next 'I' tank, the Mk IV – the Churchill (A22) – was undoubtedly the best even though it was initially plagued with difficulties and had a disastrous 'blooding' in the ill-fated Dieppe raid in August 1942. It took about a year for all the problems to be sorted, after which the Churchill became a very reliable and much loved tank. Some eleven different marks were produced with main armament ranging from 2 pdr up to 75 mm and 95 mm howitzer, and, like the Sherman, it was adapted for a wide variety of other uses such as the Crocodile flamethrower, numerous bridgelayers, mine clearing devices, AVREs (Armoured Vehicle RE), ARVs and Beach ARVs. The Black Prince (A43) was developed from the Churchill; it mounted a 17 pdr gun and had great potential, but did not reach its final trial stage until May 1945.

Prime Minister Winston Churchill inspecting a regiment of Churchill tanks on Lulworth Ranges, 6 April 1942. After its disastrous debut on the ill-fated Dieppe raid the Churchill would become one of our most reliable tanks. (IWM – BH 15707)

Most fearsome was the Churchill Mk VII Crocodile flame-thrower, which was a Churchill Mk VII (75 mm gun) with a flame gun in the bow and towing a trailer of flame fluid. (Ground Photo Recce Unit HQ Second Army, via Author's Collection)

Infantry tanks

Type	Matilda 1	Matilda 2	Valentine	Churchill
Weight (tons)	11	26.5	17	38.5–40
Length	15 ft 11 in	18 ft 5 in	17 ft 9 in	24 ft 5 in
Height	6 ft 1.5 in	8 ft 3 in	7 ft 5.5 in	10 ft 8 in
Width	7 ft 6 in	8 ft 6 in	8 ft 7.5 in	9 ft
Armour	60 mm	78 mm	65 mm 102 mm	
Armament				
Main	1 × .5 VMG	1 × 2 pdr	1 × 2 pdr–6 pdr	see below
Secondary	1 × .303 MG	1 × 7.92 MG	various	
Crew	2	4	3–4	5

These Valentine Mk IIIs and VIIIs have been fitted with DD screens etc., to be used for amphibious trials. However, in 1943 the Sherman took over the DD role. (Tank Museum)

The best of the infantry tanks was the Mk IV Churchill (A 22). This was the Mk I, with a 3 in howitzer in its nose and a 2 pdr in the turret. (Tank Museum)

Churchill Armament, etc.

Mark	Weight	Main armament	Remarks
I	38.5	2 pdr in turret and 3 in howitzer in nose	All of these had fully-exposed tracks and engine intake louvres.
II	38.5	2 pdr in turret and MG in nose	
IICS	38.5	as for Mk I but with gun positions reversed	
III	39	6 pdr in new welded turret	
IV	39	6 pdr in new cast turret	
IV (NA 75)		as above with the American 75 mm gun	
V	39	95 mm howitzer in place of 6 pdr	
VI	39	British 75 mm in place of 6 pdr	
VII	40	thicker armour, new cast/welded heavy turret, heavier suspension, better gearbox, 75 mm gun and other mods	
VIII	40	as for the Mk VII but with a 95 mm howitzer	
IX	40	up-armoured Mk II and IV	
X	40	up-armoured Mk VI	
XI	40	up-armoured and up-dated Mk V	

This is the Churchill Mk VI, which mounted a 75 mm gun instead of the 6 pdr. It saw service in NW Europe during 1944/5. (Tank Museum)

The Churchill AVRE (Armoured Vehicle Royal Engineers) was one of the most useful tanks in the British Army. Its 290 mm spigot mortar threw a 40 lb bomb some 80 yd and was used against blockhouses etc. (Tank Museum)

A graphic photograph of infantrymen sheltering from enemy fire behind the large bulk of a Churchill AVRE on the Normandy beaches on D-Day. Over to its right is an M10 tank destroyer. (Tank Museum)

Looking down from the turret into the driver's compartment of a Churchill tank. (Ministry of Information Middle East via Author's Collection)

Fitters repairing a recently knocked out Churchill in the River Orne bridgehead area. (IWM – B 9162)

Commonwealth Tanks British and American tanks were of course used by Commonwealth armoured units. However, initially these two major suppliers were not available as the UK was short of tanks having lost so many in France, while the USA had not yet geared up its industry to produce AFVs. So Canada, for example, designed and built it own cruiser tank – the Ram, Mk I and Mk II – 1,000 of which were produced but were never used in action, except as an APC (the Ram Kangaroo). The Canadian Pacific Railway Co. of Montreal also built some 1,400 Valentines and 200 Grizzlies (the Canadian version of the US M4 Sherman medium tank). Australia produced a small number of their own cruiser tanks – the Sentinel AC 1 and other models – while even New Zealand managed to build various AFVs including the Bob Semple tank – a 20–25 ton mobile pillbox!

The Ram was a Canadian cruiser tank that utilized some of the American M3 medium mechanical parts, but with a hull and turret of Canadian design. This is the Ram Mk I, which mounted a 2 pdr gun, while the Mk II had a 6 pdr. (Tank Museum)

The only Rams to see action were the turretless stripped-out Ram Kangaroos, which could hold a section of infantry and all their weapons and equipment inside their capacious 'pouches'. The Ram Kangaroo APC gave good mobility plus all round cover, but none overhead. (Tank Museum)

Canada also built their own version of the Sherman M4 tank, known as the Grizzly. Total production was 200 and they saw service with Canadian units in the UK and NW Europe. (Tank Museum)

The AC (Australian Cruiser) Sentinel was a remarkable effort for a country with such a small heavy manufacturing base. The AC 1, seen here, mounted a 2 pdr gun. There were to have been various upgunned models, but once British and American tanks became more plentiful they never got past prototype stage. (Tank Museum)

Type	Ram	Grizzly	Sentinel
Weight (tons)	29	30	28
Length	19 ft	19 ft 1 in	20 ft 9 in
Height	8 ft 9 in	9 ft 10 in	8 ft 5 in
Width	9 ft 1 in	8 ft 9.5 in 9 ft 1 in	
Armour max (mm)	87	62	65
Armament			
Main	Ram 1 – 1 × 2 pdr Ram 2 – 1 × 6 pdr	1 × 75 mm	1 × 2 pdr
Secondary	2 × MG + 1 × MG (AA)	2 × MG	2 × MG
Crew	5	5	5

SELF-PROPELLED GUNS

There were three main British SP guns designed during the Second World War, although one of them – the Avenger (A30) – did not enter service until the war had ended. The other two were both based upon the Valentine chassis, being the Bishop 25 pdr (Carrier, Valentine 25 pdr Mk I, Bishop) and the 17 pdr Archer (SP 17 pdr Valentine Mk I, Archer). The former came into being in order to meet the urgent needs of British forces in the Western Desert in 1941, for an SP weapon to provide normal artillery fire support rather than direct a tk fire. In June

A somewhat battered Bishop SP gun, in which a 25 pdr Mk I was fitted onto a Valentine chassis in a large box-like structure, with an all-up weight of some 17.4 tons. This was done in order to give British infantry the same sort of fire support the Afrika Korps had in North Africa. (Tank Museum)

The Archer also used a Valentine chassis, this time to mount the highly effective British 17 pdr a tk gun in a streamlined, open-topped compartment, becoming the British equivalent of the American tank destroyers. It was one of the best a tk guns of the war. (Tank Museum)

1941 a scheme proposed mounting a 25 pdr gun on to an existing tank chassis; the Valentine was quickly chosen and just two months later a pilot model was ready for trials. It consisted basically of a Valentine tank minus its turret, with a rigid armoured box-like structure in its place, inside which was a complete 25 pdr field gun. Trials were successful although the crew was rather cramped and the gun could not reach its maximum elevation, which limited the range to just about half of normal (6,400 yd instead of 12,000 yd). After crew protection had been improved (up to 60 mm of armour plate) it was rushed into service, an order for 100 being placed in November 1941, with a further 200 promised as a follow-up order. However, four months later the Americans produced a much better SP – namely the M7

HMC Priest – and this came into service instead of more Bishops.

Work began on the Archer in July 1942 and the pilot model was ready for trials in March 1943. The 17 pdr gun was mounted, pointing to the rear, in an open-topped superstructure. A total of 665 were built from March 1944 onwards and Archer equipped a tk battalions in British armoured divisions in NW Europe from October 1944 onwards.

Commonwealth SP – The Sexton Just as the Americans produced the M7 Priest SP version of their M3 medium tank, so the Sexton was the SP version of the Ram, but with the British 25 pdr gun instead of the American 105 mm gun. Developed during the latter half of 1942, some 2,150 were built of this highly effective SP before the end of the war.

For the Sexton SP, a British 25 pdr Mk II gun was mounted onto a Canadian Ram chassis. Over 2,000 were built and they gradually replaced the American SP Priest in British and Canadian armoured divisions SP artillery regiments. (Tank Museum)

Type	Bishop	Archer	Sexton
Weight (tons)	17.4	16.5	24.45
Length	18 ft 2 in	21 ft 11.5 in	20 ft 1 in
Width	8 ft 7.5 in	8 ft 7.5 in	9 ft
Height	9 ft 3.25 in	7 ft 4.25 in	8 ft
Armament			
Main	25 pdr	17 pdr	25 pdr
Secondary	1 × Bren .303in	LMG (AA)	2 × Bren
Armour thickness (mm)	60 mm	60 mm	25 mm
Engine	131 hp AEC	165 hp GMC	400 hp Wright
Max speed (mph)	15	15	25
Range (miles) 90	90	135	

SCOUT CARS

Daimler Scout Car The 'Dingo', as it was called, was produced after the Mechanization Board had asked Alvis, BSA and Daimler to submit prototypes for a new class of small, turretless, armoured vehicle for scouting purposes. There were five marks of this excellent little two-man vehicle (Mk I, Ia, Ib, II and III), the final version weighing 3.15 tons. A total of 6,626 of all marks were built.

Humber Scout Car Slightly larger and heavier, the Humber had a similar layout to the Daimler but could carry three men comfortably; some 4,300 were built during the war.

Type	Daimler	Humber
Weight (tons)	Mk I – 2.8 Mk III – 3.15	3.39
Length	10 ft 5 in	12 ft 7 in
Width	5 ft 7.5 in	6 ft 2.5 in
Height	4 ft 11 in	6 ft 11.5 in
Armament	1 × LMG	1 × LMG (could be a Vickers K)
Speed (mph)	55–60	60
Range (miles)	200	200
Crew	2	3

The Daimler Dingo scout car was widely used – some 6,626 being built of all Marks. It was a tiny 2.8 ton AFV, with a standard crew of two. However, as demonstrated in this photograph – taken during an exercise in the UK prior to D-Day – it could take more! (Tank Museum)

A good shot of a Daimler Dingo scout car leading a column of Recce Corps vehicles, including armoured cars and motorcyclists. It is followed by a Daimler armoured car, then a Humber, with another Dingo bringing up the rear. (Tank Museum)

The other British scout car, the Humber, was slightly larger and heavier than the Daimler. This Humber, belonging to 51st Inf (Highland) Div, has just had an argument with a Teller mine, losing a wheel. (Author's Collection)

Lynx Scout Car This was the Canadian version of the Daimler Dingo and was 1 ton heavier and 1 ft 8.5 in longer. 3,000 were built during the war. In addition to the Mk I and Mk II Lynx, there was an SP a tk version that mounted a 2 pdr. Maromon-Herrington of the USA also built a version of the Lynx.

LIGHT RECONNAISSANCE CARS
Humber produced a range of other armoured recce vehicles, such as the Humber Mk I and Ironside I. Three of these were specially modified for use by the Royal Family and cabinet ministers and were known as 'Special Ironside Saloons'. There was also the Humber Mk II Light Recce Car, which was similar to the Ironside I but had roof armour and a small, half-circular conical shield for the LMG. A total of 3,600 Humber LRCs were built (all marks). Another range of light recce cars was known as the Standard Car 4×2 (the RAF called it the Beaverette I). There was a Mk II and a Mk III (called the 'Beaverbug'). Morris also produced a light recce car (Model CS9/LAC), thirty-eight of which were taken to

Two Beaverette Mk II LRCs, belonging to 2nd Inf Div, on training in the UK. The Mk II had all round armour, while the Mk I had thick planks of wood at the rear because of the severe shortage of metal after Dunkirk. (Tank Museum)

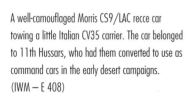

A well-camouflaged Morris CS9/LAC recce car towing a little Italian CV35 carrier. The car belonged to 11th Hussars, who had them converted to use as command cars in the early desert campaigns. (IWM – E 408)

An impressive line-up of Humber LRCs Mk III, showing their Boys A tk rifles and LMGs. (Tank Museum)

France with the BEF, while thirty more went to the Western Desert with 11th Hussars (as well as their Rolls-Royce Armoured Cars). They were followed by a large number of other Morris LRCs – Mk I and Mk II – 2,200 being built of both marks. Finally, there was a range of ad hoc armoured recce cars, based on normal civilian saloons, which were built in small garage workshops all over the UK in the dark days of 1940.

EXAMPLE LRCS

Type	Humber Mk II	Beaverette III	Morris I
Weight (tons)	3	2.6	3.7
Length	14 ft 4 in	10 ft 6 in	13 ft 3.5 in
Width	6 ft 2 in	7 ft 1 in	6 ft 8 in
Height	6 ft 10 in	5 ft 10 in	6 ft 2 in
Armament	all mounted 1 × Boys a tk rifle and 1 × Bren LMG		
Speed (mph)	40	40	50

Otter LRC The Canadians also produced an LRC – their version of the Humber Mk III, known as the Otter. Over 1,700 were built and mainly used by Canadian troops in Italy.

ARMOURED CARS

There were a number of obsolescent armoured cars in service when war was declared, including the Lanchester and Rolls-Royce (1924 pattern), the former being used in Malaya in 1941–42 against the Japanese, while the latter performed yeoman service in the Western Desert in 1940–41, and despite their age were fitted with a new turret to mount a Boys a tk rifle and an LMG.

As the German armoured cars came into prominence in the desert, so came the cry for bigger and better British armoured cars to take over reconnaissance from the light tanks. Humber, Guy, Daimler, AEC and Coventry models were all produced, their armament ranging from 2 pdr and 37 mm up to 6 pdr and 75 mm. The best and most widely used was probably the Daimler, 2,700 of which were built. They saw service in most theatres.

Fox Armoured Car Some 200 Fox armoured cars were built by GM of Canada. The Fox was the Canadian version of the Humber Mk III, but mounted Browning MGs (1 × .50 and 1 × .30) instead of Besas. There was also an SP version, mounting a 6 pdr on a Fox Mk I chassis.

Marmon-Herrington Armoured Cars South Africa produced a series of excellent armoured cars that were used widely in the Western Desert. Their engines came from the USA and their armament from the UK. A total of 5,746 were built, 1,180 of which were supplied to British and Indian armoured car regiments.

CARRIERS

One of the most widely used AFVs of the war was the British Universal Carrier, known popularly as the Bren Carrier. However, there were many varieties of this excellent 3½ ton vehicle such as: Carrier MG No. 1 and No. 2;

(text continues on page 262)

EXAMPLES OF ARMOURED CARS

Type	Humber Mk I	Guy Mk IA	Daimler Mk I	AEC Mk I	Coventry Mk I
Weight(tons)	6.85	5.75	6.8	11	11.5
Length	15 ft	13 ft 6 in	13 ft	17 ft	15 ft 6.5 in
Width	7 ft 2 in	6 ft 8 in	8 ft	9 ft	8 ft 9 in
Height	7 ft 10 in	7 ft 6 in	7 ft 4 in	8 ft 4.5 in	7 ft 9 in
Armament Main Secondary	Both had 1 × 15 mm Besa and 1 × 7.92 Besa, but the Mk IV Humber mounted a 37 mm gun		All three had 1 × 2 pdr and 1 × 7.92 Besa. However, the AEC Mk II mounted a 6 pdr and the Coventry Mk II a 75 mm gun		
Crew	3	3	3	4	4
Speed (mph)	45	35	50	36	41
Range (miles)	250	210	200	250	250

The Marmon-Herrington armoured car was built by the South Africans but saw service with the British and other Commonwealth countries as well as South Africa. This is a late model Mk II, with the octagonal turret. (Author's Collection)

The first armoured car into Tripoli was this Humber Mk II, belonging to Sgt Hugh Lyon of 11th Hussars. The Rootes Group had the major share of armoured car building during the war and most of those produced were Humbers. (IWM – E 22668)

Where's the lifeboat? This Mk IV Humber armoured car was carrying out amphibious trials at Weymouth, Dorset, on Christmas Day, 1943, but seems to be in a certain amount of trouble! (IWM – H34983)

Leading this long line of Recce Corps vehicles is a Humber Mk IV, which was the last of the line and mounted an American 37 mm gun that gave the AFV much better fire-power, but reduced the crew to three. (Tank Museum)

The design of the 6.8 ton Daimler armoured car was based upon the Daimler scout car — just larger and with a turret, mounting a 2 pdr gun and coax MG. (Tank Museum)

At 11 tons the AEC Mk I armoured car was a private venture and mounted a turret which was basically the same as that on the Valentine tank. This AEC belonged to 4 Tp, C Sqn, Royals. (Author's Collection)

The Americans designed and built the Staghound heavy armoured car, which weighed 13.7 tons. It was built originally to be used by both armies, but eventually only the British took it, 2,400 being built. (Tank Museum)

Scout carriers belonging to the BEF in France soon after their arrival in September 1939. (Tank Museum)

These scout carriers were on patrol outside the badly damaged Fort Capuzzo in the Western Desert. (Tank Museum)

This recce platoon of carriers belonged to FC/CIH Regt of the South African Armoured Corps in Italy. Note their names – Snow White and the Seven Dwarfs (plus Prince Charming in the Jeep!). (SA Official via Author's Collection)

These universal carriers belonged to an Indian infantry unit in Italy and were photographed in April 1944. (MOD New Delhi via Author's Collection)

A well-laden trio of Carriers Universal operating in Burma. Note the spare track being carried on two of the carriers. (Tank Museum)

A good layout of weapons and equipment for this universal carrier, with a Boys a tk rifle and Bren LMG, plus the vehicle tools, etc. (Tank Museum).

Scout Carrier; Carrier armoured OP (five different versions); General Service Carrier; Mortar (3 in) Carrier; Flame-thrower Carrier; MMG Carrier; Conger (exploding hose); Ambulance; Anti-aircraft (two Vickers K MG); Praying Mantis (a strange version with two remotely controlled MGs in a tower-like head that could be raised/lowered), and various others. Details of two of the most widely used carriers are:

Type	Bren No. 2 Mk I and Mk II	Carrier Scout Mk I
Weight (tons)	3.75	3.3
Armament	.303 in Bren LMG or Boys a tk rifle	Bren and Boys a tk rifle
Crew	3	3–4

Loyd Carrier The 4 ton Loyd Carrier was very similar and less complicated mechanically than the Universal Carrier and was built by Vivian Loyd & Co. Ltd and other companies such as Wolseley and Dennis (and also later by Ford of Canada). The first versions entered service in 1940 when they were used just as troop carriers (they could hold up to eight men). Later it was used as a gun tower (2 pdr and 6 pdr a tk guns), SP gun carrier (2 pdr various versions), mobile welding plant and tracked mobile bridge.

Windsor Carrier The Ford Motor Co. of Windsor, Ontario, produced their version of the Universal Carrier, which incorporated many of the Loyd Carrier components and was based upon the Universal Carrier's design. Production began in 1943 at 500 a month. However, because certain mechanical problems had then to be rectified very few entered service before the war ended.

ARMOURED COMMAND VEHICLES (ACV)

Mention must also be made of the ACV, which quickly became the ideal vehicles to control armoured formations in battle because they

An AEC 4×4 armoured command vehicle, on amphibious training at Weymouth, comes ashore from a landing craft, 16 December 1943. (IWM – H 34815)

were larger and more roomy than command tanks, could hold extra radios, mapboards, plans, files, etc., and, of course, they could house the staff officers and signallers to man the 'hub' of an armoured formation. They were also much prized by the enemy, Rommel capturing three in the Western Desert and using two of these *Mammuts* (Mammoths), as the Germans called them, as command vehicles for the DAK. Examples of these vehicles are the 4×4 AEC Mk I, built on an AEC Matador truck chassis and powered by a 95 hp diesel engine; the 6×6 AEC Mk I, which was larger and powered by a 150 hp diesel engine. Both were produced in two types – High Power (HP) and Low Power (LP) – depending upon the range of radio sets fitted.

MOTORCYCLES

PREWAR CIVILIAN MODELS

Apart from some innovations such as those miniature bikes designed for use by the airborne forces, the majority of Second World war British military motorcycles were prewar civilian models, but with such necessary additions as extra toolboxes, a pair of standard issue canvas pannier bags, a rear carrier rack and masked lighting. Painted khaki and stripped of unessential items such as kneegrips, footrests and all chrome, they were ready for military use. In the first and main category were those used for solo riding, primarily on surfaced roads, and these included the Ariel W/NG, BSA

Men of the 10th Royal Welch Fusiliers at Piddlehinton Camp, Dorset, on parade on their BSA 500 cc motorcycles. BSA built over 126,000 motorcycles during the war. (IWM – H 16609)

M20, Matchless G3 and G3L, Norton 16H and Big Four, Royal Enfield WD/C and WD/CO, Triumph 3SW and 3HW and the Velocette MAF. Tasks performed were message carrying by despatch riders (DR), reconnaissance, convoy control and MP duties. All officers up to the rank of lieutenant-colonel were expected to be able ride a motorcycle proficiently, having been taught during their officer training. Over 100,000 Nortons and 125,000 BSAs were produced during the war out of a total of 425,000 motorcycles built by British factories.

The next category included those for use with a sidecar attached – the BSA M20 and Norton 16H for example. The sidecar was a simple one, with a single seat, a stowage box at the rear and a large protective front panel.

Large handles were provided at the front and rear for manhandling the sidecar. Several thousand were produced, some being fitted with a swivel mounting for a machine gun, or the sidecar replaced by a platform to carry a 3 in mortar, tripod and two boxes of ammunition. The last category was the light models, built from 1942 onwards, such as the James ML (known as the 'Clockwork Mouse') and the Royal Enfield WD/RE (the 'Flying Flea'). Both models were used by airborne troops (about 6,000 'Mice' and 8,000 'Fleas' were built), while the tiny Excelsior Welbike (weighing only 70 lb) was packed into its own cylindrical container for parachute drops, and over 3,800 of these 'parascooters' were produced.

Signalman Jeff Orchard, a DR of 7th Armd Div Sigs, in the Western Desert astride his beloved Norton. The company produced over 100,000 motorcycles during the Second World War. (Author's Collection)

A DR's life in North Africa was an extremely hazardous one, with all manner of terrain to negotiate – even the roads were old and worn. This DR is on an ancient road in Tunisia. (BNA 629).

An impressive line-up of Norton 'Big Fours' Combination 3×2, which were used in this instance for reconnaissance. The troops are from 1st Bn Northumberland Fusiliers and are seen here in Blandford Camp, Dorset, in 1940. (IWM – H 3709)

The Recce Corps used motorcycle combinations until they were replaced by the ubiquitous American Jeep. This trio were on exercise in the UK (in the springtime by the look of the broom). (Author's Collection)

The BSA M20 provides a good example of the basic characteristics of British motorcycles of the period:

Weight	310 lb
Fuel capacity	4.3 gal approx.
Fuel consumption	46 mpg
Speed	60 mph
Range	200 miles
Engine	single cylinder

'B' VEHICLES

1¼ MILLION VEHICLES

During the interwar period the large number of 'B' vehicles that had been in service during the First World War was allowed to run down and further mechanization did not begin until the 1930s. However, once the decision to mechanize had been made, then it was embraced in Britain far more whole-heartedly than by any other country apart from the USA. The Germans, for example, continued to use a considerable quantity of horsed transport throughout the Second World War, especially on the Eastern Front. Various wheeled vehicle designs were specifically developed for the British Army – such as those in the 15 cwt 4×2, 3 ton 4×2 and 4×4 classes – but these all took time to build. Two 'instant' schemes greatly increased the numbers of trucks available at the start of hostilities; one was the impressing of civilian vehicles (see Chapter 6), the other was the hiring of military-type vehicles from two large private forestry companies. The total number of vehicles held by the War Department was thus greatly increased, so that by September 1939 they held some 55,000 and could properly equip the BEF. However, most of these were left behind in France, which created a vacuum that was partly made up by the impressing of more civilian vehicles, but slowly and steadily overcome by increased home production and imports from the USA and the Commonwealth. By the end of the war the total number of soft-skinned vehicles in use by the British armed services had risen to a staggering 1¼ million.

A distinction was made between the terms 'truck' and 'lorry'. The former was used to describe any load-carrying vehicle of 1 ton or less. 'Lorry' was used to describe any load-carrying vehicle of 30 cwt or more. In addition, the term 'van' was used to describe a truck with a fixed top, and 'tractor' a lorry used to pull or tow anything – thus all artillery prime movers were called tractors.

STAFF CARS AND LIGHT UTILITIES
A large number of saloon cars were manufactured specifically for use by the Services during the first year of the war – small cars like the civilian Austin 10, Standard 10 and Hillman Minx modified for Army use by painting them khaki, including all the chrome parts. Larger staff cars were mainly Fords and Humbers, various models of the latter being widely used – for example, the

Tripoli Victory Parade. Prime Minister Winston Churchill, accompanied by Monty, passes the tanks of 4 CLY. Their car is the Humber Snipe Mk II. (IWM – E 22280)

Snipe and Super Snipe, both saloons and open tourers, also the 4×4 heavy utility (a four-door estate that was produced in other versions as well, such as an 8 cwt truck and an ambulance). Details of the Austin 10 and Ford V8 are:

Type	Austin 10	Ford V8
Weight	0.675 ton	1.4 ton
Engine	4-cylinder	8-cylinder
Speed	33 mph	76 mph
Range (approx.)	280 miles	230 miles
Fuel tank	8.4 gal	18 gal
Fuel consumption	33 mpg	13 mpg

Another widely used, popular adaptation of civilian cars was the range of light load carriers known by one and all as 'Tillies'. The most common were the Austin 10, Hillman 10, Morris M Series and the Standard 12. They all had an open truck-type body behind the normal two-seater cab, which was covered by a canvas tilt cover supported by three metal hoops. Some had additional seats (folding) in the rear. There were a number of different models produced by all the manufacturers between 1940 and 1945 and their reliability was well known. For example, it is said that some of those 'Tillies' captured by the Germans from the BEF in 1940 and pressed

Another view of the same car in Tripoli, shortly after the Desert Rats had entered the city. The car was a militarized version of the Humber Super Snipe. (IWM – E 21587)

Montgomery, now CinC 21 Army Group, crossing the Seine at Vernon, near Beauvais, on 1 September 1944 in his Humber Tourer. (IWM – BU 551)

A Humber heavy utility 4×4 estate that belonged to 79th Armd Div. This was the most common form of this heavy car, although it was also produced as an ambulance, armd recce vehicle and 8 cwt truck. (Author's Collection)

Cherbourg during the evacuation of part of the BEF. A convoy of various heavily laden trucks and lorries moves towards the ships, presumably for loading, while a group of motorcycles and their riders is parked beside the port building on the left. In the foreground is an Austin 4×2 two seater, one of the many taken to France. (IWM – F 4862)

A Morris Commercial PU8/4, 8 cwt wireless truck, 4×4; this one was used in North Africa. (Author's Collection)

into Wehrmacht service were recaptured in 1944 and went on motoring for the rest of the war!

Light Trucks 15 cwt GS Class An important range of vehicles was the 15 cwt GS Class, for which the War Office had invited tenders in 1933. Five British manufacturers subsequently tendered: Commer, Ford, Guy, Vauxhall and Morris Commerical. The latter produced their contender first – the CS8 – which was later (in 1941) replaced by the C4. Basic details of these two 15 cwts are:

Type	CS8	C4
Date produced	1934	1941
Weight (unladen)	1 ton 18 cwt	1 ton 18 cwt
Wheelbase	8 ft 2 in	8 ft 2 in
Engine	6-cylinder	4-cylinder
	3.495 litre	3.5 litre

Both had a tarpaulin cover over the load-carrying area (roughly 6 ft wide × 6.5 ft long), which was located at the rear of the open cab (fitted with a folding canopy and two bucket-type seats and later with a windscreen and metal doors). The 15 cwt was used for a wide variety of tasks, such as load carrier, fire tender, water tanker, wireless truck and to carry light guns 'portee'.

Next on the scene was the 15 cwt Guy Ant, produced in 1935, which was similar to the CS8 but weighed 2 ton 3.5 cwt (unladen) and had an 8 ft 5 in wheelbase. It was produced as a GS truck, a wireless van and as a compressor unit. Later in the war, in 1944, came a 4×4 version, the 'Quad' Ant, the first British four-wheel drive vehicle in the 15 cwt class, derived from the Guy artillery tractor. Vauxhall Motors Bedford MW 15 cwt truck came next and was eventually

A major problem for NAAFI was getting enough water to make thousands of cups of tea! Here a NAAFI girl fills up two jerricans from a 200 gal water truck. (B 9191)

The Morris Commercial CS8 was one of the many 15 cwt light trucks that did all the jobs later taken over by the American Jeep. This one is moving along the road to Tobruk, looking rather like a tinker's cart! (IWM – BM 1472)

More CS8 15 cwts, this time in convoy near the Pyramids, 12 May 1940. (IWM – E 30)

The 15 cwt was also used by the 'Jock Columns' – the brainchild of Lt Col (later Maj Gen) Jock Campbell, VC. Here the column navigating officer, in an early Bedford 15 cwt MWD, waves his blue flag to start the column moving, July 1942. (IWM – E 14032)

It was amazing just how much kit the average 15 cwt Bedford would hold. This crew is having a quick 'forty winks' on and around its Bedford MWD truck, with the sides and rear down. (IWM – E 14042)

This Ford truck was part of RHQ 1 RTR and was photographed on exercise in the desert just before the war began. Note also the wireless lorry in the background. (Author's Collection)

produced in considerable quantity – some 66,000 MWs including water tankers (200 gal), radio trucks, a tk gun tractors (2 pdr), AA gun carriers (20 mm), enclosed trucks and standard GS. The Commer 'Beetle' was very similar in appearance to the MW and first appeared in 1939, but production was limited. Finally, there was the Fordson WOT2, which appeared in 1940, powered by the 3.6 litre V8 engine. It was the last of this class to be built in quantity.

Details of the Bedford MW 15 cwt are:

Weight	2 ton
Engine	6-cylinder
Speed	53 mph
Fuel consumption	10 mpg

Lorries 3 ton 4×2 GS and 6×2 GS At the start of the war there were plenty of lorries in the 30–40 cwt class in service, ranging from modified civilian vehicles produced by Bedford, Morris Commercial and Thornycroft to the Bedford OXD, which was a larger version of their 15 cwt. The army had some 10,000 of these lorries in September 1939, but lost at least half of them in 1940. Also in the 1930s, a range of 6×2 30 cwts had been built not only by Morris Commercial and Thornycroft but also by Crossley, Garner and Vulcan. Variants included breakdown trucks, winch vehicles and AA tractors (to tow the 40 mm Bofors). The 3 tonner was widely used by all the Services, being the heaviest type that could be mass produced – by the end of the war some 390,000[3] were in service, the most common 4×2s being the Austin K3, the Bedford OY and the Commer Q4. Details of the Bedford OY give a good example of the specifications of this, the main army load-carrier:

Engine	6-cylinder
Speed	43 mph (governed to 40 mph)
Fuel consumption	7.5 mpg
Fuel capacity	45 gal
Weight	2.6 ton

The GS body had a flat floor and a detachable canopy mounted on hoops, the internal dimensions of the cargo space being 11.5 ft long × 6.5 ft wide. The cab was enclosed, steel panelled, with two seats. The vehicle was designed to take special low-pressure tyres and to give adequate clearance for cross-country work.

Lorry 3 ton 4×4 In contrast to the USA, the use of four-wheel drive suspension had received little attention in Britain during the interwar years and America provided the UK with a fair number of both 4×4 and 6×6 vehicles via 'Lend-Lease' before they entered the war. Design work did begin with the outbreak of hostilities, but it was not until 1 February 1940 that the first prototype was ready. After trials, the army placed an initial order for just over 4,000. The new model was called a 'QL'[4] and was far larger than any of the previous Bedford lorries although still powered by the standard 3.5 litre 6-cylinder petrol engine. Vauxhall engineers were not entirely happy about this, but could not afford to delay. Between 1941 and 1945 some 52,245 QLs were built, making them the most common in the 3 ton 4×4 class that was also built by Ford and Austin. There were a number of different Bedford QLs produced, viz, 'QLB' – tractor for Bofors 40 mm AA gun; 'QLC' – lorry/tractor with semi-trailer; 'QLD' – standard 3 ton cargo;

---

3. It has to be said that not all these were built in the UK, many thousands coming from the US and Canada.

4. In his book *World War Two Military Vehicles* Mr Georgano explains that the derivation of 'QL' is possibly 'Q' for 'Quad', a common name for 4×4s, and 'L' for 'Long', as it was a full-length truck and not an artillery tractor.

'QLR' – wireless truck; 'QLT' – troop carrier; 'QLW' – winch-equipped tipper lorry.

Lorry 3 ton 6×4 Three main types were built during the war – the Austin K3 and 6, the Fordson WOT1 and the Leyland Retriever – although AEC, Albion and Thornycroft did produce them as well. Details of the K3 are:

Weight	4 ton 8 cwt
Engine	3.9 litre 6-cylinder
Wheelbase	12 ft 9 in

As well as load carriers, specialized bodies included mobile workshops, fire tenders, bulk fuel carriers, mobile offices and cranes. Later models of the Leyland Retriever – such as the 'Hippo' – were in the 10 ton class and

A Chevrolet 3 ton 4×4, towing a trailer and leading a convoy of mixed lorries, crosses a temporary bridge in Burma on the way to Rangoon. (IWM – SE 3892)

This 3 ton 6×4 (probably a Leyland Retriever Machinery lorry) has been made into a most useful early command vehicle. (Author's Collection)

This Leyland Retriever, belonging to 7th Hussars, carries a 15 cwt truck on its four-wheeled trailer. (Author's Collection)

had special bodies for carrying specialized loads such as pontoon carriers for pontoons of the Bailey bridge. Over 6,500 Retrievers were built.

Lorry 5 to 10 tons, 4×2 and 6×4 Nearly all the heavier trucks were based upon prewar models, apart from the Dennis 5 ton, Fordson Thames 7V and the Commer Q6. These larger lorries came into their own after D-Day, when vast loads of stores had to be moved so the bigger capacity per lorry the better (compare with the US Army 'Red Ball Express' system). Also used were 10 tonners with a wide range of special bodies and these remained in service for many years after the war.

AMBULANCES
The best known British ambulance of the war was the Austin K2 – known as the 'Katie' – which used the same chassis as the K3, 30 cwt lorry. Other ambulances included the Morris Commercial CS11/30F 30 cwt, which had a four-stretcher body, and the Morris TMV 10 cwt, which could carry four stretchers or eight sitting casualties.

TRACTOR/TRAILER UNITS, TANK TRANSPORTERS AND ARTILLERY TRACTORS
As well as making most use of American and Canadian tractors, the British did build a few, the most common being the Bedford OXC used

The inside of a senior officer's caravan, *c.* 1944/5. This one belonged to 79th Armd Div. (Author's Collection)

The most well known of British ambulances during the war was the Austin K2. This one belonged to 7th Armd Div in the desert war and was photographed with two of the MOs of 7 Motor Brigade. (Author's Collection)

with a Scammell semi-trailer with automatic coupling. The Bedford OXC was also used with a 40 ft low-loading trailer, known as the 'Queen Mary' because of its size (40 ft long × 12 ft 3 in wide), thus the overall length of the vehicle was some 50 ft! The most widely used tank transporter was the Scammell Pioneer 6×4 tractor, which was first built in 1927 then modernized, although only two were in service when war began. They were always in short supply, under 600 being built, so the shortfall had to be made up by using American transporters like the Diamond T. The Scammell Pioneer was also built as a heavy recovery tractor for pulling disabled vehicles. Some 1,500 were built – nearly three times the number of tank transporters and twice the number of artillery tractors.

A Scammell Pioneer recovery lorry gives a Matilda a helping hand, somewhere near Sollum. (Author's Collection)

Climbing up over the Timini Pass near Gazala is this heavy breakdown tractor, towing not only a Cranes 7½ ton light recovery trailer plus Stuart light tank but also a Scammell Pioneer. (Author's Collection)

A line of 25 pdr, Quads and limbers of 94 Fd Regt, RA, moving up towards the Rhine. The Morris Commercial C8 artillery tractors were widely used. (IWM – BU 2715)

In the 1930s Scammell, Guy and FWD all built petrol-engined tractors that were used by the army to tow field guns, while a new generation of light 4×4 tractors had entered production by the outbreak of war – such as the Guy 'Quad' Ant. These lighter tractors were suitable for towing 18 and 25 pdr field guns, while heavier tractors like the 6×4 Morris Commercial CD/SW and the 4×4 Morris Commercial C8/AT, the Bedford QL and the Austin K5 could all be used to tow the 40 mm Bofors AA gun, while the Bedford could also be used to carry a 6 pdr a tk gun (see 'QLB' above) when a blast shield over its radiator allowed the gun to be fired forward over the cab. This was also the case with the Austin K5. The AEC Matador and Thorny-

croft Amazon could also carry a tk guns – 6 and 17 pdr respectively. Their bodies were armoured and very heavy and this affected their cross-country performance, so although 175 Matadors (called the 'Deacon' when used in the SP role) were produced, the Amazon was not ordered in any quantity. The Matador was much better known as an artillery tractor, over 9,000 being produced. Some Matadors were also used to carry 25 pdrs and armoured for use as an ACV (known as the 'Dorchester', with over 400 built). The Matador was famous for its pulling power; stories (true!) are told of a Matador tow-starting a Sherman tank on a steep slope, while another tells of a Matador towing a 4×4 3 ton lorry with a Jeep inside, plus a 6×6

279

refuelling lorry and another 6×6 GS to the top of a high pass in Australia then 50 miles on to Sydney!

COMMONWEALTH VEHICLES

Of all the Commonwealth countries, Canada produced the most vehicles. Prewar, Canada had depended upon American designed commercial trucks, built by subsidiaries of Ford, General Motors and Chrysler, and these were suitably modified for military use. In addition, new standardized designs were produced to meet British Army requirements under the name 'Canadian Military Pattern' (CMP). Vehicles were produced in the 8 cwt 4×2 and 4×4 ranges, the 15 and 30 cwt 4×2 and 4×4 ranges, the 3 ton 4×2 and 4×4 ranges, the 3 ton 6×4 and 6×6 ranges, also 4×4 artillery tractors. The rest of the Canadian military vehicles were known under the category 'Modified Conventional Vehicle' and were generally similar to those made in the USA. Production of all CMP types was a staggering 409,936 out of an even more staggering total of 857,970 soft-skinned and over 50,000 armoured vehicles built in Canada. Australia, New Zealand, India and South Africa all produced smaller but significant numbers of vehicles.

Australia:	just under 60,000 all types including armoured vehicles
New Zealand:	just over 5,000 all types
India:	just under 124,000 all types including armoured vehicles
South Africa:	just under 35,000 all types

Canadian-built Chevrolet 30 cwt 4×4 trucks, as used by the Long-Range Desert Group. (IWM – E 12390)

EQUIPMENT

ENGINEER AND BRIDGING EQUIPMENT
At the start of the war the sappers had just hand tools, compressors and waterpumps. However, by 1944, they had the use of all the earth-moving and road-making equipment as used by civil engineers on both sides of the Atlantic. This included angledozers, bulldozers, excavators, ploughs, scrapers, graders, rollers, stone crushers, etc.

Boats Two main types of small boat were used by the engineers, etc. – recce/assault boats and folding boats for use in bridging. In the former category there were two types. Firstly, pneumatic boats (inflated using a foot-pump), which were 6 ft 8 in long × 2 ft 8 in wide, built in two compartments with a wooden floor-stiffener. They weighed approximately 40 lb and could carry two men. The second type, the wooden, folding assault boat, was larger – some 12 ft 1 in long × 4 ft 1 in wide

As demonstrated by these Indian sappers in North Africa, road building often had to be done with basic hand tools such as compressor drills, picks and shovels. (IWM – E 721)

Rubber boats were not used in any great numbers by the British Army – these particular ones were employed by the Chindits to ford rivers in Burma. (IWM – IND 2072)

and weighing 174 lb. It could carry nine fully armed men.

In the second category, the folding boat equipment (FBE) Mk III had a superstructure that was suitable for both bridging and rafting use. It was also used to carry trestles, anchors, anchor stores, auxiliary rafting, gear, etc. The boats could be made up into rafts, or used as single boats to carry sixteen armed men as well as the commander and boat crew of four men. These boats were 21 ft 10 in × 6 ft 8 in and weighed 870 lb.

Roughly some thirty recce and seventy assault boats were carried for each division (armoured and infantry), although the assault boats were normally held by the Corps Bridging Company, RASC, which also held more recce boats as well as other bridging equip-

ment. The recce boat allocation allowed for one per engineer recce officer, plus a reserve of twelve with the field park company/squadron.

Bridging The early war situation was that there were seven types of bridge in use (as well as rafts): a light assault footbridge up to some 520 ft in length; the FBE Mk III; small box-girder (SBG) bridge Mk III; Mk V pontoon bridge; equipment; Inglis bridge Mk III; Hamilton bridge and lastly, the Bailey bridge. By 1944 in NW Europe, there were two types in everyday use as well as the bridge-laying tanks (three included in each armoured brigade by 1944), plus of course the special devices in 79 Armd Div (dealt with below).

Assault pontoons being unloaded from a lorry before crossing the Seweli River. (IWM – SE 1829)

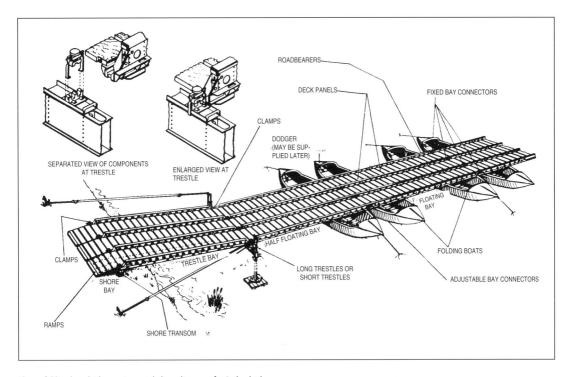

Above, folding boat bridge equipment; below, diagram of a Bailey bridge.

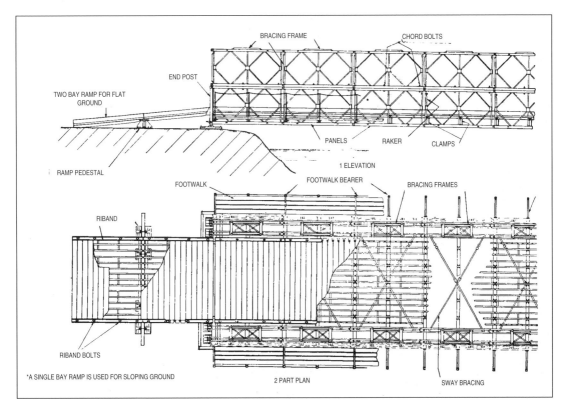

Engineers rafting a Covenanter tank across a river during an exercise in the UK. (Tank Museum)

Equipment being transported across the Irrawaddy by an ad hoc raft and small native boats. (IWM – SE 870)

Engineers rafting a Sherman tank on a Class 40/70 raft in Italy. (IWM – NA 10957)

A convoy moving across a completed pontoon bridge. (Tank Museum)

The two main types of bridging were the FBE which was limited to 9 ton loads,[5] and the Bailey, which could be built to take loads of up to 70 tons. The light, quickly built FBE bridge was usually the first to be

5. The British Army used a load classification system in which they gave all their vehicles (and the bridges they used), a 'classification number', that represented (on the vehicle) its weight when fully loaded, and meant that it could safely be taken over any bridge bearing a corresponding or higher classification number.

constructed after an assault crossing of a river had established a bridgehead and it could take most of the vehicles on charge to the infantry division. As soon as practicable, this was usually supplemented by a 40 ton Bailey, thus allowing the main supply routes (MSR) in the divisional area to be developed for 40 ton loads. This would cover all AFVs and soft-skinned vehicles apart from loaded transporters that needed 70 ton routes and, normally, one of these was developed in every army area. The versatile Bailey had a standard single span capacity of 190 ft for

40 ton loads and 150 ft for 70 ton. With the addition of pontoons and a few extra parts, the sappers could construct robust, floating bridges, capable of operating across the broadest river despite wide fluctuations in the water level.

Between D-Day and the breakout, 10,000 ft of equipment bridges were built in the 21 Army Group area, the largest obstacle being the River Orne, over which three Bailey pontoon bridges were built across tidal gaps of 250–300 ft, while fourteen fixed bridges were constructed over the river as a whole. Between the Orne and the Somme the main problem was enemy demolitions rather than river obstacles, some 3,000 ft only were built. Across the Seine, three FBE and eight Bailey pontoon bridges were built, over gaps ranging between 450 and 750 ft, four of these being in tidal water. Each Bailey was built by two or three field companies and took between 14 and 34 hours to construct.

Almost there. Sappers building a pontoon bridge in Burma. (IWM – SE 2830)

Madras sappers and miners built this bridge across the River Pegu to replace one blown by the retreating Japanese. (IWM – MUL 2925)

A heavy girder bridge under construction on the Caen–Cherbourg railway line. (IWM – B 8992)

SIGNAL EQUIPMENT

As the war progressed, the speed with which the wireless set could be got into action made it the primary means of communication for mobile operations, especially where it was necessary to establish links from the ground to ships at sea and aircraft in the air. It was also an invaluable standby for long distance links in more static operations, until line, with its greater traffic capacity, could be laid or repaired. In the forward areas the manpack radio sets were the WS 18 and 38, while the WS 19 and 22 were normally

The 18 set was designed for short-range communications in forward areas, in particular between an infantry Bn HQ and its sub-units. (R Sigs Museum)

The 38 set was another widely used man-pack radio set. (R Sigs Museum)

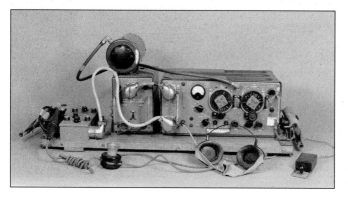

One of the best AFV radio sets of the war, the 19 set was three sets in one (A, B & IC). (R Sigs Museum)

Maintenance work on a signal cable in Normandy, 11 August 1944. (IWM – B 9079A)

Infantrymen using a man-pack radio set on D-Day. (IWM – B 5076)

Two BEF signallers using a field telephone. (IWM – F 4616)

Cable laying in the Western Desert at Agedabia. (IWM – E 20899)

This 9 set was an early AFV set, mounted in an armoured car and used for communications within 7th Armd Div in the desert. (Author's Collection)

Wearing his 'Bombay Bloomers', this signals operator switches to 'send' and talks into the microphone of his 11 set. (Author's Collection)

fitted into vehicles. The 18 set weighed 30 lb (complete with 'battle battery') and had a maximum range in good conditions of some 5 miles and was the main means of communication between infantry companies and their Battalion HQ. The 38 was a few pounds lighter and had a range of only 2 miles, so was used within the company and for infantry–tank co-operation. The 19 set was designed for use by armour and comprised three sets in one: 'A' set for ranges of some 10 miles while on the move (15 using a morse key); 'B' set for talking between tanks over short distances; 'IC' to enable the crew to converse. The 22 set was similar but had a longer range (15 miles on speech and 30 on key) and was chiefly found at brigade and divisional level and in artillery units. Appendix 5 gives full details of all types of ground radio sets.

SPECIALIZED ARMOURED EQUIPMENT

Although tanks have been dealt with earlier in this chapter, the various items of specialized equipment, based on the Churchill tank, deserve their own place and brief description.

Churchill AVRE This was a Churchill Mk III or IV tank that had been converted to serve as an RE vehicle and weighed some 40 tons with a crew of commander, driver, demolition engineer, wireless operator, mortar gunner, and co-driver (who also acted as mortar loader). Its main armament was a specially designed 290 mm calibre Petard spigot mortar, capable of firing a 26 lb demolition charge (known as a 'Flying Dustbin') out to a range of 80 yd. Other items carried/fitted on occasions were cables

The Churchill Great Eastern, with the ramps in the travelling position. (Author's Collection)

The Great Eastern was able to bridge a gap that was wider and/or higher than the gap a normal Churchill ARK could manage. (Author's Collection)

to fire hand-placed explosive charges (also carried); bridging, carpet-laying, mechanical charge placing and other devices. These included a brushwood fascine about 8 ft in diameter, made of 12–14 ft faggots bound together around three or four lengths of piping. This would be dropped into a ditch to enable it to be crossed – the piping providing a freeway for any water flowing in the ditch.

Churchill AVRE Carpet-layer Known also as 'Bobbins', they carried lengths of interlocking flexible trackways that could be laid on soft ground for vehicles – this was ideal for wheels but was badly damaged by tanks. There were various models of these 'carpet-layers'.

SBG Assault Bridge Also carried by a Churchill AVRE, this was a single span that could either cover a 30 ft gap or enable a 14 ft high wall to be crossed. It could take a 40 ton load. The bridge was either carried on the front of the vehicle or towed, mounted on a two-wheeled axle or carried as a folding SBG bridge, which reduced the height when travelling.

A Churchill AVRE towing an engineless universal carrier, fitted with the Conger 2 in Mk I (Line Charge) for quickly clearing a narrow lane through a minefield. The rocket propelled the empty hose across the minefield. It was then pumped full of explosive and detonated. (Author's Collection)

Log Carpet Device Designed to enable AFVs to cross soft ground, the log carpet was made of tree trunking about 14 ft long and 27 in in girth, linked together with a 2 in wire rope.

Skid Bailey Bridge The bridge was made out of normal Bailey panels, transoms and deck units with special skids under each panel that were pushed across the crater. In ideal conditions some 70 ft of Bailey bridge could be pushed across a crater (up to 40 ft wide).

Churchill ARK This was an 'Armoured Ramp Carrier' comprising a unturreted tank with timbered trackway on the hull top, with either one or two ramps. It was driven into the obstacle, then sat in the bottom with the ramps opened on both sides, so that vehicles could drive over.

Churchill Crocodile Extensive use was made of these mobile flame-throwers, the flame gun being fitted in the co-driver's position, while the flame fuel (400 gal) was carried in a trailer towed behind the tank. Fighting range was 90 yd and maximum about 120 yd. Eighty one-second bursts could be fired. Total production was 800, of which some 250 were kept for use against Japan but never used.

A Churchill Mk II ARK, with ramps raised. (Tank Museum)

Two Churchill Mk I ARKs in a deep gulley – one on top of the other to bridge the formidable gap. (Tank Museum)

Bullshorn Plough This type of mine-clearing device was used in small numbers in action, but proved to be unreliable compared with the Sherman Crab. Its name derived from the divisional insignia.

Miscellaneous A wide range of other devices, especially mine rollers, were trialled using the Churchill, but never saw action, because the Sherman Crab was so effective.

CHAPTER 10

TACTICS

A New Beginning

Although the British Army of 1939 had embraced mechanization, its tactical thinking was still steeped in the slow, ponderous tactics of the trench warfare of the First World War – and it was not helped by the fact that its major ally, France, had firmly opted for static warfare with its enormous commitment to the Maginot Line.[1] Small wonder that the free-wheeling 'Blitzkrieg' tactics of the Panzerwaffe sliced through those static positions so easily in May 1940. It was a sadder and wiser army that took stock of the situation in June 1940, as it doggedly prepared to defend Great Britain against the coming German invasion. It was still basically an infantry-heavy army, so it is relevant that in this short tactical survey, we examine first of all what came to be the cornerstone of infantry tactics, namely Battle Drill.

Battle Drill

'YOU PROVIDE THE ORCHESTRATION'

It was not until after Dunkirk, when most of the BEF had arrived back in the UK with minimal weapons, vehicles and equipment, that a new conception of realistic training began to emerge. It began in the units of a few of the BEF divisions and its name was simply 'Battle Drill'. Soon all infantry divisions, now rejuvenated, had established their own battle schools, with a central establishment at Barnard Castle to train instructors. Many thought that the new tactics were something quite revolutionary and that everything from the past must be abandoned. Yet it was nothing of the kind because all it did was to popularize the best of the old ideas and provide those under training with a clear aim and greater realism. It gave the junior leader a series of simple, but elastic rules for minor tactics, which had been devised within the field force from their battle experience and not just laid down by the War Office from above. This is how the opening address to new arrivals at the battle schools began:

'We are not proposing to return to the tactics of the Peninsular War, nor to abandon the principles which the Germans have shown us to be applicable still. Our aim is to teach the basic ploys so that they become second nature to you all. Then the leaders – junior and senior – can develop their own ideas and methods. We give you the theme, you provide the orchestration.'[2]

1. The Maginot Line was named after André Maginot, the French Minister for Defence in the late 1920s, and was first occupied by troops in 1936. It was a system of fortifications in Lorraine along the Franco-German border, extending for 87 miles and costing seven billion francs to build. Considered impregnable, it proved to be a 'white elephant' and was easily bypassed by the Germans in 1940.

2. As quoted in *Infantry Tactics 1939–45* by A. Farrar-Hockley (Almark Publishing Co., 1976)

First Drills The method of initially teaching the basic battle drills began on the barrack square, with the lowest common denominator – the infantry section – formed up in a line. On a command from the instructor, each man would call out his individual task, viz, 'Section Commander' – 'No. 1 on the Bren', 'No. 2 on the Bren' – 'Section 2IC' – 'No. 1 rifleman (sniper)' – 'No. 2 rifleman (bomber)' – 'No. 3 rifleman' – 'No. 4 rifleman (rearguard)'. Next would come the order 'Observe' and each man would turn to cover his allotted arc, chosen so as to give all round cover and with sufficient overlap so as to allow for casualties. The order 'Advance' would then be given, the instructor also telling the section what type of ground they were in – open fields, woods, streets, etc. Next the instructor would call out 'Under fire!' and the section would shout together 'Down – crawl – observe – take up fire positions' (often abbreviated to 'sights'), taking the appropriate action as they shouted. The section commander then had to work out his plan and shout out orders to put it into effect, for example, 'We will attack left flanking – Bren group take up position there [point]; Rifle group give covering fire'. Then, when the Bren group was in position, 'Bren group give covering fire, remainder follow me!' One of the main aims of battle drill was to convince those under instruction that battles were really won by small numbers of men – platoons or even sections – who continued to fight to the best of their ability even when cut off. This determination applied in all tactical manoeuvres and all situations.

Having established the pattern at section level then platoons would be trained collectively in much the same way, the platoon commander having to go through, step by step, how he would carry out a manoeuvre to deal with the scenario set by the instructor, his entire platoon first acting out their tasks on the barrack square, then

applying the drill in the field. In this phase all aspects of basic fieldcraft had to be observed and mistakes pointed out and rectified. It was possible to make such training both highly realistic and enjoyable, so that everyone, even the slowest thinking soldier in the platoon, eventually caught on. Such manoeuvres soon became second nature, so that without realizing it, everyone developed a better eye for ground, a swifter response and, above all, did everything they could to maintain the security of their own little group.

There were simple drills laid down for every manoeuvre – defence, withdrawal, advance, attack, etc.; drills in support of armour; others for street fighting and patrolling. In fact, every aspect of the infanteer's craft that could be practised in this way was practised, building up confidence, quick reaction time and team spirit. Larger-scale manoeuvres were not always so successful, some umpires still finding it difficult to forget the 'old school approach'. Nevertheless, the new battle drills undoubtedly gave everyone a tremendous 'lift', which was translated into success on the battlefield.

THE ALL-ARMS TEAM

ALL-ARMS CO-OPERATION

The basic reason why the German 'Blitzkrieg' tactics were so successful was that they encouraged the co-operation of all arms, working together (including air support). This was nothing new – it had been the British interwar experiments with similar mechanized formations of all arms, staged on Salisbury Plain between the wars, that the Germans had copied. However, to be able to get full and continual battlefield co-operation between armour, infantry, gunners, engineers and all the rest, took time, effort and continual practice. Realistic collective training therefore became the 'norm', some of which involved using live ammunition, making it possible for troops who had never been in action to get a good idea of what the real thing would be like.

Changes in the Use of Armour   After breaking the old, hidebound notions that the tank was merely there to support infantry at walking pace, the new 'wonder weapon' – the cruiser tank – was used in purely armoured formations, relying on its shock action to win battles. However, these fast, lightly armoured, 'armour heavy' formations soon proved ineffective, basically because they were highly vulnerable to dug-in a tk guns and could not capture and hold ground on their own. The tanks needed the infantry just as much as the infantry needed the tanks, but both had to be able to go everywhere and do everything in partnership. Both also required immediate artillery support on call, together with the expertise of all the other 'teeth arms' – the sappers and the signallers, plus of course the continual support of the Services – to keep them resupplied and repaired, etc. With ground attack aircraft 'on call' to provide close and devastating support – thanks to reliable ground to air communications – the result was a highly effective and balanced battle-winning team. What made one of the major differences was, of course, good, mobile voice communications by radio, so that all members of the team could speak to one another and, most importantly, so that the commander could command every aspect of the battle, imposing his will on his team and able to give immediate orders to counter any happening without delay.

Another important aspect was infantry/tank co-operation and this did not come without continual practice and, of course, the ability of the infantry to travel cross-country at the same speed as the tanks. The motor battalion of the armoured brigade was probably the most skilled at this type of co-operation, their half-tracks being able

to go everywhere the tanks could go. What they still lacked was a similar degree of protection, but with a few notable exceptions (see the 'Kangaroo' in Chapter 9) this was not achieved until after the war. It was equally important for the other Arms and Services to be just as mobile, so the amount of self-propelled artillery increased and specialized armour such as the AVRE and the ARV (manned by REME fitters from the unit LAD) became essential rather than just desirable elements of the combat team/battle group. If one were challenged to describe all this new realism in one word, then perhaps 'Professionalism' would be the correct one. By 1944 the British Army had learned its trade the hard way, up against some of the toughest and most professional fighting men in the world, and had proved themselves superior. New weapons, vehicles and equipment made a considerable difference, but training and experience were essential as was the new-found spirit of all-arms co-operation that now reigned.

STANDING OPERATING PROCEDURES (SOPS)

Most units used SOPs to lay down the way units/sub-units would operate in a given situation. SOPs also included such details as the composition and grouping of sub-units, the composition of orders groups, orders of march for road movement, etc., in fact, any standard drills that could be formulated and practised until they became second nature in order to speed up operations, cut out errors and help tired men to do the right thing under stress. The outline events of any battle scenario also followed a recognizable sequence, in which well-used terms made the procedure easier to follow. However, it was essential that these did not become too hidebound, and commanders at all levels had to be ready for the unexpected and able to use their initiative accordingly.

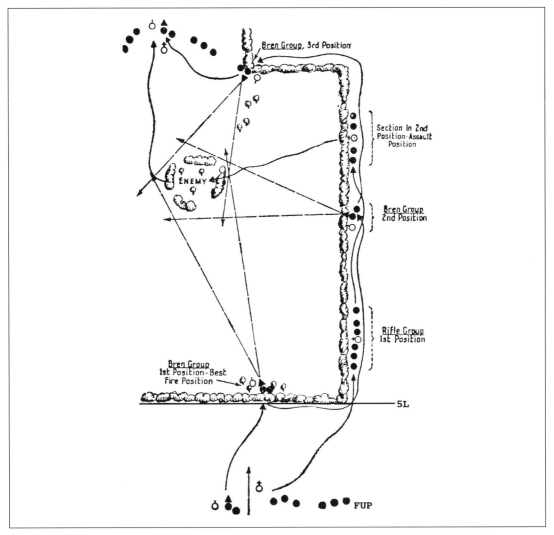

Infantry section in the attack.

The Attack The outline steps in any attack, for example, followed a set procedure, which began in moving the assault force into a concentration area(s) (see diagram), possibly after an advance to contact had been carried out by other forces. At the same time as the main bodies of the units involved in the attack were moving into their hidden concentration areas, commanders at all levels would be carrying out reconnaissance, working out their plans and then giving out orders – either in person or over the radio. Of course, security was paramount and might well include wireless silence, so that important information was not given away or units located by enemy direction finding equipment. From the concentration area troops would move forward into an assembly area, where final adjustments to weapons, topping up of vehicles, etc., would take place, still under strict wireless silence.

Hopefully the troops would not spend too long in the assembly areas, which might

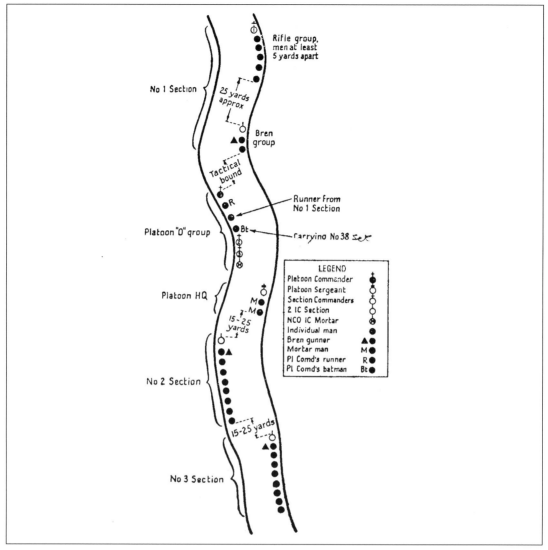

Infantry platoon advancing along a road.

be some miles back or just a few thousand yards from the enemy. The next move, to the forming up place (FUP) would be made just before H hour. Ideally, the FUP would be in dead ground, still hidden from enemy view so that the troops could 'marry up' without enemy interference. It was essential for the tanks and infantry to carry out this 'bonding' so that communications between the two could be effective at the very lowest level, such as tank troop to infantry platoon, individual tank to infantry section, using small manpack radios (see Appendix 5) or the infantry/tank telephone that was fitted in a metal box on the rear end of every tank. Sadly, these methods were notoriously ineffective, and then the infantry would have to resort to climbing up on the tank or the tank commander would climb down, both actions liable to draw enemy fire. The attack

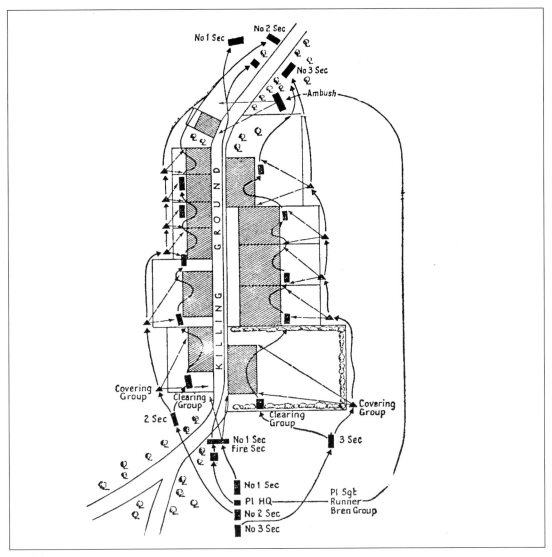

Street fighting.

would start at H hour, which was usually when the leading troops crossed the start line (SL), so time had to be allowed for any movement necessary from the FUP to the SL, also for any pre-H hour barrages, etc. Timings leading up to such events were stated as being 'H minus', while after H hour all timings were 'H plus'. The assaulting force might be supported by a separate supporting fire force in static positions, or elements of the assault force might support each other forward (compare with the fire and movement of basic battle drill), the tanks and artillery firing at suspected a tk and machine gun positions, the infantry remaining mounted as long as possible before assaulting known enemy positions. Tanks usually tried to work forward from fire position to fire position, where the ground gave protection to their vulnerable belly and tracks. However, part of the tank force at least would motor right on to the objective, with the dismounted infantry, firing their turret guns (main and coax) in support.

Having cleared the enemy off the objective, the assaulting force had to be ready for an immediate counter-attack – it was usual for troops in defence to keep part of their armour uncommitted and ready so that they could be launched before the attacker had gone firm. Once this immediate counter-attack had been dealt with, then the victorious force could start to dig in and consolidate. Slit trenches were normally dug to hold two or four men maximum (where possible with some over-head cover), while tanks would adopt hull/turret down positions using the natural cover that the ground afforded, or sometimes, if bulldozer blades were fitted, dig tank scrapes. Resupply might then be possible – especially of ammunition – from the A1 echelon, whose ammo and POL trucks would have been located not far behind the 'F' (Fighting) echelon.

Defence   From El Alamein (October 1942) onwards, it is perhaps true to say that in general terms the Allies were constantly on the offensive in most theatres, so the need for permanent defensive lines was a thing of the past. However, from time to time it was necessary to adopt a defensive posture (for example, at Anzio and Arnhem) and the rules of all-round defence, the keeping of part of the force in reserve for counter-attack purposes, etc., all still applied.

THE EFFECT OF NEW WEAPONS ON TACTICS
Commanders at all levels had to adapt to the advent of new weapons on both sides, out-standing examples being:

(a).   **Anti-tank   weapons**   Hand-held   a tk weapons, like the German panzerfaust,

the American bazooka and even the British PIAT, had a great effect on the ability of the lone infantryman to deal with AFVs, being far superior to the obsolete Boys a tk rifle. In addition, as the firepower and protection of tanks improved so a tk guns became larger – from 2 pdr, to 6 pdr, to 17 pdr. The towed varieties were more difficult to move and conceal (although the ubiquitous American Jeep could tow most of them), although SP tank destroyers, like Valentine Archer and the Sherman Firefly, both of which mounted the highly effective British 17 pdr, could move about on the battlefield under their own power and, despite not having the same built-in protection as the enemy heavy tanks, were really the only weapons capable of dealing with the dreaded German Tiger.

(b).   **Small-arms**   The   British   Army   had begun the war with very similar weapons to those it had used during the First World War, for example, the .303 SMLE rifle, the Lewis gun and the Mills No. 36 fragmentation grenade. New weapons like the Bren light machine gun had made their appearance in the 1930s, replacing most of the outdated Lewis guns, but machine carbines and automatic rifles would not be adopted by the British during the war with the exception of the easy to manufacture Sten gun. So, while such weapons did improve, they were not really on a par with those of either the enemy (German machine guns and machine carbines in particular) or the Americans and Russians.

(c).   **Tanks**   By the time the Second World War ended the tank was undoubtedly 'Queen of the Battlefield' with the lion's share of credit for victory and an awe-inspiring catalogue of success, which imbued the more powerful German tanks with a reputation for invincibility that still persists today.

On the Allied side, the tank did not succeed simply because of the superior number possessed by the British, but also because of its versatility, particularly of ARVs such as the Churchill, which was the basis of so much of the specialized armour in the amazing 79 Armd Div and which is but one example of the adaptability and ingenuity of such machines.

(d). **Air support** In a book about the British Army one cannot afford to give too much space to the other Services. However, one of the major factors that heralded success in NW Europe was undoubtedly the close ground–air co-operation that existed. The RAF not only 'closed out' the Luftwaffe most of the time, but also made enemy ground daylight movement extremely hazardous if not impossible. No better example can be given than the dramatic turn-around of the totally unexpected German offensive in the Ardennes in the winter of 1944/5, and the effect the clearing skies and subsequent release of Allied aircraft had on German fortunes.

(e). **Amphibious operations** Never before had tri-service co-operation been put to a more significant test than in the series of amphibious operations that became a major feature of the Second World War. Debacles like Norway and the Dieppe raid were followed, for example, by successful amphibious landings in North Africa (*Torch*), Sicily (*Husky*), Italy (*Baytown* and *Avalanche*) and Normandy (*Overlord*), all of which required troops at all levels to learn and practise new skills and new tactics, although the basic ones still remained once the amphibious assault had been completed.

CHAPTER 11

VEHICLE MARKINGS, FLAG CODES AND CAMOUFLAGE

VEHICLE MARKINGS

NATIONAL IDENTIFICATION MARKS

Although there were no official instructions on vehicle markings issued before the introduction of the Allied White Star in 1943, there were some markings in common use on British Army vehicles well before that date, such as:

(a). A white patch (12 in × 15 in approx.) painted on the front hulls of AFVs sent to France with the BEF. 'B' vehicles had the same patch on their left front mudguard, while carriers had it on their sides.

(b). A broad white band around the lower edge of the turret on some tanks in the UK after Dunkirk. This was not widely used and may have been unofficial.

(c). A white/red/white patch (18 in square) on tanks in various positions was used in the Western Desert from late 1941 (compare with similar marking used in the First World War) to distinguish them from those captured British tanks being used by the enemy. From March 1942 a rectangular patch, with the colours reversed and only 10 in high was introduced in the UK and became known as the 'RAC Patch'. It was also used on some tanks in Tunisia in 1943 and up to late 1944 in Italy despite the introduction of the Allied white star.

(d). The Allied white star. This was used sometimes with a stripe, sometimes within a circle and sometimes on its own. Official instructions issued at the time stated that:

'A white five-pointed star will be the national symbol for *all* motor vehicles assigned to tactical units. Administrative motor vehicles operating in an active theatre of operations will be similarly marked when directed by theatre commanders. Whenever requirements for camouflage and concealment outweigh the requirements for recognition, the national symbol may be covered by lusterless olive-drab gasoline solvent paint, camouflage nets, oil and dirt, etc., or will be removed.'

Despite these instructions, British AFVs in NW Europe rarely carried the star, while 'B' vehicles carried them only on their sides. However, in the Far East the rules were more closely followed, although AFVs still only had them on the hull and turret sides.

(e). Union Jack. Towards the end of the war in some areas, the Union Flag was painted on to some vehicles although this was rare.

AIRCRAFT RECOGNITION SYMBOLS

Early in the war various coloured symbols were placed/painted on the upper surfaces of vehicles, including yellow fabric triangles, white edging to the turret, white St Andrew's crosses, even the white/red/white painted around the edges of turret tops. Later, an RAF-type roundel was introduced (blue outer, then white, red in centre, sometimes with a further

The national identification star is very visible on the side of this universal carrier (with a specially heightened hull for wading) being unloaded in Normandy. (IWM – B 5393)

An aircraft recognition 'roundel' is very clear on the roof tarpaulin of this vehicle, one of a convoy on the coast road in North Africa. (IWM – E 21250)

outer yellow ring). In Normandy, from D-Day onwards, AFV crews used coloured plastic panels (pink and yellow), laid out in a haphazard sequence that was issued daily with other code information. This system had two advantages: the panels could be quickly removed if an enemy aircraft approached; it was difficult for the enemy to copy it in order to protect his own tanks as it was unlikely that he would know the code for the day. The white star, already mentioned, also provided an aircraft recognition symbol.

BRITISH RANK AND SIGNAL FLAGS

A prewar system of flags was in use in armoured units when the war began and was extensively used on AFVs in the early fighting

in the Western Desert. These included rank flags and signal flags. The *rank flags* are shown in the top row of the accompanying drawings: 1. Brigade command (1 ft × 3 ft); 2. Regiment/Battalion command (1.5 ft × 3 ft); 3. Squadron/Battalion command (9 in × 1.5 ft); 4. Troop/Platoon command (9 in × 13 in). The *signal flags* are shown in the bottom row: 5. 'Rally' (red over white over blue); 6. 'Come on' (green/white); 7. 'out of action' (red/yellow). 8. The eighth drawing consists of a blue pennant with a red disc on it. This was not a rank or signal flag but was carried by all RAOC recovery and repair vehicles; it was phased out when the REME was formed.

All these flags were flown from vehicle wireless aerials.

BRITISH RANK AND SIGNAL FLAGS.

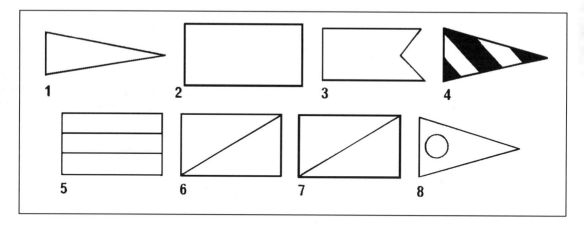

Notes on the drawings:

1. No markings, colour chosen by brigade.
2. In regiment colour (brown, red and green horizontal stripes for the RTR, green uppermost) with unit serial number superimposed in white.

3. Coloured: red for A Sqn/Coy, yellow for B Sqn/Coy, blue for C Sqn/Coy, with the squadron/company letter/number superimposed in white.
4. Black with two coloured stripes: red for 1 Tp/Pl, yellow for 2 Tp/Pl, blue for 3 Tp/Pl, green for 4 Tp/Pl and white for 5 Tp/Pl.

Friend from Foe   There was also a system of coloured pennants used to distinguish friend from foe by some armoured units in 1941 (see Annex 'A' for details).

FORMATION SIGNS

Coloured formation signs were stencilled/ hand painted on to all British vehicles through-out the war in most theatres. These signs were normally *exactly* the same as the insignia worn by the soldiers on their battledress. Details of formation signs are to be found in Appendix 1 (Divisional signs) and in other appropriate chapters (Army Group, Army, Corps, etc.). All these were stencilled on to the nearside front mudguard of *all* types of vehicles and where no mudguard existed then it would be stencilled in a corresponding location on the body of the vehicle itself. They were not applied to motorcycles however. In general terms div-isional signs were carried on the vehicles of all units that were permanently part of that division, while corps and above signs were only carried by those units that were corps troops, etc. Certain exceptions were allowed for specialized units such as independent brigades. However, as one might have ex-pected, regulations were not always followed!

Visit to Wakefield in September 1941. The Daimler Dingo and Valentine tank are both painted olive green, and the formation signs on the scout car show up well. 'GO' was the insignia of 8th Armd Div, while the '61' indicates one of the armoured regiments. (Tank Museum)

Tactical serial numbers and coloured flashes were also painted on to all vehicles with different numbers for each and every unit (serial number and flash). For obvious security reasons details of serial numbers were not included in wartime pamphlets, but rather issued on a limited circulation. On occasions during the war, these serial numbers were changed, again for security, and sometimes varied between theatres. Details of examples are attached at Annex 'B' to this chapter. These numbers and flashes were painted on to the opposite mudguard to the formation sign.

CAMOUFLAGE

PERSONAL CAMOUFLAGE

Uniform colours were now khaki for battledress, sand coloured or Jungle Green for the lighter weight uniforms worn in the Middle and Far East respectively. In 1941 the first item of camouflaged clothing, the

These infantrymen in the Western Desert are using natural camel thorn to garnish their netting. Also note how the hessian covers prevent shine in contrast with the uncovered steel helmet. (IWM – E 13831)

These infantrymen of 2nd Seaforths have made no attempt at personal camouflage, but have used natural foliage and other vegetation to camouflage their Bren position in France, 1940. (IWM – F 4626)

Glider-borne troops in Normandy, 6 June 1944, have used sticks from a nearby woodpile to camouflage their foxholes. (IWM – B 5051)

Denison[1] smock, was issued to airborne forces. Few items of camouflage clothing were in general issue, while pieces of dyed netting, which could be worn over the head

1. Named after its designer, Capt Denison, who served in a camouflage unit commanded by the distinguished stage designer, Oliver Messel.

and shoulders to dull light reflection, were normally only issued to snipers. On more general issue were dark brown, green and black sticks of camouflage cream for smearing on to faces and necks, while steel helmet nets were provided, into which live foliage or hessian camouflage strips (scrim) could be threaded. However, it has to be said that personal camouflage was not regarded as

PREPARE FOR BATTLE

1. The helmet still shines through the net.

3. Too little – dome and rim still show.

5. Just right – dome shape and shadow disappear.

7. Crossed strings hold natural garnish on the flap.

2. Dark hessian cover, hessian knots and string laced round in 2-in. loops.

4. Too much – rim not broken, and large foliage shines.

6. Square shape and shiny gas-cape are obvious.

8. Use the personal net when observing.

9. Small screen with hessian and natural garnish give excellent cover against a good background. Fire beneath it.

Helmet
Hessian knots plus natural garnish to break the dome and shadow under the rim.

Face, Neck, and Hands
Highlights darkened with camouflage cream, soot, dark blanco, or cocoa.

Rifle
Darken shiny metal with matt paint. Dark hessian cover conceals shiny butt-plate.

Webbing
Dark blanco No. 1A or 3. All brass painted with dark paint.

Haversack
String holds hessian. Knots, plus natural garnish, to destroy square shape.

Respirator
Dark blanco.

Boots
Dubbined.

Medium Regt gunners on the Imphal Plain have made good use of a scrimmed camouflage net to hide their gun/howitzer from enemy view. (IWM – IND 3377)

very important in the British Army during the Second World War.

VEHICLE CAMOUFLAGE

In general terms army vehicles were painted drab brown (later drab olive green) in temperate theatres, sand coloured in the Middle East and Jungle Green in the Far East. The canvas tilts on trucks and lorries were usually manufactured in olive drab colour. However, the painting of vehicles in disruptive patterns was not entirely neglected. Military Training Pamphlet No. 26 *Notes on Concealment and Camouflage*, issued in 1939, did include some examples of camouflage painting schemes for vehicles, although it dealt mainly with concealment of troops and vehicles through dispersal, the concealment of static weapon pits and buildings with netting and painting and the use of netting on vehicles. Camouflage nets, made of suitably coloured string, with pieces of scrim inserted and tied on to the netting, were widely used for camouflaging both 'A' and 'B' vehicles, especially later in the war. Similar netting was also used for camouflaging guns in firing positions etc., while natural foliage, even mud, was also widely used. In winter, during very snowy weather, vehicles might be daubed with whitewash to make them blend with their white background. In some cases sand was mixed with paint and stuck on to vehicles to make them 'disappear' into the desert. Perhaps one of the most cunning forms of camouflage used were the tank 'sunshades' of the desert war, which very successfully turned tanks into lorries (and sometimes vice versa). Dummy vehicles were also used by both sides on a few occasions.

Later in the war a pamphlet entitled *Vehicle Marking 1943* was published, which included charts showing how to camouflage-paint cars and lorries in a basic dark matt brown with a jagged black disruptive

Natural camouflage was useful on vehicles, provided it was renewed and appropriate – it is starting to wilt a little on these Priest SP guns in Normandy. (IWM – 5032)

Camouflage painting schemes were sometimes used, as evident on these 'I' tanks on parade in the UK, July 1941. The nearest tank mounts a 3 in howitzer. (IWM – H 11654)

These Churchills in North Africa have a somewhat bizarre camouflage pattern, which was not used again after Tunisia. (Tank Museum)

This strange patterned camouflage was used in Malta, to blend with the stone walls! (IWM — GM 845)

'foliage' pattern. Finally, ACI 533 of 12 April 1944 stated that 'Olive Drab will be adopted as the basic camouflage colour for all army equipments, in lieu of Standard Camouflage Colour No. 2 (Brown) and certain new equipments painted Olive Drab will shortly be received by units.' However, the instruction went on to emphasize – with typical War Office canniness – that the ACI did not automatically authorize units to re-paint their vehicles until '. . . re-painting is due and necessary, and all stocks of Standard Camouflage Colour No. 2 in unit or RAOC

charge have been exhausted.' In their book *British Military Markings*, Peter Hodges and Michael Taylor provide a most useful overall summary of British Army wartime camouflage:

Interwar Years – all vehicles painted mid-green with a gloss finish.

May 1938 – progressive application of matt finish on all unit equipments.

February 1939 – appearance of Khaki Green No. 3 as a single standard colour.

When is a tank not a tank? This 'deceptive device' turned a cruiser tank into a lorry, to fool passing aircraft. (Author's Collection)

June 1939 – adoption of two-tone disruptive painting.

May 1940 – two-tone green camouflage scheme officially sanctioned for all WD equipments.

August 1941 – Dark Tarmac No. 4 is an established disruptive colour in conjunction with Khaki Green No. 3, but the very dark brown Standard Camouflage Colour (SCC) 1A is authorized to replace the Dark Tarmac disruptive colour.

November 1941 – two concurrent officially accepted schemes: Khaki Green No. 3 with Dark Brown SCC 1A; Brown SCC 2 also

with SCC 1A. However, both schemes still sanction the Dark Tarmac No. 4 and Black SCC 14 as alternatives to SCC 1A.

May 1942 – Brown SCC 2 with Dark Brown SCC 1A patterning becomes the officially sanctioned colour scheme.

October 1943 – black again becomes the preferred disruptive pattern colour with SCC 14 the preferred type on the basic brown.

April 1944 – Olive Drab becomes the basic colour, with by inference Black SCC 14 for disruptive patterning.

August 1944 – disruptive painting on Olive Drab painted vehicles officially discontinued.

And of course there were dummy tanks made out of hessian and wood, Western Desert, March 1941. (Author's Collection)

ANNEX 'A'

1st Armoured Division pennants as used in the Middle East, *c.* 1941

Units	Colour of flags	Units	Colour of flags
2nd Armd Bde		22nd Armd Bde	
Queen's Bays	Red	Royal Glos Hussars	Red
9th Lancers	Yellow	3rd CLY	Yellow
10th Hussars	Blue	4th CLY	Blue
1st Rifle Bde	Green	2nd KRRC	Green
Div Units			
12th Lancers	White		
1st Fd Sqn, RE	Red		
7th Fd Sqn, RE	Yellow		

(Note: 'HQ' was also carried on the pennants of Sqn HQ vehicles.)

ANNEX 'B'

Examples of vehicle markings – serial numbers and arm of Service coloured flash

Serial numbers and flashes for armoured divisions as used in NW Europe in 1944–45

Units	Serial	Flash	Units	Serial	Flash
Div HQ			2 × Fd Sqns, RE	41, 46	Blue
& Employment Pl	40	Black	Fd Pk Sqn, RE	42	Blue
Div Fd Security Sec	40	Black	Div Bridging Tp,		
HQ RA	40	Red/blue	RE	52	Blue
HQ RASC	80	Red/green	Armd Div adopt number of unit		
HQ RAOC	40	Blue/red/blue	Sigs to which they have		
HQ REME	40	Blue/yellow/red	been attached		White/blue
Div Provost Coy,			Armd Bde Coy,	81	Red/green
CMP	43	Black	RASC		
Armd Recce Regt	45	Green/blue	Inf Bde Coy, RASC	83	Red/green
HQ Armd Bde	50	Red	Div Tps Coy, RASC	84	Red/green
3 × Armd Regts[1]	51, 52, 53	Red	Tpt Coy, RASC	82	Red/green
Motor Bn	54	Red	Lt Fd Amb, RAMC	89	Black
HQ Inf Bde	60	Green	Fd Amb, RAMC	90	Black
3 × Inf Bns[1]	61, 62, 63	Green	Fd Hygiene Sec	92	Black
Indep MG Coy	64	Black	FDS, RAMC	93	Black
2 × Fd Regts,			Ordnance Fd Pk,		
RA/RHA	74, 76	Red/blue	RAOC	97	Blue/red/blue
Atk Regt	77	Red/blue	Armd Bde Wksp,		
LAA Regt	73	Red/blue	REME	99	Blue/yellow/red
Counter Mortar Bty	78	Red/blue	Inf Bde Wksp, REME	100	Blue/yellow/red

1. The three numbers were allocated by order of regiment/battalion seniority in the Order of Precedence.

Serial numbers and flashes for infantry divisions for 1940–42, UK

Unit	Serial	Flash	Unit	Serial	Flash
Div HQ	40	Black	HQ RE	40	Blue
HQ Inf Bde	81	Red	3 × Fd Coys RE	49, 50, 51	Blue
3 × Inf Bns	55, 56, 57	Red	Fd Pk Coy	48	Blue
HQ Inf Bde	87	Green	Div Sigs	52	White/blue
3 × Inf Bns	60, 61, 62	Green	HQ RASC	40	Red/green
MG Bn	53	Red	3 × RASC Coys	70, 71, 72	Red/green
Armd Car Regt	41	Blue/green	Wksp Coy	84	Black
HQ Div Arty	40	Red/blue	3 × Lt Amb Coys	75, 76, 77	Black
Atk Regt	46	Red/blue	Fd Postal Unit	80	Blue
3 × Fd Regts RA	42, 43, 44	Red/blue	Provost Unit	79	Black
LAA Regt	47	Red/blue			

Serial numbers and flashes for 1st Airborne Division, 1944–45

Unit	Serial	Flash	Unit	Serial	Flash
Div HQ & Def Pl	40	Black	Fd Pk Sqn RE	49	Blue
Indep Para Coy	50	Black	Div Sigs	40	White/blue
HQ Para Bde & Def Pl	81	Red	HQ RASC	40	Red/green
			3 × Lt Coys		
3 × Para Bns	55, 56, 57	Red	RASC	70, 71, 73	Red/green
HQ Para Bde & Def Pl	87	Green	2 × Fd Amb	75, 76	Black
			Air Ldg Fd Amb	77	Black
3 × Para Bns	60, 61, 62	Green	Div RAOC	92	Blue/red/blue
HQ Air Ldg Bde & Def Pl	94	Brown	HQ REME	40	Blue/yellow/red
			REME Wksp	40	Blue/yellow/red
3 × Air Ldg Bns	67, 68, 69	Brown	5 × Air Ldg LADs	47, 81, 87, 94, 95	Blue/yellow/red
Air Ldg Recce Sqn	41	Green/blue	Provost Coy	79	Black
HQ Div RA	40	Red/blue	Postal Unit	80	Black
Air Ldg Lt Regt RA	46	Red/blue	HQ Indep Para Bde	109	Black
Air Ldg Atk Regt RA	47	Red/blue			
HQ Div RE	40	Blue	3 × Para Bns	110, 111, 112	Maroon
Para Sqn RE	48	Blue			

CHAPTER 12

ATS AND OTHER WOMEN'S CORPS

MOBILIZING WOMENPOWER

Mobilizing women was extremely effective in the UK during the Second World War, so that by the autumn of 1943 it was estimated that some 7,750,000 women were in paid employment that was in some way connected with the war effort. Of these, about 470,000 were in the Women's Services or the forces nursing services, while a similar number were full or part-time members of the Civil Defence, Home Guard, Royal Observer Corps or Women's Land Army.

ATS/FANY

FORMATION OF THE ATS

War scares in 1938 and the need to make use of the skills of the entire population had resulted in the Committee of Imperial Defence (CID) changing its mind about not recruiting women. It was Army Order 199/38, dated 9 September 1938, that promulgated the Royal Warrant under which the Auxiliary Territorial Service (ATS) was formed. Its ancestry can be traced directly back to the Women's Army Auxiliary Corps (WAAC), which had been formed in July 1917 to undertake non-combatant duties behind the lines in France, although there had been dissenting voices, including that of the CinC, Douglas Haig. In April 1918 they had been renamed the Queen Mary's Army Auxiliary Corps, and by the end of the war their numbers had risen to 40,850. Two

years later, on 1 May 1920, the QMAAC were officially disbanded. Responsibility for forming the ATS rested on three voluntary women's services – the First Aid Nursing Yeomanry (FANY), the Women's Legion and the Emergency Service. They provided an officer cadre. Once established, then further officers came from the ATS rank and file. There was a rush of volunteers – some 17,000 women had enlisted by September 1939. When the National Service Act was followed by a second Act in 1941, women were made liable for military service, so that when the war was at its peak just under half a million women were serving in all the British armed forces. At the same time they were also given full military status.

First in Combat At peak strength approximately 250,000 women were serving in the ATS during the Second World War, in some eighty different army trades, the largest contingents being office, mess and telephone orderlies. Next came cooks and cookhouse staff, drivers and postal workers, and then storekeepers working in depots and other storehouses. Other ATS gave valuable service as butchers and bakers, ammunition inspectors and military police. About a quarter of all ATS served in AA Command, in anti-aircraft batteries where they came under fire but did not, in theory anyway, fire the guns, because the Royal Warrant that had brought the ATS into being limited the

Members of the Bovington ATS contingent wearing the 1941 ATS service dress outside their 'married quarter' in Higher Wood, which was taken over to house all the ATS contingent. (Author's Collection)

women to non-combatant duties. Despite this, the CinC of AA Command, Gen Sir Frederick Pile, described his ATS gunners as being 'the first women to take their place in a combatant role in any army in the world'[1]. The Americans, who never used their Women's Ambulance Corps (WACs) in this role, were most intrigued by these 'Co-ed Gun Girls' as they called them. The ATS operated search-lights, predictors, kine-theodolite (height and range finders) and radar sets, remaining calm and efficient in action, despite being bombed on numerous occasions.

1. The tradition that banned women from combat was also broken by the Special Operations Executive, who trained women in the use of weapons and explosives, sending fifty women agents into occupied France. They got around regulations by enrolling them in the FANY!

Helping the RASC Special mention must also be made of the wartime assistance given to the RASC by the ATS. In order to relieve the manpower problems, the ATS provided drivers, clerks and 'housekeeping personnel' in many static establishments. The RASC had, of course, a direct interest in the ATS. For many years prewar, it had undertaken the technical training and general sponsoring of FANY – an unoffical body that, although never fully recognized by the War Office, had still managed to maintain an identity from Boer War days up to 1939, carrying out annual camps at their own expense, with the loan of WD equipment. Most of the officers of the MT branch of the ATS were drawn from the FANY, which in wartime was amalgamated with the ATS. Other voluntary organizations, some of which have already been mentioned, were also attached to the

ATS (but not under the Army Act); these included the Motor Transport Corps (MTC), the American WAC, and the Women's Legion.

Other Arms and Services   In addition to the RASC, the ATS were to be found in considerable numbers in the RE and in the R Sigs as has already been covered in another chapter. However, these were by no means the only Arms and Services to benefit from their assistance. For example:

(a).   RAOC involvement. One of the earliest and largest ATS/FANY operations was staffing a large part of the vehicle side of the Command Ordnance Depot (COD) at Chilwell, to which all kinds of vehicles and spare parts were collected from industry. From there they were delivered all over the country and to ports of embarkation to bring units up to their mobilization scales. The companies deployed there were originally mixed companies without drivers, while the FANY driver companies did not have any clerks or cooks supporting them, so rapid changes of employment had to be effected. Civilian volunteer drivers were apt to be swiftly enrolled and kitted out as best they could be, but there was a great shortage of everything in the winter of 1940, especially greatcoats! The ATS took over the whole

The first members of the Canadian Women's Army Corps to land in France are seen here in Bainville, 30 July 1944. (National Archives of Canada – PA 132838)

ATS NCOs enjoying a break in a NAAFI canteen. (Author's Collection)

process – receiving unit indents, preparing the demanded vehicles for the road (for example, if they were going overseas, stripping them down and putting all 'attractive' stores into packing cases and nailing them down, to prevent theft), preparing all the paperwork (including vehicle documents) and then delivering them to the FANY drivers in full running order. Altogether the RAOC employed 22,648 ATS, of whom 18,199 were tradeswomen, 6,212 were specialist 'Clerks RAOC' and 9,855 were trade-trained storewomen. Among the non-tradeswomen there were 294 ordinary storewomen and 1,983 drivers.

(b). REME involvement. They employed a smaller contingent – just 6,208, of whom 2,643 belonged to skilled trades, such as radio-mechanics, motor-mechanics, welders, turners, tinsmiths, electricians, draughts-women (for machine drawings) and coach-trimmers. However, after 1944 training for all REME trades was discontinued.

(c). CMP involvement. In January 1942 the provost branch of the ATS was formed, with training at the CMP depot at Mytchett and by 1943 their strength in the UK alone was 752.

(d). Intelligence work. The first detachment of ATS to be sent out from England to Cairo in December 1940 comprised twenty ATS officers who had been trained in technical intelligence duties for employment in the

Combined Services Detailed Interrogation Centre at Maadi, just outside Cairo. They were accompanied by a small contingent of cooks and mess orderlies.

(e). RAPC. The Pay Corps employed both officers and ORs in the Pay Services.

(f). RACh D. Chaplains Assistants (women) were posted over to the Continent for service with the ATS.

Within the ATS itself, there were 24,121 women employed in the ATS schools and training units, while small numbers were PT instructors, tailors, hairdressers and even chiropodists.

ORGANIZATION OF THE ATS

At the top of the ATS was the Director (DATS), in the rank of Chief Controller (equated to Major General). Unlike other Directors of Arms and Services, she was not responsible for technical proficiency, which remained the responsibility of the Directorate of Military Training. Instead, she and her officers were responsible for the morale, welfare, well-being, tone and public image of the ATS. This last responsibility was a difficult one to put across because, unlike nurses, whose role of caring for the sick and wounded had long been accepted by the public as a traditional and feminine one, it was this new

'. . . "army of women", dressed and behaving like soldiers, that caught public attention and anxiety, in spite of the fact that they could claim with pride that as far as they were soldiers there were no others in the Army quieter, better behaved and better disciplined.'[2]

2. *The Women's Royal Army Corps* by Shelford Bidwell (Leo Cooper, 1977)

The largest ATS administrative unit was known as a 'Group' and comprised any number of ATS companies, each being made up of two or three platoons. Examples of ATS companies were Motor Transport (MT) drivers, Clerical, Signal, Kine-Theodolite and General Duties (GD) such as cooks, orderlies, storekeepers and clerks.

Ranks Pre-1941 ATS other ranks were known as Volunteer (Pte), Chief Volunteer (LCpl), Sub-Leader (Cpl), Section Leader (Sgt) and Senior Leader (WO2), but thereafter they adopted normal army nomenclature. However, for the officers, the ranks remained unique to the ATS. Below the rank of Chief Controller (Major General), there were seven other commissioned ranks:

ATS	Abbreviation	Army Equivalent
Chief Controller	C Contr	Major General
Senior Controller	S Contr	Brigadier
Controller	Contr	Colonel
Chief Commander	C Comd	Lieutenant Colonel
Senior Commander	S Comd	Major
Junior Commander	J Comd	Captain
Subaltern	Sub	Lieutenant
Second Subaltern	2nd Sub	Second-lieutenant

The women officers' badges of rank were the same as for the men. Women addressed their superior officers as 'Ma'am'. In general their pay was only two-thirds that of the equivalent male ranks.

Uniforms Initially, the military had been unprepared for the sudden influx of females, so uniforms were in short supply and it was quite common to see ATS still in civilian clothes apart from an arm brassard with 'ATS' on it. From the service's formation in 1938, early uniforms were heavily influenced by the existing FANY uniform and were made of good quality khaki serge. The 1941 pattern

ATS Service Dress was really just a utility version of the earlier uniform, with less 'frills' – for example, the breast pockets of the belted tunic had no pleats and single rather than three-point flaps. All ranks wore a similar uniform over a khaki shirt with collar and tie, full-panel skirt, greatcoat, service dress cap with soft visor or a chocolate brown field cap that was piped with green and an ATS capbadge. Officers sometimes wore the Sam Browne belt. FANY wore the same uniform with the FANY badge at the top of coat sleeves and slight alterations to the headgear. Later in the war a further utility uniform was

ATS in shirt sleeves, battledress trousers, boots and gaiters, putting the finishing touches to a marquee. (IWM – B 5806)

A bevy of ATS officers wearing battledress and steel helmets. (IWM – B5679)

issued with plastic green buttons replacing brass ones on the tunic, except for the lower pockets which had no buttons at all. That indispensable accessory the ATS handbag was introduced from 1943, with room for personal items such as cosmetics, which were tolerated in moderation. Some ATS, especially on gunsites, wore specially tailored ATS battle-dress, while there were brown ATS shoes, ATS leather jerkins, ATS PT kit, ATS overalls, etc., plus Khaki Drill and Jungle Green for wear in the appropriate theatres. Mention must also be made of ATS Provost staff, who wore the highly recognizable red covers on their caps, a blue brassard with 'MP' in red on it and, in some cases, a blue on red 'PROVOST' sleeve title.

Strengths At the outbreak of war the whole ATS was only some 17,000 (914 officers and 16,000 rank and file). By December 1940 its numbers had doubled, while three years later it had reached 207,492.

QAIMNS

NURSES
Although there have been female nurses in the British Army for hundreds of years, having been officially included, for example,

ATS wearing bush jackets; one carries her bush hat on her shoulder and all wear normal ATS headgear. It is difficult to tell whether they were Khaki Drill or Jungle Green uniforms, although they look too light to be the latter. (IWM – SE 4314)

in the campaign in Portugal in 1762–63, it was not until the Crimean War that Florence Nightingale brought military nursing to the fore. However, until 1914, it had always remained on an auxiliary basis. The FANY, as already mentioned, had been originally proposed as bands of mounted nurses who would ride out to scenes of action. The Voluntary Aid Detachment (VAD) Organization, which came into existence in 1910, the Queen Alexandra's Imperial Military Nursing Service (QAIMNS) and the Territorial Force Nursing Service, were able to muster 3,000 military nurses by the outbreak of the First World War. They continued to give sterling

service throughout the Second World War, being employed in hospitals in every theatre of operations.

When the Second World War began there were less than 700 regulars in the QAIMNS. However, under the guidance of the Matron-in-Chief at the War Office, the Reserve and the Territorial Army Nursing Service (TANS) were swiftly mobilized and merged into the QAIMNS. A group of QAs were thus able to sail to France with the BEF. Although they had little to do during the 'Phoney War', after the German assault they nursed both troops and refugees during the trek to the coast. Well over 1,000 QAs (including

Reserves and TANS) returned to the UK in the evacuation. Thereafter QAs served all over the world, being shelled and bombed on land and on hospital ships, putting on their 'battle bowlers' when necessary, but as always ministering to the sick and wounded with great devotion. Some were taken prisoner – for example, by the Japanese, who refused to recognize the fact that QAs were of officer status and rank. They had to endure long years of hardship, illness, grief, hunger and hard work before they were eventually freed. As Juliet Piggott says in her history of the QARANCs:

'Such were the many facets of the war in which the QAs had taken such a varied and encompassing part. They had seen every kind

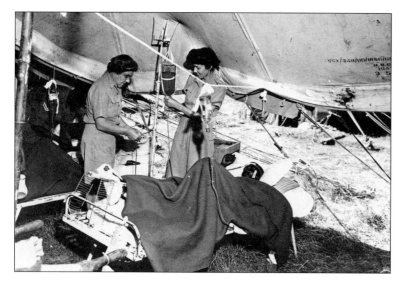

Nursing officers adjusting suction apparatus in a post-operative tent of a field hospital in Burma. Both wear khaki drill shirts and long trousers. (IWM – SEU 1951)

These Canadian nurses, coming ashore at Arromanches, belong to No. 10 RCAMC. The nurse on the left carries an ATS handbag. (National Archives of Canada – PA 108174)

of bestiality, every kind of wound, both to the body and to the mind, and not the least, to the spirit.'[3]

Ranks Members of the QAIMNS ranked with the officers of the army, having been granted officer status in 1904. However, it was not until 1941 that they were granted Emergency Commissions and were allowed to wear the appropriate badges of rank. The rank structure was then:

QAIMNS	Army
Matron-in-Chief (at the War Office)	Brigadier
Chief Principal Matron	Colonel
Principal Matron	Lieutenant Colonel
Matron	Major
Senior Sister	Captain
Sister/staff nurse	Lieutenant

Dress QAs initially wore their familiar grey and scarlet cotton dresses and red capes at all times. However, these became increasingly difficult to obtain, rationing having taken its toll of all available fabric. Therefore, with effect from 1 January 1944, it was decided that all army nurses would wear the same khaki uniform as worn by ATS officers, but with their own cap and collar badges, plus a lanyard in the nursing services' scarlet and grey. Ward dress for normal daily work in temperate climates away from the battlefield still consisted of a grey smock-type dress (with a detachable starched white collar), on top of which was worn a white apron and traditional veil-type headdress, while the scarlet QAIMNS tippet/cape (with shoulder boards bearing the badges of rank) was still worn. When available, the long 'corridor

Wearing grey ward dress, with her scarlet and grey tippet of the QAIMNS(R) – the QAIMNS was all scarlet – this nurse was serving in the Middle East. She also wears the sterling silver 'badge of office' of the QAIMNS(R) on the right corner of her tippet. (Author's Collection)

cape' would replace the tippet. In 1944 a revised ward dress was introduced, which required less laundering and maintenance, this being an all grey cotton dress with detachable sleeves, known as the 'Field Force Dress'. Where the normal ward dresses were totally unsuitable, then nurses wore battle-dress – either ATS or men's pattern, depending upon availability, or KD/Jungle Green, with such refinements as 'Spats, Mosquito, Nursing Officers' or 'Hoods Mosquito', 'anti-mosquito gloves' and 'individual insecticide sprayers (DDT)', added to taste!

3. *Queen Alexandra's Royal Army Nursing Corps* by Juliet Piggott (Leo Cooper, 1975)

BRITISH ARMY DIVISIONS OF THE SECOND WORLD WAR

ARMOURED

1. **Guards Armoured** Formed on 17 June 1941 in the UK, where it served until 27 June 1944, then in NW Europe until 12 June 1945, when it was redesignated and reorganized as the Guards Division. INSIGNIA: A blue shield edged with red with a white eye in its centre.

2. **1st Armoured** This was a regular division in existence in September 1939, formerly being called the Mobile Division. It was disbanded in Italy on 11 January 1945, after service in the UK, France, the UK, Egypt, North Africa, Libya and Italy. INSIGNIA: A standing white rhino on a green background (later on a black oval). From early 1942 the rhino was charging.

3. **2nd Armoured** Formed in the UK on 15 December 1939, it served in the UK, Egypt and Libya, where its HQ was captured on 8 April 1941. INSIGNIA: A white plumed helmet on a red background.

3rd, 4th and 5th Armoured Divisions were never formed.

4. **6th Armoured** Formed on 12 September 1940 in the UK and still in existence after the war ended. Served in the UK, North Africa, Italy, Austria. INSIGNIA: A white clenched mailed fist on a black background.

5. **7th Armoured** It was in existence as a regular division in Egypt and was designated as the Armoured Division (Egypt) having previously been named the Mobile Division. On 16 February 1940 it was redesignated as 7th Armoured Division and served in Egypt, Libya, North Africa, Italy, the UK and NW Europe. It was still in existence after the war ended. INSIGNIA: Initially a white disc on a red background, which later had a red jerboa superimposed upon it. From 1944 the jerboa was larger, in brown, outlined in white and on a black rectangular background.

6. **8th Armoured** Formed in the UK on 4 November 1940, it was disbanded in Egypt on 1 January 1943, after service in the UK and Egypt, but was never deployed as a complete division. INSIGNIA: 'GO' in black on a green disc within a black square.

7. **9th Armoured** Formed in the UK on 1 December 1940, it never served outside the UK and was disbanded on 31 July 1944. INSIGNIA: A panda's head – no background.

8. **10th Armoured** Formed in Palestine on 1 August 1941 by designation and reorganization of 1st Cavalry Division. Disbanded in Egypt on 15 June 1944 after service in Palestine, Egypt, Palestine, Syria and Egypt. INSIGNIA: A red fox's mask on a black or yellow disc.

9. **11th Armoured** Formed in the UK on 9 March 1941, it was still in existence when the war ended, having served in the UK and NW Europe. INSIGNIA: A charging black bull with red hooves, eyes and horns, on a yellow background.

12th to 41st Armoured Divisions were never formed.

10. **42nd Armoured** Formed in the UK on 1 November 1941 by the conversion of 42nd Infantry Division. Served in the UK only and was disbanded on 17 October 1943. INSIGNIA: A white diamond on a red diamond.

11. **79th Armoured** Formed in the UK on 14 August 1942, then in April 1943 it was reorganized and its composition was changed to specialized armour known as the 'Funnies'. It served in the UK and NW Europe and was broken up at the end of the war. INSIGNIA: A bull's head on a yellow, inverted triangle, edged in black on a larger inverted white triangle.

ARMOURED DIVISIONS

Guards

1st
(and 2nd Armoured Brigade until the end of the war)

1st
(in Italy 1944)

2nd

6th

7th
(First Style)

7th
(Second Style)

8th

9th

10th
(also with yellow instead of black)

11th

42nd

79th

CAVALRY

1. **1st Cavalry** Formed in the UK on 31 October 1939, it served in the UK and Palestine, Transjordan, Iraq and Syria. It was reorganized and redesignated as 10th Armoured Division on 1 August 1941 in Syria. INSIGNIA: Not recorded.

INFANTRY

1. **1st Infantry** A regular division prior to the war, it was reorganized as a Mixed Division in June 1942 but reverted to a normal infantry division in November 1942. It served in the UK, France and Belgium, the UK, North Africa, Pantelleria, North Africa, Italy and Palestine. INSIGNIA: A white triangle.

2. **1st London/56th (London)** In September 1939 it was a First Line TA Division organized as a motor division, then in June 1940 it was reorganized as an infantry division and on 16 November 1940 it was redesignated as 56th (London) Division. It served in the UK, Iraq, Palestine, Egypt, Libya, North Africa, Italy, Egypt and Italy. INSIGNIA: A black cat (sitting down) on a red rectangle.

3. **2nd Infantry** A regular infantry division prior to the war, it served in the UK, France and Belgium, the UK, India, Burma and India. INSIGNIA: Two crossed white keys on a black square.

4. **2nd London/47th (London)/47th Infantry (Reserve)** In September 1939 it was a second line TA division organized as a motor division – a duplicate of 1st London Division. In June 1940 it was reorganized as an infantry division and on 21 November 1940 it was redesignated 47th (London) Division. In December 1941 it was placed on lower establishment (LE) and then on 15 August 1944 commenced dispersing – completed by 31 August. On 1 September 1944 the division was reformed as 47th Infantry (Reserve)

Division. It served only in the UK. INSIGNIA: 'Bow bells', that is, two red bells joined by a red bow on a black background.

5. **3rd Infantry** In September 1939 it was a regular infantry division, but was reorganized as a mixed division in June 1942 and again in April 1943 as an infantry division. It served in the UK, France and Belgium, the UK and NW Europe. INSIGNIA: A red inverted triangle with three black triangles attached to each side, forming an equilateral triangle.

6. **4th Infantry** In September 1939 it was a regular division, but was, like the 3rd Division, reorganized as a mixed division in June 1942 and again in December 1943 as an infantry division. It served in the UK, France and Belgium, the UK, North Africa, Egypt, Italy and Greece. INSIGNIA: Fourth quadrant of a circle in red, later a red disc with the fourth quadrant protruding from the disc on a white background.

7. **5th Infantry** In September 1939 it was a regular division, its two infantry brigades going to France in October 1939 as independent infantry brigades. In December 1939, Divisional HQ crossed to France and the division was reformed. In April 1942, 13th and 17th Infantry Brigades plus a proportion of divisional troops were detached to Force 121 for operations in Madagascar. The division was not complete again until August 1942. In addition it served in India, Iraq, Persia, Syria*, Egypt*, Sicily, Italy, Egypt, Palestine, Italy and NW Europe (* = in transit). INSIGNIA: A white 'Y' on a khaki background.

8. **6th Infantry** Formed in Egypt on 3 November 1939 by redesignation of 7th Infantry Division (see next serial). On 17 June 1940 Divisional HQ became HQ Western Desert Force and the division ceased to exist. Reformed in Egypt on 17 February 1941, it moved to Tobruk in October 1941, having been redesignated as 70th Infantry Division on 10 October 1941.

INFANTRY DIVISIONS

1st   2nd   3rd   4th   5th   6th

8th   9th   12th   15th   18th   23rd

36th   38th   40th   42nd   43rd   44th

45th   46th   47th   48th   49th   50th

51st   52nd   53rd   54th   55th   56th

59th   61st   66th   76th   77th   78th

80th

AIRBORNE

1st and 6th
(Same insignia)

Tobruk Fortress ceased to exist on 13 December 1941. On 6 September 1943 it started to reorganize for the Long Penetration role and on 25 October 1943 handed over its formations and units to Special Forces. INSIGNIA: A red four pointed star on a white background.

9.   **7th Infantry**   In August 1939 it was a regular division in Palestine on Internal Security (IS) duties, but on 3 November 1939 it was redesignated as HQ 6 Infantry Division. INSIGNIA: Not recorded.

10.   **8th Infantry**   In September 1939 it was a prewar regular division on Palestine IS duties, but was disbanded there on 28 February 1940. INSIGNIA: A red Cross of St George on a blue shield.

11.   **9th/51st (Highland) Infantry**   In September 1939 it was a second line TA division, a duplicate of 51st Infantry Division, embodied in the UK. On 7 August 1940, it was redesignated as 51st (Highland) Infantry Division after the original 51st had been captured in France (see serial 28 Infantry). INSIGNIA: As 9th Infantry – A silver thistle on a dark blue background.

10th and 11th Infantry Divisions were not formed.

12.   **12th (Eastern) Infantry**   A second line TA division formed in September/October 1939, which moved to France in April 1940 to join the BEF for training and labour duties, leaving certain RA, Signals and administrative units behind. Disbanded in the UK on 11 July 1940. INSIGNIA: A white diamond.

Note: The title '12th Division' was also given to the 1st Sudan Defence Force Brigade for deception, admin and IS reasons, when it was under command of HQ BTE. Then in December 1942 it came under Eighth Army (for LofC duties between Tobruk and Tripoli) until February 1943. Thereafter it was under Tripolitania Base Area

until 12 January 1945 when it was redesignated 'Sudan Defence Force Group (North Africa)'.

13th and 14th Infantry Divisions were not formed.

13.   **15th (Scottish) Infantry**   In September 1939 it was a second line TA division and was placed on LE in November 1941, then raised to higher establishment (HE) in March 1943 and reorganized as a mixed division. In September it was reorganized as an infantry division and fought in NW Europe from 14 June 1944 onwards. INSIGNIA: A red rampant Scottish lion on a yellow disc edged in white on a black square.

16th and 17th Infantry Divisions were not formed.

14.   **18th Infantry**   Formed on 30 September 1939 as a second line TA division, it served in the UK, India and Malaya until 15 February 1942 when it was captured and was never reformed. INSIGNIA: A black diagonal cross overset with a black diamond, all on an orange background.

19th to 22nd Infantry Divisions were not formed.

15.   **23rd (Northumbrian) Infantry**   Formed on 2 October 1939 as a second line TA division, it served in the UK until moving to France in April 1940 to join the BEF for training and labour duties, leaving all its RA, most of its Signals and admin units behind. Disbanded in the UK on 30 June 1940. INSIGNIA: A white Tudor rose on a blue background.

25th to 35th Infantry Divisions were not formed.

16.   **36th Infantry**   Formed on 1 September 1944 by the redesignation of 36th Indian Infantry Division in Burma. Served in Burma and India. INSIGNIA: White and red interlinked circles on a black background.

37th Infantry Division was not formed.

17. 38th (Welsh) Infantry In September 1939 it was a second line TA division, but was placed on LE on 15 August 1941. On 15 August 1944 it ceased to command formations and units and began to disperse. On 1 September 1944, Divisional HQ was reorganized and redesignated HQ 38th Infantry (Reserve) Division. It served only in the UK. INSIGNIA: A yellow St David's Cross on a black shield on a khaki background.

39th Infantry Division was not formed.

18. 40th Infantry HQ formed in Sicily by redesignating HQ 43rd Infantry Brigade for deception purposes. On 17 June 1944 it ceased to exist. INSIGNIA: An acorn on a white background.

41st Infantry Division was not formed.

19. 42nd (East Lancashire) Infantry In September 1939 it was a first line TA division and on 1 November 1941 it was reorganized and re-designated 42nd Armoured Division. INSIGNIA: An equal-sided white diamond within a red diamond.

20. 43rd (Wessex) Infantry In September 1939 it was a first line TA division, organized in June 1942 as a mixed division, then in September 1943 it was reorganized as an infantry division. It served in the UK and NW Europe. INSIGNIA: A gold heraldic wyvern on a dark blue square.

21. 44th (Home Counties) Infantry In September 1939 it was a first line TA division, which served in the UK, France and Egypt and was disbanded in North Africa on 31 January 1943. INSIGNIA: A red horizontal oval.

22. 45th Infantry In September 1939 it was a second line TA division and in December 1941 was placed on LE. In August 1944 the division was dispersed and ceased to exist. However, on 1 September 1944 it was reformed in the UK as HQ 45th (Holding) Division from personnel of 77th (Holding) Division, then on 1 December 1944 its title was changed to 45th Infantry Division. INSIGNIA: A Drake's drum on a khaki background.

23. 46th Infantry In October 1939 it was a second line TA division, which in April 1940 went across to France to join the BEF for training and labour duties. It subsequently saw service in the Middle East (Tunisia), Italy and Greece. It was still operating at the end of the war. INSIGNIA: An oak tree edged in white on a black background.

24. 47th Infantry – see serial 4 Infantry.

25. 48th (South Midland) Infantry In September 1939 it was a first line TA division, then in November 1941 it was placed on LE, but on 20 December 1942 it was redesignated 48th (Reserve) Division and remained in the UK thereafter throughout the rest of the war. INSIGNIA: A blue macaw on a red diamond within a blue oval.

26. 49th (West Riding) Infantry A first line TA infantry division in September 1939, it ceased to function as a division in April 1940, when its HQ became HQ AVONFORCE (Norway) then HQ ALABASTERFORCE (Iceland). It was reconstituted on 26 April 1942 and became an infantry division once again, fighting in NW Europe. INSIGNIA: A white polar bear on a black background.

27. 50th (Northumbrian) Infantry In September 1939 it was a first line TA division, organized as a motor division. It fought in France and Belgium, then in June 1940 was reorganized as an infantry division and saw service in the UK, the Middle East (N Africa, Cyprus, Sicily), then the UK and over to NW Europe. It moved to Norway in August 1945 and assumed the title HQ British Land Forces Norway. INSIGNIA: Linked red 'T's (representing the Rivers Tees and Tyne) on a black square.

28. **51st (Highland) Infantry** In September 1939 it was a first line TA division and was captured in France on 12 June 1940 (less 154 Brigade). Reconstituted from 9th (Highland) Infantry Division on 7 August 1940 (see serial 11). Fought in North Africa, Sicily and NW Europe. INSIGNIA: Red letters 'HD' linked together within a red circle on a blue background.

29. **52nd (Lowland) Infantry** In September 1939 it was a first line TA division that was trained in mountain warfare between May 1942 and June 1944, but was never used in this role. In August/September 1944 it trained in airlanding operations but was not used in this role either. It fought in France in 1940 and in NW Europe. INSIGNIA: A cross of St Andrew on a blue shield. A scroll with the word 'MOUNTAIN' was added below in about 1942.

30. **53rd (Welsh) Infantry** In September 1939 it was a first line TA division, reorganized as a mixed division in May 1942, then in October 1943 as an infantry division. It fought in NW Europe. INSIGNIA: A red 'W' standing on a red bar, on a black background.

31. **54th (East Anglian) Infantry** In September 1939 it was a first line TA division. It was placed on LE in January 1942 and on 14 December 1943 was redesignated HQ LofC (54th Division). It did not serve outside the UK. INSIGNIA: The letters 'JP' with a common vertical in blue on a red disc. It stood for the initials of Maj Gen J. Priestman, the first divisional commander.

32. **55th (West Lancashire) Infantry** In September 1939 it was a first line TA division, organized as a motor division. In June 1940 it was reorganized into an infantry division. It was placed on LE in January 1942 and raised to HE in May 1944. It did not serve outside the UK. INSIGNIA: A red rose of Lancashire with two sets of five leaves (representing '55').

33. **56th (London) Infantry** – see serial 2 Infantry.

34. **57th Infantry** HQ was formed on 9 November 1943 by redesignating HQ 42 Infantry Brigade for deception purposes. It ceased to exist on 29 July 1944.

58th Infantry Division was never formed.

35. **59th (Staffordshire) Infantry** In September 1939 it was a second line TA division, organized as a motor division, then in June 1940 it was reorganized as an infantry division. It fought in NW Europe and on 19 October 1944 it was placed in suspended animation. INSIGNIA: Red pithead gear against a black slagheap on a blue background.

60th Infantry Division was never formed.

36. **61st Infantry** In September 1939 it was a second line TA division and on 15 April 1940 the divisonal commander and his staff formed HQ MAURICE FORCE and went to Norway. A new commander and staff were appointed on 26 April 1940 and the division remained in the UK. In August 1945 it was reorganized as a light division. INSIGNIA: A red diamond on a blue background.

62nd to 65th Infantry Divisions were never formed.

37. **66th Infantry** In September 1939 it was a second line TA division but was disbanded on 23 June 1940 having never moved from the UK. INSIGNIA: A light blue triangle with a horizontal yellow bar across its middle.

67th to 69th Infantry Divisions were never formed.

38. **70th Infantry** – see serial 8 Infantry.

71st to 75th Infantry Divisions were never formed.

39. **76th Infantry** Formed in the UK on 18 November 1941 on LE by the redesignation of the Norfolk County Division. Redesignated on 20 December 1942 as the 76th Infantry (Reserve) Division and reorganized. Disbanded in the UK on 1 September 1944. INSIGNIA: A Norfolk 'wherry' (sailboat) in red on a black background.

40. **77th Infantry** Formed in the UK on 1 December 1941 on LE by the redesignation of the Devon and Cornwall County Division. Redesignated on 20 December 1942 as the 77th Infantry (Reserve) Division and reorganized. On 1 December 1943 it was redesignated 77th Holding Division and reorganized for sorting, retraining and holding personnel temporarily, due to disbandments, medical or other causes. Disbanded in the UK in 1 September 1944. INSIGNIA: A red 'Excalibur' sword held aloft by a white arm emerging from the water (three blue wavy lines) on a black background.

41. **78th Infantry** Formed in the UK on 25 May 1942 (Divisional Commander assumed command on 14 June 1942). Served in the UK, N Africa, Sicily, Italy and Austria. INSIGNIA: A yellow battleaxe on a black background.

79th Infantry Division was never formed.

42. **80th (Reserve) Infantry** Formed on 1 January 1943 in the UK. Served only in the UK, disbanded on 1 September 1944. INSIGNIA: A red ocean liner, blue sea and light blue funnel smoke, all in a light blue border.

COUNTY DIVISIONS

There were also ten county divisions that were static formations established for the defence of the coasts of the UK, commanding independent infantry brigades (home) stationed on the coast. There were no basic divisional troops, all being on loan from other divisions. The County Divisions were:

Devon and Cornwall County Division – became 77th Infantry Division on 1 December 1941

Dorset County Division – disbanded 31 December 1941

Durham and North Riding County Division – ceased to function on 1 December 1941

Essex County Division – disbanded 7 October 1941

Hampshire County Division – disbanded 31 December 1941

Lincolnshire County Division – disbanded 3 December 1941

Norfolk County Division – became 76th Infantry Division on 18 November 1941

Northumberland County Division – ceased to function on 1 December 1941

West Sussex County Division – redesignated Essex County Division on 18 February 1941

Yorkshire County Division – redesignated East Riding District on 1 December 1941

AIRBORNE

1. **1st Airborne** Formed in the UK in November 1941. Served in the UK, Sicily and NW Europe, then Norway. Between 21 May and 24 August 1945 it was designated HQ Norway Command. INSIGNIA: Bellerophon astride Pegasus in pale blue on a maroon background.

2. **6th Airborne** Formed in the UK in May 1943 and brought up to full war establishment on 23 September 1943. Served in the UK and NW Europe. INSIGNIA: As for 1st Airborne Division.

Source: Extracted from Joslen, *Orders of Battle of the Second World War, 1939–1945*.

MILITARY SYMBOLS

MILITARY SYMBOLS

(For use on maps, sketches or aerial photographs. When the symbols are coloured RED is used to denote British and friendly installations, BLUE for the enemy and GREEN for demolitions, craters, mines and minefields.)

(1) *Topographic.*—(a) *Anti-tank obstacles:*

    1. Projected anti-tank ditch

    2. Anti-tank ditch under construction

    3. Completed anti-tank ditch

    4. Anti-tank ditch facing both ways

    5. Anti-tank obstacle

    6. Tank trap

    7. Road block

    8. Areas strewn with rocks or boulders of 18-inch or greater diameter

(b) *Bridges:*

    1. Weight capacity of bridges and culverts is given in tons (British maps give weight in long tons.)

    2. Bridge demolitions   proposed

    3. Bridge demolitions   charged

    4. Bridges blown

(c) *Craters:*

    1. Site for

    2. Charged

    3. Blown

(d) *Embankments and cuttings (cuts).*—Height of embankment in feet

(e) *Flame traps*

(f) *Inundations:*

    1. Projected

    2. Under construction

    3. Completed

(g) *Mines:*

    1. Mine

    2. Mine field

    3. Beach mines:

        Electrically fired

        Contact

(h) *Water:*

    1. Width of waterway in feet

    2. Depth of waterway in feet

(i) *Wire entanglements:*
    1. Abatis _____

    2. Single (on posts) _____ XXXXXXXXXXXXXXXX

    3. Multiple (on posts) _____

    4. Coiled or Dannert _____

    5. Chevaux de frise _____ —X—X—X—X—X—X—X-

(j) *Woods:*
    1. Average diameter of trees in inches _____ *5d*

    2. Average spacing of trees in feet _____ *10S*

(2) *Special military.* —(a) *Anti-aircraft:*
    1. Section of guns _____

    2. Machine gun _____

    3. Searchlight _____

    4. Visual plotting station _____

Nature of AA guns to be stated, i.e., 3.7″, 3″, or B (Bofors).

(b) *Anti-tank:*   No concrete Concrete
    1. Projected anti-tank gun emplacement _____

    2. Anti-tank gun emplacement under construction _____

    3. Completed anti-tank gun emplacement _____

    4. Artillery anti-tank guns _____

    5. Cavalry or infantry anti-tank guns _____

    6. Anti-tank rifle _____

(c) *Batteries and gun emplacements.* —General _____

No concrete Concrete

(d) *Bren guns:*
    1. Projected Bren gun emplacement _____

    2. Bren gun emplacement under construction _____

    3. Completed Bren gun emplacement _____

(e) *Dumps:*

    1. Supply -   S

    2. Petrol (gasoline), oil, and lubricants (POL) - - - - - - - - - - - - -   P

    3. Ammunition -   A

    4. Engineer -   E

(f) *Gas.*—Gassed areas (shaded yellow if possible) - - - - - - - - - - - - -   Mustard

(g) *Hospital, clearing station, or aid post* -

(h) *Machine guns:*

                                                                No concrete   Concrete

    1. General symbol -

    2. Symbol for use on maps of 1:25,000 and larger, especially in field sketching -

    3. Projected machine gun emplacement - - - - - - - - - - - - - -

    4. Machine-gun emplacement under construction - - - - - - -

    5. Completed machine-gun emplacement - - - - - - - - - - - - -

(i) *Mortars:*

    1. Mortar emplacement projected - - - - - - - - - - - - - - - - - - -   ○M   Nature

    2. Mortar emplacement under construction - - - - - - - - - - -   ◔M2″   of mortar

    3. Mortar emplacement completed - - - - - - - - - - - - - - - - - -   ●M3″   to be shown

(j) *Observation post:*

                                               No concrete   Concrete

    1. Projected -   ⊙OP   ⊙OP

    2. Under construction -   ◔OP   ◔OP

    3. Completed -   ●OP   ●OP

(k) *Railway stop* -   ✕

(l) *Searchlight* -

(m) *Shelters:*

    1. Dugouts -

    2. Hutments (cantonments) -

(n) *Signal symbols:*

	No concrete	Concrete
1. Telephone or telegraph office _____	⊖T	 ▣T
2. Wireless-telegraph station _____	⊕W/T	
3. Radio-telephone station _____	⊕R/T	
4. Beam station _____	⊕B	
5. Direction-finding (DF) station _____	⊕D/F	
6. Visual signaling station _____	✗✗	

(o) *Tanks.* Special symbols are used for drill formations of light tanks. When distances and intervals are shown, they are in paces for dismounted drill and in yards for mounted drill.

1. Regimental commander (in armoured force vehicle) _____

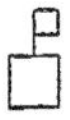

2. Squadron leader (in AFV) _____

3. Troop leader (in AFV) _____

4. Tank _____

5. Carrier _____

6. Squadron (etc.) leader (dismounted) _____

7. Troop (etc.) leader (dismounted) _____

8. Crew commander (dismounted) _____

9. Crew of leader's tank (dismounted) _____

10. Men (dismounted) _____

339

(p) *Trenches:*

1. Projected __ ------------------------------------

2. Under construction---------------------------------

3. Completed --------------------------------

4. System of trenches (old or disused trenches
are shown dotted) -------------------------------

(q) *Troops and headquarters.*—Titles will be written alongside the appropriate
symbol and the authorized abbreviations used.

1. Units ----------

	Cavalry	Artillery	Infantry	Tanks	Armoured Cars or Carriers	Transport	
						HT	MT
Individual ------							
General --------							
Column of route_							

(Insert (M) against mechanized units.)

2. Parachute troops (frame enclosing area in which parachute
troops have been reported) ------------------------------------ **P**

3. Air-borne troops (frame enclosing area in which air-borne troops
have landed) -- **A**

4. Headquarters:

Example:

GHQ   Brig (Cav or Inf)   5 Inf Bde

Army   Regt, Bn, or Arty Regt   5 R Tks

Corps   Sq, Co, or Btry   B Coy

Division   Tr or Plat   5 Pl

AA Div   AA Brig   AA Regt, Bn   AA Btry, Co

5. Boundaries:
Inter-army ------------------------------------
Inter-corps------------------------------------
Inter-division--------------------------------
Inter-brigade --------------------------------
Inter-battalion-------------------------------

APPRECIATIONS OF THE SITUATION AND OPERATION ORDERS

APPRECIATIONS

The term 'appreciation of the situation' is nothing more than the orderly sequence of reasoning that leads to the best solution to a problem. The basic sequence is covered by the following headings:

(a). Aim.
(b). Factors (for example, enemy courses of action, relative strengths, ground, time and space, administrative considerations, air situation, climatic conditions, assessment of tasks, etc.).
(c). Own Courses.
(d). Plan (based upon course selected).

The commander would try to do this at an OP from where he could see the ground, or if that were impossible he would have to make his appreciation using a map. Having decided upon his plan the commander would then work out his orders – possibly with the assistance of his staff – so that he was able to pass on his plan to his subordinates, either verbally or in writing. This process involved the giving out of an Operation Order.

OPERATION ORDERS

Orders were issued in one of two main ways:

(a). **Verbally** By the commander to those subordinates who made up his Orders Group ('O'

Group)[1]. This took place either at his HQ or, if the situation allowed, at a suitable vantage point from where all could see the ground. Essential members of his staff would also be present, so that they could brief the 'O' Group on specific matters such as the up-to-date enemy situation. They would also take note of any alterations to the plan which were agreed at the 'O' Group, so that they could be included in any subsequent written orders. As the war progressed and operations became more fluid, then orders for small operations were increasingly given out over the radio. This was done mainly when time was of the essence and it was impossible to hold verbal orders. It was a quick and easy way for the commander not only to get across his orders without going through the time-consuming business of holding an 'O' Group, but also to impress his personality upon his subordinates. Care had to be taken not to give away anything to the enemy, so either codes had to be used and/or the operation, such as mounting an assault, put into effect immediately – for example, an armoured battle group being briefed for a quick attack from the line of advance. A variation might be the issue of orders by telephone if line had been laid, but

1. Members of the 'O' Group would normally include sub-unit commanders, representatives of Arms and Services, selected staff officers, LOs (to take orders to those unable to attend). Clearly the list of those to attend could be a long one at larger HQs and when the situation demanded a full and formal 'O' Group.

radio orders came to be much more the 'norm' in armoured formations, especially at low level.

(b). **Written** Usually as formal orders or as confirmation of verbal orders, if the situation demanded it – for example, when there was a great deal of detail to be covered. Written orders had to be date/timed (see below) and properly signed by the issuer. They might well be delivered in person by a Liaision Officer (LO) who, having been briefed by the commander or his immediate staff, could explain/amplify any points raised by the recipient.

No matter how orders were issued or at whatever level they were given, they *always* followed a laid-down sequence,[2] so that nothing important was forgotten and they could be followed easily. Here, by way of example, is the sequence for an Operation Order that had been written down. Those attending had to ensure that their maps were properly folded, and that they had notebooks, pencils, etc.

SECRET

. . . .(Formation/Unit)   Operation Order No . . . .

Copy No . . . .

Ref Map . . . .   Date . . . .

ORDERS IN CONFIRMATION OF VERBAL ORDERS GIVEN BY . . . .[Comd]
ON . . . .[Date] AT. . . . .[Location – usually a Grid Reference]
AT . . . . HRS [Time]

INFORMATION
(a).   **Regarding the Enemy** – a summary of up-to-date and relevant information about the enemy, from which the commander had made his plan. This information must be on a 'need to know basis'.
(b).   **Regarding Own Troops** – a summary of the situation and intentions of neighbouring troops, whose actions might affect the recipient of the order, bearing in mind at all times the interests of security.

INTENTION
This had to be a clear, concise and decisive statement of what the command intended to achieve. It had to be expressed in the future imperative tense, i.e. 'will' had to be used.

METHOD
Again a clear, concise statement on how the operation would be carried out, in sufficient detail so that everyone knew what they had to do. It would cover such subjects as (in an attack) the allocation of troops to tasks, attachments and detachments, the order of march to the forming up point (FUP) and from there to the start line (SL) and then on to the objective, the location of the SL, all timings (including ZeroHour – all timings then expressed as either plus or minus of Z hr), the fire plan (including AA and a tk), any special engineer tasks, action on consolidation, etc. If the fire plan were very detailed then it might be the subject of a special appendix, or perhaps given/issued separately by the CRA or his representative.

---

2. The British Army wartime sequence was very similar to, but worded slightly differently from that used by the US Army. Their headings were: INFORMATION, DECISION OR MISSION, TACTICAL MISSIONS FOR SUBORDINATE TROOPS, ADMINISTRATIVE MATTERS AND SIGNAL COMMUNICATIONS. Postwar, all NATO troops standardized their Orders as part of their Staff Duties.

ADMINISTRATION

A statement of the general administrative arrangements, again on a 'need to know' basis. It might be more convenient to issue the administrative details separately, either as an appendix or in a separate administrative order. One would expect to cover (at the appropriate level) all the matters that are dealt with by the A & Q Staff and the Services (for example: (a). **Supplies & Transport** – POL, rations and transport; (b). **Medical** – locations and allotment of medical services; (c). **Ordnance** – issues of ammunition and ordnance stores; (d). **REME** – repair and recovery; (e). **Provost** – CMP matters as necessary, etc.). Note: At unit level, care had to be taken to restrict this paragraph only to those points that affected everyone in the tactical operation, such as ammunition resupply and medical arrangements.

INTERCOMMUNICATIONS

The type of information to be included was:

(a).   Location of HQ.

(b).   Routes to be followed, with codewords etc., as mentioned in the 'Method' paragraph and possibly supplied as a 'trace' to be put onto the 'O' Group's maps, or members of the sub-unit commander's staff might be on hand to mark up individual maps.

(c).   Wireless details – special frequencies, codes, etc., to be used if different from standard daily issues.

(d).   Any prearranged verey light or other signals, to indicate such items as: Z hr, successful capture of successive objectives, end of artillery/mortar concentrations, indication of targets, SOS signal for immediate artillery fire on a prearranged location.

ACKNOWLEDGE

. . . .

[Signature, rank & appointment of officer signing the order]

METHOD OF ISSUE

TIME OF SIGNATURE

Time was described by reference to the 24-hour clock. Groups of four figures followed by 'hrs' were used – the first two representing the hour and the last two the minutes past the hour. For example:

(a).   One minute past midnight – 0001hrs   (c).   Noon – 1200hrs
(b).   Nine o'clock in the morning – 0900hrs   (d).   Twenty minutes to five in the afternoon – 1640hrs

DISTRIBUTION

A list of everyone who was being issued with the orders went to all addressees so they could see who had been sent them, the number of copies being carefully listed (all copies were classified as appropriate and numbered, that number being kept as low as possible). However, distribution might well include, in addition to the 'O' Group personnel of flanking formations, higher headquarters, plus of course copies for the file and war diary.

QUESTIONS AND SYNCHRONIZE

In the case of verbal orders the commander will ask the members of the 'O' Group if they have any questions and finally, all would synchronise their watches.

REMIND ALL OF TIME OF ZERO HOUR

NORMAL BREAKDOWN OF PERSONNEL IN AN INFANTRY BATTALION (CIRCA 1944)

There were normally four groups: 'R' = Recce Gp; 'O' = Orders Gp; 'F' = Fighting Gp;
'T' = Transport Gp:

Gp	Bn	Coy	Pl
'R'	CO IO Sig Offr 2 × DR 1 × Sig (c/w wrls set) Comds of any SP arms	Coy Comd Batman 2 × runners Comds of any SP wpns alloted to coy	Pl Comd Batman NCO i/c Mor
'O'	As for 'R' plus Adjt Coy Comds Pl Comds of Mor Pl, Carr Pl, A tk Pl & Pnr Pl MO Comds of SP arms*	Coy Comd Batman 2 × runners Pl Comds CSM Comds of secs of SP Coy Pls if alloted	Pl Comd Batman Sec Comds NCO i/c Mor Orderly
(*Note: Comds of SP arms may be attending their own 'O' Groups, leaving LOs to represent them.)			
'F'	2IC Bn Bn HQ Sig Pl Pls of SP Coy Rifle Coys 'F' Ech Tpt	2IC Coy Coy HQ Pls	Pl Sjt Pl HQ Secs
'T'	Tpt Offr 'A' Ech Tpt Men of HQ Coy not req in 'F' Gp	CQMS Coy tpt (not req in 'F' Tpt)	

COMPOSITION OF 21 ARMY GROUP

The following table shows all British and Canadian Troops engaged on the Continent between 6 June 1944 and 31 August 1944.

Note: This is not a complete Order of Battle as it does not include the many essential specialist and administrative units that have had to be omitted to save space and because of the great variety of their tasks.

Source: Joslen, *Orders of Battle of the Second World War, 1939–45*

TWENTY-FIRST ARMY GROUP
General Sir Bernard L. Montgomery
Commander-in-Chief
Major-General Sir Francis W. de Guingand
Chief of Staff

G.H.Q. AND ARMY TROOPS
79th Armoured Division
Major-General Sir Percy C. S. Hobart

30th Armoured Brigade
22nd Dragoons
1st Lothians and Border Horse
2nd County of London Yeomanry
(Westminster Dragoons)
141st Regiment R.A.C.

1st Tank Brigade
11th, 42nd and 49th Battalions
R.T.R.

1st Assault Brigade R.E.
5th, 6th and 42nd Assault
Regiments R.E.

79th Armoured Divisional Signals
1st Canadian Armoured Personnel Carrier Regiment

Independent Brigades

4th Armoured Brigade
The Royal Scots Greys
3rd County of London Yeomanry
(Sharpshooters) (to 28.7.44)
3rd/4th County of London Yeomanry (Sharpshooters) (from 29.7.44)
44th Battalion R.T.R.
2nd Battalion The King's Royal Rifle Corps (Motor)

6th Guards Tank Brigade
4th Tank Battalion Grenadier Guards
4th Tank Battalion Coldstream Guards
3rd Tank Battalion Scots Guards

8th Armoured Brigade
4th/7th Royal Dragoon Guards
24th Lancers (to 29.7.44)
The Nottinghamshire Yeomanry
13th/18th Royal Hussars (from 29.7.44)
12th Battalion The King's Royal Rifle Corps (Motor)

27th Armoured Brigade (to 29.7.44)
13th/18th Royal Hussars
1st East Riding Yeomanry
The Staffordshire Yeomanry

31st Tank Brigade
7th Battalion R.T.R. (to 17.8.44)
9th Battalion R.T.R. (to 31.8.44)
144th Regiment R.A.C.
(23–31.8.44)

34th Tank Brigade
107th and 147th Regiments R.A.C.
153rd Regiment R.A.C. (to 24.8.44)

33rd Armoured Brigade
1st Northamptonshire Yeomanry
144th Regiment R.A.C. (to 22.8.44)
148th Regiment R.A.C. (to 16.8.44)
1st East Riding Yeomanry
(from 16.8.44)

2nd Canadian Armoured Brigade
6th Armoured Regiment
(1st Hussars)
10th Armoured Regiment (The Fort Garry Horse)
27th Armoured Regiment (The Sherbrooke Fusiliers Regiment)

H.Q. Anti-Aircraft Brigades
74th, 76th, 80th, 100th, 101st, 105th, 106th and 107th
Heavy Anti-Aircraft Regiments
60th, 86th, 90th, 99th, 103rd, 105th, 107th, 108th, 109th, 112th, 113th, 115th, 116th, 121st, 146th, 165th and 174th; 2nd Canadian
Light Anti-Aircraft Regiments
20th, 27th, 32nd, 54th, 71st, 73rd, 93rd, 109th, 112th, 113th, 114th, 120th, 121st, 123rd, 124th, 125th, 126th, 127th, 133rd, 139th and 149th
Searchlight Regiments
41st

56th Infantry Brigade
(Became integral part of the 49th Division from 20.8.44)
2nd Battalion The South Wales Borderers
2nd Battalion The Gloucestershire Regiment
2nd Battalion The Essex Regiment

1st Special Service Brigade
Nos. 3, 4 and 6 Commandos
No. 45 (Royal Marine) Commando

4th Special Service Brigade
Nos. 41, 46, 47 and 48 (Royal Marine) Commandos.

Other Formations and Units

Armoured

G.H.Q. Liaison Regiment R.A.C. ('Phantom')
2nd Armoured Replacement Group
2nd Armoured Delivery Regiment
25th Canadian Armoured Delivery Regiment (The Elgin Regiment)

Artillery

H.Q. Army Groups Royal Artillery: 3rd, 4th, 5th, 8th and 9th; 2nd Canadian

Heavy Regiments: 1st, 51st, 52nd, 53rd and 59th

Medium Regiments: 7th, 9th, 10th, 11th, 13th, 15th, 53rd, 59th, 61st, 63rd, 64th, 65th, 67th, 68th, 72nd, 77th, 79th, 84th, 107th, 121st and 146th; 3rd, 4th and 7th Canadian

Field Regiments: 4th R.H.A., 6th, 25th, 86th, 147th, 150th and 191st; 19th Canadian

Engineer

H.Q. Army Groups Royal Engineers: 10th, 11th, 12th, 13th and 14th; 1st Canadian

G.H.Q. Troops Engineers: 4th, 7th, 8th, 13th, 15th, 18th, 48th and 59th

Airfield Construction Groups: 13th, 16th, 23rd, 24th and 25th

Army Troops Engineers: 2nd, 6th and 7th; 1st and 2nd Canadian

2nd and 3rd Battalions Royal Canadian Engineers

Signal

Twenty-First Army Group Headquarters Signals
Second Army Headquarters Signals
First Canadian Army Headquarters Signals
Air Formation Signals, Nos. 11, 12, 13, 16, 17 and 18
1st Special Wireless Group

Infantry

4th Battalion The Royal Northumberland Fusiliers (Machine Gun)
First Canadian Army Headquarters Defence Battalion (Royal Montreal Regiment)

Royal Marine

Armoured Support Group: 1st and 2nd Royal Marine Armoured Support Regiments

Army Air Corps

Glider Pilot Regiment: 1st and 2nd Glider Pilot Wings

Special Air Service

1st and 2nd Special Air Service Regiments
3rd and 4th French Parachute Battalions

European Allies

1st Belgian Infantry Brigade
Royal Netherlands Brigade (Princess Irene's)

ARMIES, CORPS AND DIVISIONS

Second Army

Lieutenant-General Sir Miles C. Dempsey
General Officer Commanding-in-Chief
Brigadier M. S. Chilton
Chief of Staff

First Canadian Army

Lieutenant-General H. D. G. Crerar
General Officer Commanding-in-Chief
Brigadier C. C. Mann
Chief of Staff

I Corps

Lieutenant-General J. T. Crocker

The Inns of Court Regiment R.A.C. (Armoured Car)
62nd Anti-Tank, 102nd Light Anti-Aircraft, 9th Survey Regiments R.A.
I Corps Troops Engineers   I Corps Signals

VIII Corps

Lieutenant-General Sir Richard N. O'Connor

2nd Household Cavalry Regiment (Armoured Car)
91st Anti-Tank, 121st Light Anti-Aircraft, 10th Survey Regiments R.A.
VIII Corps Troops Engineers   VIII Corps Signals

XII Corps

Lieutenant-General N. M. Ritchie

1st The Royal Dragoons (Armoured Car)
86th Anti-Tank, 112th Light Anti-Aircraft, 7th Survey Regiments R.A.
XII Corps Troops Engineers   XII Corps Signals

XXX Corps

Lieutenant-General G. C. Bucknall (to 3.8.44)
Lieutenant-General B. G. Horrocks (from 4.8.44)

11th Hussars (Armoured Car)
73rd Anti-Tank, 27th Light Anti-Aircraft, 4th Survey Regiments R.A.
XXX Corps Troops Engineers.   XXX Corps Signals

II Canadian Corps

Lieutenant-General G. G. Simonds

18th Armoured Car Regiment (12th Manitoba Dragoons)
6th Anti-Tank, 6th Light Anti-Aircraft, 2nd Survey Regiments R.C.A.
II Canadian Corps Troops Engineers   II Canadian Corps Signals

Guards Armoured Division

Major-General A. H. S. Adair

5th Guards Armoured Brigade

2nd (Armoured) Battalion Grenadier Guards
1st (Armoured) Battalion Coldstream Guards
2nd (Armoured) Battalion Irish Guards
1st (Motor) Battalion Grenadier Guards

32nd Guards Brigade

5th Battalion Coldstream Guards
3rd Battalion Irish Guards
1st Battalion Welsh Guards

Divisional Troops

2nd Armoured Reconnaissance Battalion Welsh Guards
Guards Armoured Divisional Engineers

55th and 153rd Field, 21st Anti-Tank and 94th Light Anti-Aircraft Regiments R.A.
Guards Armoured Divisional Signals

7th Armoured Division

Major-General G. W. E. J. Erskine (to 3.8.44)
Major-General G. L. Verney (from 4.8.44)

22nd Armoured Brigade

4th County of London Yeomanry (Sharpshooters) (to 29.7.44)
1st and 5th Battalions R.T.R.
5th Royal Inniskilling Dragoon Guards (from 29.7.44)
1st Battalion The Rifle Brigade (Motor)

131st Infantry Brigade

1/5th, 1/6th and 1/7th Battalions The Queen's Royal Regiment

Divisional Troops

8th King's Royal Irish Hussars
7th Armoured Divisional Engineers
7th Armoured Divisional Signals

3rd and 5th Regiments R.H.A.; 65th Anti-Tank and 15th Light Anti-Aircraft Regiments R.A.

11th Armoured Division
Major-General G. P. B. Roberts

29th Armoured Brigade
23rd Hussars
2nd Fife and Forfar Yeomanry
3rd Battalion R.T.R.
8th Battalion The Rifle Brigade (Motor)

159th Infantry Brigade
3rd Battalion The Monmouthshire Regiment
4th Battalion The King's Shropshire Light Infantry
1st Battalion The Herefordshire Regiment

Divisional Troops
2nd Northamptonshire Yeomanry (to 17.8.44)
15th/19th The King's Royal Hussars (from 17.8.44)
11th Armoured Divisional Engineers

13th Regiment R.H.A.; 151st Field, 75th Anti-Tank and 58th Light Anti-Aircraft Regiments R.A.
11th Armoured Divisional Signals

3rd Division
Major-General T. G. Rennie (to 13.6.44)
Brigadier E. E. E. Cass (acting)
Major-General L. G. Whistler (from 23.6.44)

8th Brigade
1st Battalion The Suffolk Regiment
2nd Battalion The East Yorkshire Regiment
1st Battalion The South Lancashire Regiment

9th Brigade
2nd Battalion The Lincolnshire Regiment
1st Battalion The King's Own Scottish Borderers
2nd Battalion The Royal Ulster Rifles

185th Brigade
2nd Battalion The Royal Warwickshire Regiment
1st Battalion The Royal Norfolk Regiment
2nd Battalion The King's Shropshire Light Infantry

Divisional Troops
3rd Reconnaissance Regiment R.A.C.
3rd Divisional Engineers
3rd Divisional Signals

7th, 33rd and 76th Field, 20th Anti-Tank and 92nd Light Anti-Aircraft Regiments R.A.
2nd Battalion The Middlesex Regiment (Machine Gun)

6th Airborne Division
Major-General R. N. Gale

3rd Parachute Brigade
8th and 9th Battalions The Parachute Regiment
1st Canadian Parachute Battalion

5th Parachute Brigade
7th, 12th and 13th Battalions The Parachute Regiment

6th Airlanding Brigade
12th Battalion The Devonshire Regiment
2nd Battalion The Oxfordshire and Buckinghamshire Light Infantry
1st Battalion The Royal Ulster Rifles

Divisional Troops
6th Airborne Armoured Reconnaissance Regiment R.A.C.
6th Airborne Divisional Engineers

53rd Airlanding Light Regiment R.A.
6th Airborne Divisional Signals

15th (Scottish) Division
Major-General G. H. A. MacMillan (to 2.8.44)
Major-General C. M. Barber (from 3.8.44)

44th (Lowland) Brigade
8th Battalion The Royal Scots
6th Battalion The Royal Scots Fusiliers
7th Battalion The King's Own Scottish Borderers

46th (Highland) Brigade
9th Battalion The Cameronians
2nd Battalion The Glasgow Highlanders
7th Battalion The Seaforth Highlanders

227th (Highland) Brigade
10th Battalion The Highland Light Infantry
2nd Battalion The Gordon Highlanders
2nd Battalion The Argyll and Sutherland Highlanders

Divisional Troops
15th Reconnaissance Regiment R.A.C.
15th Divisional Engineers
15th Divisional Signals

131st, 181st and 190th Field, 97th Anti-Tank and 119th Light Anti-Aircraft Regiments R.A.
1st Battalion The Middlesex Regiment (Machine Gun)

43rd (Wessex) Division
Major-General G. I. Thomas

129th Brigade
4th Battalion The Somerset Light Infantry
4th and 5th Battalions The Wiltshire Regiment

130th Brigade
7th Battalion The Hampshire Regiment
4th and 5th Battalions The Dorsetshire Regiment

214th Brigade
7th Battalion The Somerset Light Infantry
1st Battalion The Worcestershire Regiment
5th Battalion The Duke of Cornwall's Light Infantry

Divisional Troops
43rd Reconnaissance Regiment R.A.C.
43rd Divisional Engineers
43rd Divisional Signals

94th, 112th and 179th Field, 59th Anti-Tank and 110th Light Anti-Aircraft Regiments R.A.
8th Battalion The Middlesex Regiment (Machine Gun)

49th (West Riding) Division
Major-General E. H. Barker

70th Brigade (to 20.8.44)
10th and 11th Battalions The Durham Light Infantry
1st Battalion The Tyneside Scottish

146th Brigade
4th Battalion The Lincolnshire Regiment
1/4th Battalion The King's Own Yorkshire Light Infantry
Hallamshire Battalion The York and Lancaster Regiment

147th Brigade
11th Battalion The Royal Scots Fusiliers
6th Battalion The Duke of Wellington's Regiment (to 6.7.44)
7th Battalion The Duke of Wellington's Regiment
1st Battalion The Leicestershire Regiment (from 6.7.44)

56th Brigade (from 20.8.44)
See under GHQ Troops (page 523)

Divisional Troops
49th Reconnaissance Regiment R.A.C.
49th Divisional Engineers
49th Divisional Signals

69th, 143rd and 185th Field, 55th Anti-Tank and 89th Light Anti-Aircraft Regiments R.A.
2nd Princess Louise's Kensington Regiment (Machine Gun)

50th (Northumbrian) Division
Major-General D. A. H. Graham

69th Brigade
5th Battalion The East Yorkshire Regiment
6th and 7th Battalions The Green Howards

151st Brigade
6th, 8th and 9th Battalions The Durham Light Infantry

231st Brigade
2nd Battalion The Devonshire Regiment
1st Battalion The Hampshire Regiment
1st Battalion The Dorsetshire Regiment

Divisional Troops
61st Reconnaissance Regiment R.A.C.
50th Divisional Engineers
50th Divisional Signals

74th, 90th and 124th Field, 102nd Anti-Tank and 25th Light Anti-Aircraft Regiments R.A.
2nd Battalion The Cheshire Regiment (Machine Gun)

51st (Highland) Division
Major-General D. C. Bullen-Smith (to 26.7.44)
Major-General T. G. Rennie (from 27.7.44)

152nd Brigade
2nd and 5th Battalions The Seaforth Highlanders
5th Battalion The Queen's Own Cameron Highlanders

153rd Brigade
5th Battalion The Black Watch
1st and 5th/7th Battalions The Gordon Highlanders

154th Brigade
1st and 7th Battalions The Black Watch
7th Battalion The Argyll and Sutherland Highlanders

Divisional Troops
2nd Derbyshire Yeomanry R.A.C.
51st Divisional Engineers
51st Divisional Signals

126th, 127th and 128th Field, 61st Anti-Tank and 40th Light Anti-Aircraft Regiments R.A.
1/7th Battalion The Middlesex Regiment (Machine Gun)

53rd (Welsh) Division
Major-General R. K. Ross

71st Brigade
1st Battalion The East Lancashire Regiment (to 3.8.44)
1st Battalion The Oxfordshire and Buckinghamshire Light Infantry
1st Battalion The Highland Light Infantry
4th Battalion The Royal Welch Fusiliers (from 5.8.44)

158th Brigade
4th and 6th Battalions The Royal Welch Fusiliers (to 3.8.44)
7th Battalion The Royal Welch Fusiliers
1st Battalion The East Lancashire Regiment (from 4.8.44)
1/5th Battalion The Welch Regiment (from 4.8.44)

160th Brigade
2nd Battalion The Monmouthshire Regiment
4th Battalion The Welch Regiment
1/5th Battalion The Welch Regiment (to 3.8.44)
6th Battalion The Royal Welch Fusiliers (from 4.8.44)

Divisional Troops
53rd Reconnaissance Regiment R.A.C.
53rd Divisional Engineers
53rd Divisional Signals

81st, 83rd and 133rd Field, 71st Anti-Tank and 116th Light Anti-Aircraft Regiments R.A.
1st Battalion The Manchester Regiment (Machine Gun)

59th (Staffordshire) Division
Major-General L. O. Lyne

176th Brigade (to 26.8.44)
7th Battalion The Royal Norfolk Regiment
7th Battalion The South Staffordshire Regiment
6th Battalion The North Staffordshire Regiment

177th Brigade (to 26.8.44)
5th, 1/6th and 2/6th Battalions The South Staffordshire Regiment

197th Brigade (to 26.8.44)
1/7th Battalion The Royal Warwickshire Regiment
2/5th Battalion The Lancashire Fusiliers
5th Battalion The East Lancashire Regiment

Divisional Troops
59th Reconnaissance Regiment R.A.C. (to 31.8.44)
59th Divisional Engineers
59th Divisional Signals

61st, 110th and 116th Field (to 31.8.44), 68th Anti-Tank (to 26.8.44) and 68th Light Anti-Aircraft (to 22.8.44) Regiments R.A.
7th Battalion The Royal Northumberland Fusiliers (Machine Gun) (to 24.8.44)

4th Canadian Armoured Division
Major-General G. Kitching (to 21.8.44)
Major-General H. W. Foster (from 22.8.44)

4th Armoured Brigade
21st Armoured Regiment (The Governor General's Foot Guards)
22nd Armoured Regiment (The Canadian Grenadier Guards)
28th Armoured Regiment (The British Columbia Regiment)
The Lake Superior Regiment (Motor)

10th Infantry Brigade
The Lincoln and Welland Regiment
The Algonquin Regiment
The Argyll and Sutherland Highlanders of Canada (Princess Louise's)

Divisional Troops
29th Reconnaissance Regiment (The South Alberta Regiment)
4th Canadian Armoured Divisional Engineers

15th and 23rd Field, 5th Anti-Tank and 8th Light Anti-Aircraft Regiments R.C.A.
4th Canadian Armoured Divisional Signals

2nd Canadian Division
Major-General C. Foulkes

4th Brigade
The Royal Regiment of Canada
The Royal Hamilton Light Infantry
The Essex Scottish Regiment

5th Brigade
The Black Watch (Royal Highland Regiment) of Canada
Le Régiment de Maisonneuve
The Calgary Highlanders

6th Brigade
Les Fusiliers Mont-Royal
The Queen's Own Cameron Highlanders of Canada
The South Saskatchewan Regiment

Divisional Troops
8th Reconnaissance Regiment (14th Canadian Hussars)
2nd Canadian Divisional Engineers
2nd Canadian Divisional Signals

4th, 5th and 6th Field, 2nd Anti-Tank and 3rd Light Anti-Aircraft Regiments R.C.A.
The Toronto Scottish Regiment (Machine Gun)

3rd Canadian Division

Major-General R. F. L. Keller (to 8.8.44)
Major-General D. C. Spry (from 18.8.44)

7th Brigade	8th Brigade
The Royal Winnipeg Rifles	The Queen's Own Rifles of
The Regina Rifle Regiment	Canada
1st Battalion The Canadian Scot-tish Regiment	Le Régiment de la Chaudière
	The North Shore (New Brunswick) Regiment

9th Brigade

The Highland Light Infantry of Canada
The Stormont, Dundas and Glengarry Highlanders
The North Nova Scotia Highlanders

Divisional Troops

7th Reconnaissance Regiment (17th Duke of York's Royal Canadian Hussars)	12th, 13th and 14th Field, 3rd Anti-Tank and 4th Light Anti-Aircraft Regiments R.C.A.
3rd Canadian Divisional Engineers	The Cameron Highlanders of Ottawa (Machine Gun)
3rd Canadian Divisional Signals	

1st Polish Armoured Division

Major-General S. Maczek

10th Polish Armoured Brigade	3rd Polish Infantry Brigade
1st Polish Armoured Regiment	1st Polish (Highland) Battalion
2nd Polish Armoured Regiment	8th Polish Battalion
24th Polish Armoured (Lancer) Regiment	9th Polish Battalion
10th Polish Motor Battalion	

Divisional Troops

10th Polish Mounted Rifle Regiment	1st and 2nd Polish Field, 1st Polish Anti-Tank and 1st Polish Light Anti-Aircraft Regiments
1st Polish Armoured Divisional Engineers	1st Polish Armoured Divisional Signals

LINES OF COMMUNICATION AND REAR MAINTENANCE AREA

Headquarters Lines of Communication

Major-General R. F. B. Naylor

Nos. 11 and 12 Lines of Communication Areas
Nos. 4, 5 and 6 Lines of Communication Sub-Areas
Nos. 7 and 8 Base Sub-Areas
Nos. 101, 102 and 104 Beach Sub-Areas
Nos. 10 and 11 Garrisons

Engineers

Nos. 2, 3, 5 and 6 Railway Construction and Maintenance Groups
No. 3 Railway Operating Group
No. 1 Canadian Railway Operating Group
No. 1 Railway Workshop Group
Nos. 2, 6, 8, 9, 10 and 11 Port Operating Groups
Nos. 1, 2, 4 and 5 Port Construction and Repair Groups
Nos. 3 and 4 Inland Water Transport Groups
No. 2 Mechanical Equipment (Transportation) Unit

Signals

Nos. 2 and 12 Lines of Communication Headquarters Signals
No. 1 Canadian Lines of Communication Headquarters Signals

Infantry

5th and 8th Battalions The King's Regiment
7th Battalion The East Yorkshire Regiment
2nd Battalion The Hertfordshire Regiment
6th Battalion The Border Regiment
1st Buckinghamshire Battalion The Oxfordshire and Buckinghamshire Light Infantry
5th Battalion The Royal Berkshire Regiment
18th Battalion The Durham Light Infantry

GROUND RADIOS

This chart appeared in *The History of the British Army Signals in the Second World War*, by Maj Gen R.F.H. Nalder CB, OBE and appears here with the kind permission of the Royal Signals Institution.

Type of Set	Type of transmission	Frequency Range in Mc/s From	To	Power Output, Watts	Comn. Range, stationary (a) CW (b) RT miles	Associated Aerial	Remarks
1. LONG RANGE (All static except where otherwise stated)							
No. 5 HP	CW MCW	2.4	20	2,000	World wide	Array	
No. 6	CW	3	25	1,500	World wide	Array	
Marconi Sender, SWB 8E ...	CW	3	22.2	3,500	5,000	Rhombic	Used in Golden Arrow mobile station for high speed keying.
Marconi Sender SWB 11E ...	CW	3	22.2	10,000	World wide	Rhombic	Used as static station for high speed keying.
2. MEDIUM RANGE (All mobile except where otherwise stated)							
No. 3	CW RT	1.36	3.33	400	(a) 100 (b) 50	24-ft. rod	Modified locally in Middle East to work in HF band.
No. 5 LP	CW MCW RT	2.4	20	500	(a) 600 (b) 200	Simple Dipole	Transportable station.
No. 12 HP	CW MCW RT	1.2	17.5	250 (RT)	(a) 500 (b) 100	14-ft. rod	
No. 33	CW MCW RT	1.2	17.5	250 (CW) 65 (MCW and RT)	(a) 1,000 (b) 60	Dipole	
No. 52	CW MCW RT	1.75	16	100 (CW) 70 (MCW and RT)	(a) 500 (b) 60	14-ft. rod	Canadian type.
No. 53	CW MCW RT	1.2	17.5	250	(a) 500 (b) 100	14-ft. rod	
No. 63	Teleprinter	3	20	1,000	500–1,000	Dipole	Transportable station.
No. 76	CW	2	12	9	(a) 300	Long wire	Has 6 crystal channels.
HS 1	CW MCW RT	2.5	14	200	(a) 100 (b) 60	14-ft. rod	
3. SHORT RANGE (Vehicle Stations)							
No. 1	CW RT	4.2	6.66	0.5	(a) 8 (b) 3.5	9-ft. rod	
No. 2	CW MCW RT	1.875	5	10	(a) 10 (b) 5	9-ft. rod	
No. 11 LP	CW RT	4.2	7.5	2	(a) 10 (b) 5	9-ft. rod	
No. 11 HP	CW RT	4.2	7.5	6	(a) 20 (b) 10	9-ft. rod	Also used in tanks.
No. 12 LP	CW MCW RT	1.2	17.5	25 (CW) 7 (RT)	(a) 60 (b) 15	9-ft. rod	
No. 21	CW MCW RT	(i) 4.2 (ii)19	7.5 31	1.5 0.8	(b) 5 (b) 1	9-ft. rod	
No. 22	CW MCW RT	2	8	1.5 (CW) 1 (RT)	(a) 20 (b) 10	12-ft. rod	3-men pack load.
No. 62	CW RT	1.6	10	1.5 (CW) 1 (RT)	(a) 20 (b) 14	14-ft. rod	2-men pack load.

Type of Set	Type of transmission	Frequency Range in Mc/s		Power Output, Watts	Comn. Range, stationary (a) CW (b) RT miles	Asso-ciated Aerial	Remarks
		From	To				
4. SHORT RANGE MAN-PACK							
No. 8	RT	6	9	0.25	(b) 2-5 1-3	6-ft. rod ground	
No. 18. Mks. II and III	CW RT	6	9	0.25	(a) 4 (b) 2.5	6-ft. rod	
No. 31	RT (FM)	40	48	0.5	(b) 3	10 ft. 8 in. rod	British version of US.SCR 300.
No. 38	RT	7.3	8.8	0.2	(b) 0.75	4-ft. rod	
No. 46	MCW RT	(i) 3.4 (ii) 5 (iii) 6.4 (iv) 7.9	4.3 6 7.6 9.1	1.5	(b) 4-10	6-ft. rod	Crystal controlled and waterproofed.
No. 48	CW RT	6	9	0.25	(a) 4 (b) 2.5	6-ft. rod	US manufactured version of No. 18.
No. 58	CW RT	6	9	0.25	(a) 4 (b) 2.5	6-ft. rod	Canadian version of No. 18.
No. 68 P	CW RT	1.75	2.9	0.25	(a) 10 (b) 5	11-ft. rod	
No. 68 R } No. 68 T }	CW RT	} 3	5.2	0.25	(a) 10 (b) 5	11-ft. rod	
No. 78	RT	2	10	0.2	(b) 1.5	4-ft. rod	Three types each with 8 crystal con-trolled frequencies.
5. ARMOURED FIGHTING VEHICLE TYPES							
No. 7	CW RT	1.875	5	5	(b) 3-5*	6-ft. rod	*Between moving vehicles.
No. 9	CW MCW RT	1.875	5	10	(b) 8*	6-ft. rod	
No. 11 HP	CW RT	4.2	7.5	6	(b) 6*	6-ft. rod	
No. 19 A Set	CW MCW RT	2	8	12	(a) 15* (b) 10*	8-ft. rod	
No. 19 HP	CW MCW RT	2	8	30	(b) 25-50*	12-ft. rod	
6. ARMOURED FIGHTING VEHICLE INTERCOMMUNICATION							
No. 14	RT	0.29	0.41	5	(b) 0.4*	6-ft. rod	*Between moving vehicles.
No. 19 B Set	RT	229	241	3	(b) 1*	Half wave	
7. RADIO LINK							
No. 10	Pulse	5,000 band		0.2	Full optical	Special reflector	Gives 8 duplex speech channels.
No. 26	RT	(i) 85 (ii) 230	95 255	100 65	(b) 30-50 optical	Koomans arrays	Gives 5 duplex speech channels.
No. 57	RT	85	95	7-10	(b) 30-40 optical	Rhombic	Gives 1 duplex speech channel.
8. ANTI-AIRCRAFT							
No. 17	RT	46	64	0.75	(b) 8	Special dipole and reflector	For searchlight communications.
No. 36, Sender	CW MCW RT	10	60	25	(b) 25	Horizontal dipole	For broadcasting from G.O.Rs.
No. AD77	CW MCW RT	(i) 0.273 (ii) 2.875 (iii) 5.000	0.545 5.455 8.570	40-50	(a) 400	Rhombic	For point to point communications.
9. GROUND TO AIR							
TR.1143	RT	100	124	2	(b) 50†	Special Dipole	For Air support and Artillery Recon-naissance.
Burndept CN 348	RT	100	120	4	(b) 50†	Dipole	†To aircraft at 11,000 ft.

PERSONALITIES

Note: In order to keep this appendix short and to the point *only* that part of the personalities' career concerned with their service during the Second World War is covered. (Those names given in bold are also listed; * = illustrated on page 355).

*Alexander, Harold (1891–1969) Immaculate, aristocratic British general, who served as a field commander throughout the war. Brilliant and always diplomatic, he first came to prominence when covering the withdrawal from France in 1940; he then took command in Burma in 1941. In August 1942 he replaced **Auchinleck** as commander of British and Allied forces in the Western Desert. He was appointed Supreme Commander Middle East in 1943 and remained in command in Italy until the end of the war.

Anderson, Kenneth (1891–1959) British general, he commanded 11th Infantry Brigade – part of **Montgomery**'s 3rd Infantry Division – in France. Later, in the UK, he rose to command the 3rd Division, then a corps and finally Eastern Command. After becoming the senior British officer in Eisenhower's planning HQ for the invasion of North Africa (Operation Torch), he went on to command the British First Army there, but fell out with Montgomery. After returning to the UK he took over the British Second Army, but was replaced in January 1944 by **Dempsey** and given Eastern Command instead, followed by East African Command.

Auchinleck, Claude (1884–1981) British general, probably one of the most underestimated commanders of the war. At the start of the war he was in India but flew back to the UK to command VIII Corps was about to join the BEF in 1940 but was instead appointed GOC Northern Norway. After that fiasco he returned to India as CinC, then in June 1941 became CinC Middle East vice **Wavell**. The 'Auk' fought a series of difficult campaigns against Rommel that ended with the First Battle of Alamein in July 1942. Differences of opinion with Churchill led to his removal and subsequent return to India, again as CinC, where he remained for the rest of the war.

Blamey, Thomas (1884–1951) Australian general who was heading the Australian Manpower Commission at the beginning of the war. He was appointed CinC Australian Army in 1942 and personally took command of Australian operations in New Guinea. Later he was CinC Allied Land Forces in the SW Pacific. He received the Japanese surrender in 1945.

Brooke, Alan Francis (1883–1963) British field marshal. He was CIGS from 1941, having come to prominence while commanding II Corps in France in 1940. After Dunkirk he became CinC Home Forces, but found his metier as CIGS. Greatly respected by Churchill, he was appointed chairman of the Chiefs of Staff Committee in June 1942 and remained in that post until the end of the war.

Browning, Frederick 'Boy' (1896–1965) British general who, in 1940, was selected to head an experimental airborne formation that became 1st Airborne Division, then Airborne Command. Joined Eisenhower's staff for planning the airborne invasion of Sicily. This was followed by command of the airborne corps in Normandy, after which he was second in command of the First Allied Airborne Army. Following the abortive Arnhem operation he went on to SEAC as Mountbatten's CofS.

Calvert, 'Mad Mike' (1913–) British brigadier. After seeing action in Norway, then training commandos, he led a Chindit column under **Wingate**. A brigadier at the age of thirty, he commanded 77 Brigade in the liberation of Burma. Afterwards he led SAS forces in Belgium, Holland and Norway.

Campbell, John 'Jock' (1894–1942) Extremely brave RHA officer who invented the 'Jock' Columns in the desert, won a VC at Sidi Rezegh, but was killed in a car crash near Halfaya Pass on 26 February 1942, soon after taking over command of 7th Armoured Division.

Crerar, Henry (1888–1965) Canadian general, he was the Canadian CGS in 1940, but resigned his post in order to take a field post as commander of Canadian I Corps in Italy in 1943. He commanded the Canadian First Army in NW Europe and was responsible for the encirclement of all German forces in the Netherlands.

Cunningham, Alan (1887–1983) British general who was appointed GOC East African Forces in late 1940, carrying out a masterful and highly successful campaign against the Italians. He next succeeded **O'Connor** as Commander Eighth Army but was soon out of his depth against Rommel as he lacked experience in armoured warfare. Replaced by **Ritchie**, he left North Africa to become commandant of the Camberley Staff College, then GOC N Ireland until 1944, when he returned to East Africa. In late 1945 he went to Palestine as high commissioner and CinC.

***Dempsey, Miles** (1896–1969) British general who came to prominence as a staunch supporter of **Montgomery**. He commanded the BEF's 13th Infantry Brigade in 1940 and was awarded a DSO. He commanded the Eighth Army's XIII Corps from the closing stages of the North African campaign going on to Sicily and Italy, then returned with **Monty** for the Normandy invasion, where he commanded the British Second Army.

Dill, John (1881–1944) British field marshal. Initially, he commanded I Corps in the BEF, but was recalled in April 1940 to become Vice CIGS, then CIGS, despite his age (he was sixty in 1941). However, because of his undoubted ability he was appointed head of the British military mission to the USA, where he was described by Roosevelt as being the 'most important figure in the remarkable accord which had been developed in the combined operations of our two countries'. He died in USA on 4 November 1944 and is buried in Arlington National Cemetery.

Fryberg, Bernard (1889–1963) New Zealand general and fearless soldier (he had won a VC in the First World War). Churchill likened him to a salamander because he 'thrived on fire'. He commanded all NZ forces throughout the war and was responsible for the heroic defence of Crete in May 1941. He commanded 2nd NZ Division for five years, in North Africa and Italy.

Giffard, George (1886–1964) British general, he was military secretary to the war minister when war began, then went to Palestine and on to be CinC West Africa. In 1943 he became GOC Eastern Army in India, then CinC 11 Army Group with Slim's Fourteenth Army under command. Sacked at the height of the Imphal battle by Mounbatten for differences of opinion, he was vindicated before a relief arrived.

***Gort, John** (1886–1946) British field marshal of legendary courage (VC, three DSOs and the MC all awarded in the First World War). Appointed CIGS in 1937, he then went to France to command the BEF. Later he was governor of Malta during its siege and high commissioner in Palestine.

Gott, William 'Strafer' (1897–1942) British general who commanded 7th Armoured Division then XIII Corps in North Africa against first the Italians then the Germans. He was promoted to Lt General and selected to command the Eighth Army. However, he was killed on 7 August 1942 when his plane was shot down while en route to Cairo.

*Harding, John (1896–1989) British general who Montgomery called 'that little tiger'. BGS to O'Connor in 1940–41, he commanded X Corps (Monty's *corps de chasse*), then became CofS 15 Army Group in Italy and later commanded XIII Corps.

*Hobart, Percy (1885–1957) British major general. Brilliant but irascible, he was one of the greatest trainers of armoured soldiers and his specialized armoured force – 79th Armoured Division, 'The Funnies' – was a major factor in the Allied success during the amphibious landings on D-Day.

Hore-Belisha, Leslie (1893–1957) British politician. Impatient, intolerant but highly effective Secretary of State for War from 1937 onwards, he was responsible for stimulating recruiting (by better pay and conditions) and revitalizing the British Army. He was forced to resign in January 1940 after criticizing Lord Gort and his BEF for slowness.

*Horrocks, Brian (1895–1985) British general, he commanded XII, then later IX and X Corps in the desert. Badly wounded in 1943 he recovered to command XXX Corps in NW Europe. He was criticized by some for apparent inaction during the Arnhem battle after a spectacularly fast advance through Belgium and Holland.

Ironside, Edmund (1880–1959) British field marshal. Immensely experienced, having fought in both the Boer War and the First World War, he was CIGS in the early months of the Second World War, then CinC Home Forces. He retired in 1941.

Ismay, Lionel (1887–1965) British general, he was Churchill's CofS from May 1940. All papers between the PM and the service chiefs went through him and his greatest talent was 'minimizing friction' between them!

Laycock, Robert (1907–1968) British general, 'Lucky' was one of the first commando leaders ('Layforce' in the Middle East), whose exploits included the abortive attempt to assassinate Rommel. He eventually became Chief of Combined Operations.

Leese, Oliver (1894–1978) British general, he led XXX Corps in North Africa, Sicily and Italy, then succeeded Montgomery to command the Eighth Army in Italy until November 1944, when he became CinC Allied Land Forces in SEAC.

Messervy, Frank (1893–1973) British general, he commanded 4th Infantry, then 7th Armoured Divisions in the desert. He was captured by Rommel's offensive in May 1942, but escaped some eighteen hours later. He returned to India and, after various appointments, took over 5th Indian Infantry Division in the Arakan. Later he commanded IV Corps in the liberation of Burma and was finally GOC Malaya.

McCreery, Richard (1898–1967) British general who, after Dunkirk, went out as armoured adviser to Auchinleck, but disagreed with him and lost his post. He was then CofS to Alexander, who thought highly of him. He commanded X Corps at Salerno and against Cassino. He became the last commander of the Eighth Army after Leese.

Montgomery, Bernard (1887–1976) British field marshal. He was one of the longest serving and most successful senior Allied field commanders of the war. He came to prominence when he took over the Eighth Army in North Africa and subsequently won the Battle of El Alamein. His success in North Africa, Sicily and Italy led him to be chosen to command 21 Army Group in NW Europe. He was appointed field commander for all the land forces taking part in the Normandy invasion. He continued to command 21 Army Group throughout the battle in Europe, but his somewhat abrasive, self-confident attitude made him a difficult person for the Americans to deal

Gen (later FM) Sir Harold Alexander. (IWM – NA 16130)

Gen Miles Dempsey.

FM Lord Gort. (IWM – F 3987)

Gen John Harding. (IWM – NA 14669)

Maj Gen P.R.C. Hobart. (Tank Museum)

Gen Brian Horrocks. (IWM – B9642)

FM Archibald Wavell and Gen Richard O'Connor. (IWM – E 1547)

Lt Gen (later FM) Sir William Slim. (IWM – SE 3311)

FM Jan Smuts. (South African War Museum via Author's Collection)

with. The Arnhem debacle was totally out of character as he was normally a careful, detailed planner who did not take risks.

Morgan, Frederick (1894–1967)   British general. After serving with the BEF and then commanding 1st Corps District in Yorkshire, he joined Eisenhower's planning staff to become COSSAC (Chief of Staff, Supreme Allied Commander), planning the Normandy landings, etc.

*O'Connor, Richard (1889–1981)   British general. A brilliant field commander, he led the Western Desert Force against the Italians, defeating their Tenth Army at Beda Fomm in February 1941. Captured by the Germans in April 1942, he escaped from POW camp in Italy in September 1943 and later commanded VIII Corps, but found he was then too old for field operations. In December 1944 he went to India and commanded the NW Army.

Paget, Bernard (1887–1961)   British general. He came to prominence as the 'Hero of Trondheim', extricating British and French troops from the hopeless situation in Norway in 1940. Having formed and trained 21 Army Group (and hailed as the greatest trainer since Sir John Moore), he was passed over in favour of **Montgomery** to command them in the field and instead became CinC Middle East.

Pile, Frederick (1884–1976)   British general. Took over AA Command in 1939, which was responsible for supporting the RAF during the Battle of Britain, and defending Britain against the Luftwaffe during the Blitz and the later V bomb raids. He worked closely and harmoniously with Churchill.

Platt, William (1885–1975)   British general. Best remembered for his successful campaigns in East Africa and Madagascar. After these campaigns, he became GOC East Africa for the rest of the war.

Ritchie, Neil (1897–1983)   British general who came to prominence when he was appointed to command Eighth Army in North Africa by **Auchinleck**. Totally unused to armoured warfare, he was thoroughly beaten by Rommel and was relieved of his command in June 1942. Later he commanded XII Corps in NW Europe.

Scobie, Ronald (1893–1969)   British general. He relieved Australian forces in Tobruk in October 1941, then made some limited objective attacks from Tobruk in the offensive that followed. CofS Middle East Command in 1943, he led British troops to Greece the following year to reinstall the king, later putting down the communist insurrection there.

Scones, Geoffrey (1893–1975)   British general who was director operations and intelligence on the CinC India's staff in 1939. Commanding IV British Corps, he conducted a classic defence/offence strategy in the Kohima–Imphal area. Later promoted to the head of Central Command.

*Slim, William (1891–1970)   British general. He was commanding 10th Indian Infantry Brigade in East Africa in 1939, then 10th Infantry Division in Syria. In March 1942 he went to command BURCORPS in the retreat from Rangoon, then in October 1943 he was given command of the newly formed Fourteenth Army, which cleared the Japanese out of Burma. He then became CinC SEAC vice **Leese**.

*Smuts, Jan (1870–1950)   South African field marshal and prime minister. Thanks to him, South Africa gave its full support to Britain during the Second World War. Churchill had a very high opinion of him and from June 1940 he was appointed CinC SA Forces and was made an honorary British field marshal.

Stopford, Montague (1892–1971)   Commanded XXX Indian Corps in the defence of Assam in early 1944, then led them in the liberation of Burma. He succeeded Slim as Fourteenth Army commander in May 1945.

*Wavell, Archibald (1883–1950) British field marshal who did not fulfil his true greatness because he fell out with Churchill. He defeated the Italians in 1940 in the Western Desert, then was moved to the Far East where, once again, he was presented with a disaster-laden scenario, having to pull out of the Dutch East Indies, Malaya and Burma. He invariably got little help from the PM and much criticism. In June 1943 he was made Viceroy of India, so ceased to exercise a combat command. Silent and withdrawn, he was nevertheless loved and respected by all who served under 'The Chief', as he was called.

Wilson, Henry (1881–1964) British general, 'Jumbo' held high commands in the Middle East and Mediterranean throughout the war. For example, he took over from **Alexander** as CinC Middle East in February 1943, then in January 1944 replaced Eisenhower as Allied CinC Mediterranean Theatre (SACMED). In December 1944 he handed over to **Alexander** and became Head of the British Joint Staff Mission in the US when **Dill** died.

Wingate, Orde (1903–1944) Brilliant, unorthodox British general who was personally selected by **Wavell** to help the Emperor of Abyssinia to organize a revolt against the Italians in 1940, which he did most successfully. However, he came to prominence organizing and commanding his Chindit operations in Burma against the Japanese. He was killed in an aircrash in Assam in March 1944.

BIBLIOGRAPHY

This bibliography has been made as complete as possible so that anyone wishing to study the subject further will know where to look for information.

Ansell, David. *The Illustrated History of Military Motorcycles*, Osprey Automotive, 1996

Bidwell, Shelford. *The Women's Royal Army Corps*, Leo Cooper, 1977

Boyd, Derek *The Royal Engineers*, Leo Cooper, 1975

Brayley, Martin and Richard Ingram. *WWII British Women's Uniforms*, Windrow & Greene, 1995

Chamberlain, Peter and Terry Gander. *WW2 Fact Files* (set of eleven volumes), Macdonald and Jane's, 1975–76

Cole, Howard N. *The Story of the Army Catering Corps and its Predecessors*, ACC Association, 1984

Crew, Graham. *The Royal Army Service Corps*, Leo Cooper, 1970

Davis, Brian L. *British Army uniforms & insignia of WWII*, Arms & Armour, 1983

Farrar-Hockley, Anthony. *Infantry Tactics 1939–45*, Almark Publishing Co., 1976

——. *The Army in the Air*, Sutton Publishing Ltd, 1994

Fernyhough, Brig A.H. *A Short History of the Royal Army Ordnance Corps*, CB Printers Ltd, 1965

Forgrave, Lt Col B.T.G. *A History of the RAVC*, privately published pamphlet, 1987

Forty, George. *The Encyclopedia of 20th Century Conflict Land Warfare*, Arms & Armour, 1997

——. *World War Two Tanks*, Osprey Automotive, 1995

——. *World War Two AFVs*, Osprey Automotive, 1996

Georgano, G.N. *World War Two Military Vehicles*, Osprey Automotive, 1994

Gibb, Lt Col J.W. *The Second World War – Training in the Army*, unpublished (typed copy held in MoD Library)

Gibbs, N.H. *History of the Second World War – Grand Strategy*, Volume 1, HMSO, 1976

Guingand, Maj Gen Sir Francis de. *Operation Victory*, Hodder & Stoughton, 1947

Hodges, Peter and Taylor, Michael D. *British Military Markings 1939–45*, Cannon Publications, 1971

Joslen, Lt Col H.F. *Orders of Battle of the Second World War, 1939–1945*, Volumes 1 and 2, HMSO, 1960

Kennett, B.J. and Patman, J.A. *Craftsmen of the Army*, Leo Cooper, 1970

Makepiece-Warne, Maj Gen Antony. *Brassey's Companion to the British Army*, Brassey's (UK), 1995

Mackenzie, Col L.H.M. (ed.). *The History of the RAPC*, Combined Printing Undertakings Ltd, 1951

Macksey, Maj (Retd) Kenneth, MC. *History of the Royal Armoured Corps and its Predecessors 1914–1975*, Newtown Publications, 1983

McLaughlin, Redmond. *The Royal Army Medical Corps*, Leo Cooper, 1972

Nalder, Maj Gen R.F.H. *The History of the British Army Signals in the Second World War*, Royal Signals Institution, 1953

Oldfield, Lt Col E.A.L. *History of the Army Physical Training Corps*, Gale & Polden, 1955

Piggott, Juliet. *Queen Alexandra's Royal Army Nursing Corps*, Leo Cooper, 1975

Rhodes-Wood, Maj E.H. *A War History of the Royal Pioneer Corps 1939–45*, Gale & Polden Ltd, 1960

Sheffield, G.D. *The Redcaps*, Brassey's (UK), 1994

Smythe, Brig The Rt Hon Sir John, Bt. *In This Sign Conquer*, A.R. Mowbray & Co. Ltd, 1968

Sutton, John and Walker, John. *From Horse to Helicopter*, Leo Cooper, 1990

Vanderveen, Bart. *Historic Military Vehicles Directory*, After the Battle, 1989

White, Col A.C.T. *The Story of Army Education 1643–1963*, George C. Harrap & Co. Ltd, 1963

Wise, Terence. *WW2 Military Vehicle Markings*, Patrick Stephens, 1981

PAMPHLETS

TM 30–410: Technical Manual *Handbook on the British Army, with supplements on the Royal Air Force and Civilian Defense Organizations*, US Government Printing Office, 30 September 1943. (Graded as 'CONFIDENTIAL' when issued but subsequently downgraded to 'UNCLASSIFIED')

Note: This pamphlet was re-published in slightly abridged form by Arms & Armour Press in 1976 and edited by Chris Ellis and Peter Chamberlain.

Various organization tables for armoured, artillery, infantry, etc., units, as appropriate.

INDEX

Note: The index covers the text only. Relevant illustrations will often be found within a page or two of the text reference.